Hypermedia Systems and Applications:
World Wide Web and Beyond

Springer
Berlin
Heidelberg
New York
Barcelona
Budapest
Hongkong
London
Mailand
Paris
Santa Clara
Singapur
Tokio

Jennifer A. Lennon

Hypermedia Systems and Applications

World Wide Web and Beyond

Foreword by Hermann Maurer

 Springer

Dr. Jennifer A. Lennon
University of Auckland
Dept. of Computer Science
Private Bag 92019
Auckland 1, New Zealand

With 93 Figures

Library of Congress Cataloging-in-Publication Data

Lennon, J. (Jennifer), 1939-
    Hypermedia systems and applications: World Wide Web and beyond/
J. Lennon.
        p.   cm.
    Includes bibliographical references and index.
    ISBN 978-3-540-62697-8   e-ISBN-13: 978-3-642-60759-2
    DOI: 10.1007/978-3-642-60759-2
    1. Interactive multimedia.   2. World Wide Web (Information
retrieval system)   I. Title.
QA76.76.I59L46   1997
006.7--dc21   97-13552
                                                                   CIP

© Springer-Verlag Berlin Heidelberg 1997

Cover Design: Künkel + Lopka Werbeagentur, Heidelberg
Typesetting: Camera ready by the author
SPIN 10551998   45/3142 – 5 4 3 2 1 0 – Printed on acid-free paper

To Michael and Rae

Foreword

It is a pleasure and an honor to write a foreword for Jennifer Lennon's book *Hypermedia Systems and Applications: World Wide Web and Beyond*. I am fortunate to have been able to follow the development of this book from an excellent Ph.D. thesis to what I would consider one of the best and most comprehensive books in the area. It has a good chance to become a *must* for teachers, researchers, and practitioners.

For the sake of this foreword let us combine the phenomena hypermedia, the Internet, and the WWW by just calling them the *Web*. Well, this Web surely has become one of the "super hot topics", from both a scholarly and a commercial point of view! We have a saying that the Web is like a dog: one year's development of the Web corresponds to seven human years.

You will be familiar with Murphy's law: "Anything that can go wrong will go wrong", and with a plethora of derivatives or specializations thereof like: "If you are in an otherwise empty locker room, the only other person there is bound to have a locker just on top of yours"; or: "If traffic is moving slowly, you are always going to be in the slowest moving lane", and so on. Well, I have coined a version that applies to the Web: "Whenever you have understood an important new development concerning the Web you can be sure that it is obsolete".

Putting all this together, it is clearly a formidable task to try to write a comprehensive book on such a rapidly moving target. Dr Lennon has done a great job and has done it in an ingenious way.

She has divided the book into three parts. The first one, *Introduction to Hypermedia Systems and their Applications*, contains a review of fundamental ideas and of some historical aspects. It therefore has a good chance of withstanding the winds of time for an extended period. The second part, *Web Technologies*, is certainly more prone to obsolesence, but Dr Lennon cleverly manages to minimize this danger by (i) discussing very much state-of-the-art work not even known to many insiders yet, and (ii) by using many pointers to the literature and to Web sites that deal with relevant topics: the latter pointers will ensure that the material remains topical for some time! Finally, the third part, *Advanced Applications and Developments*, is just that: a look ahead into the (near?) future of electronic publishing, Web based training and teaching, new aspects of interactivity on the Web, personal assistants, and new symbolisms for improved communication. All of the chapters in this third part offer intriguing insights in what is going to (or might) happen, and present much food for thought and research.

I have used a preliminary version of the book in a 3-hour, one-semester course, "Networked Multimedia Systems". I got permission from Springer-Verlag to use the electronic version for my class (as part of a closed user group) and installed it on a Hyperwave server (http://www.hyperwave.com; these servers are free of charge for universities). This enabled students to comment on any page of the book they wanted, so that the comments were visible to all other students, myself, and all my tutors, who could then continue this "asynchronous discussion" at leisure. It was interesting to see how the discussion developed, how students added references they detected, what questions were asked, and how well the material was accepted. I have thus found this book to be excellent material for such a (third year) course. Clearly, I could not cover all the material in Part 3 to the extent that would have been justified, but I feel that the book could be used both earlier and later in a suitable curriculum. The availability of the whole book in electronic form even encouraged students to discuss topics outside the "exam-relevant material", and I consider this a compliment to both the book and the style of teaching used.

Summarizing, my congratulations go to Dr Jennifer Lennon for the excellent and careful compilation of this book, and to Springer for its timely publication. I am sure the book will prove helpful to many of the myriads of persons who are interested in the Web!

May 1997   Hermann Maurer,
                                  Head, Institute for Information Processing
                                         and Computer Supported Media,
                                                          Graz, Austria,
                                                        hmaurer@iicm.edu

Preface

Now that Hypermedia and the Web are becoming an everyday part of life and work, there is a need of a book that will describe these new phenomena comprehensively, convering in one volume the services they render, their technical aspects, and their potential future. This book is designed for that purpose.

Of course, no single volume can entirely fulfil the needs of all enquirers. Accordingly I have given references to a wide array of papers, Web documents, and other sources of information available at the time of writing. The book itself includes those areas which I see as essential knowledge for people who are, or will be, affected by the Web. However, I have also included certain leading edge research initiatives which show exciting potential – where imagination and lateral thinking are in demand.

This book is divided into three parts. Part I is a general overview of Hypermedia and the World Wide Web, taking both topics from the earliest beginnings to a discussion of current problems and applications. Part II covers technical aspects of the use of Hypermedia on the World Wide Web; it is intended to give not only the theory, but also the detail needed for hands-on development. Part III covers some of the major new developments and applications of Hypermedia. Some of these are firmly established, such as Digital Libraries, while others are more speculative, such as the development of a new visual languge, "MUSLI".

Any book that attempts to depict in real time the world of the Web must inevitably be the work of a team of people. This book is no exception. It would remain little more than a series of notes if it were not for the dedicated work of all my colleagues at the HyperMedia Unit at the University of Auckland.

First and foremost, I must thank the founding director of the HyperMedia Unit: Professor Hermann Maurer. It was his inspiration and encouragement that led me to embark on the project and then follow it through.

I am also indebted to each of the following members of the HyperMedia Unit for their significant contributions:

- Chris Anderson for his work on the JPEG and MPEG sections;
- Chris Burns for work on Teleteaching;
- David Congerton for his splendid work on the pictures;
- Bob Doran for time and encouragement;
- Mike Joblin for much painstaking editing;

- Michael Klemme for the chapter on HyperWave;
- Mattias Moser for work supporting document annotation;
- Richard Persché for work on student/lecturer interaction applets;
- Carolyn Sanders for the important section entitled "A snapshot of the 90s";
- Peter Shields for technological magic.

I would particularly like to thank the people at Springer-Verlag, especially Hans Wössner and Andy Ross, for the professional expertise with which they helped me polish the many rough spots in my manuscript.

In conclusion, as the long List of URLs indicates, I would like to thank the contributors, many of them anonymous, to the vast treasure trove of information I have mined from the Web.

April 1997   Jennifer Lennon

Table of Contents

List of Figures

Part I

Introduction to Hypermedia Systems
and Their Applications

1. Introduction

1.1 Overview

The various applications discussed in this book are exciting achievements that have become possible only because of recent advances in technology. Film, television, video, and computer technologies are converging rapidly. We see competing thrusts from interactive TV, VideoTex, both orthodox and unorthodox [Maurer and Sebestyen, 1982], video-on-demand, and CD-ROM technology, driven by an increased demand for more user interaction. As we shall find again and again throughout this book, the Internet and the World Wide Web are driving the convergence even closer.

1.2 Definition of Hypermedia

The term "hypermedia" was first coined by Theodor Nelson in a 1965 paper entitled "A File Structure for The Complex, The Changing and the Indeterminate" [Nelson, 1965]. In this paper he describes "Films, sound recordings, and video recordings... arranged as non-linear systems...." [Nelson, 1965]. However, since there is currently much confusion, even amongst experts, about the interrelation of terms such as multimedia, hypertext and hypermedia, we shall begin by clarifying the meanings of these terms as they will be used throughout this book.

1.2.1 The Usual Definition of Multimedia

Usually, "multimedia" has meant a mix of media, where "media" has meant a rich combination of text, graphics, pictures, video and audio, in digitised form. The definition provided by Newcomb is this: "a parcel of information intended for human perception that uses one or more media in addition to written words and graphics. The presentation of the added media may occupy time, space, or both" [Newcomb et al., 1991].

Modern computers can store huge amounts of information in the form of text documents, graphs and diagrams, as well as the digitised information of photos, paintings, music, video clips, etc. Electronic information systems range from single documents, to large multi-volume encyclopedia sets, to distributed databases. The information can be accessed, updated, and used for many purposes: the dissemination of information (e.g., advertising and public relations efforts), desktop publishing, presentations, video conferencing, research, computer-aided instruction and a whole new virtual world of simulations. Multimedia systems incorporating new sophisticated search techniques can help users gain control of the information explosion in more efficient, productive, and yet interesting and stimulating manners.

However, as we shall elaborate in Section 1.3, this definition needs to be broadened considerably.

1.2.2 Hypertext

Hypertext is non-sequential writing. The term was introduced by Theodor Nelson [Nelson, 1965] as "a body of written or pictorial material interconnected in such a complex way that it could not conveniently be presented or represented on paper". Nelson used the term "hyper" in the sense of "extension" and "generality", which he compares to "hyperspace". (It is unfortunate that it is frequently confused with the more common meaning of "abnormal excess".)

In Chapter 2 we give several examples of early hypertext systems, but basically they are, as described by Nelson, "text chunks connected by links which offer the reader different pathways" [Nelson, 1965]. Nelson uses a very good analogy when he describes hypertext documents as containing both new material and "windows" through to other documents.

A rather more precise definition is given in [Newcomb et al., 1991]: "A hypertext document is a parcel of written and graphic information intended for human perception, which can be explored and presented in a variety of sequences, using a set of traversable connections usually called 'links'..."[Newcomb et al., 1991]. This is shown diagrammatically in Figure 1.1.

It is significant that in neither of the above definitions is there any mention of time-based media such as video.

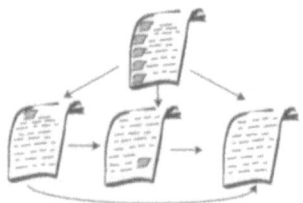

Fig. 1.1. A Simple Hypertext System

1.2.3 A Working Definition of Hypermedia

We shall start with the following rather simplistic definition of "hypermedia": multimedia, with links, embedded in a network.

That is, a networked system supporting the storage and retrieval of linked multimedia and the real-time transfer of this data among the terminals in the network. We are using the term "network" in its most generic form – whether metropolitan area (MAN), wide area (WAN), or local area (LAN) (see Section 3.2.3).

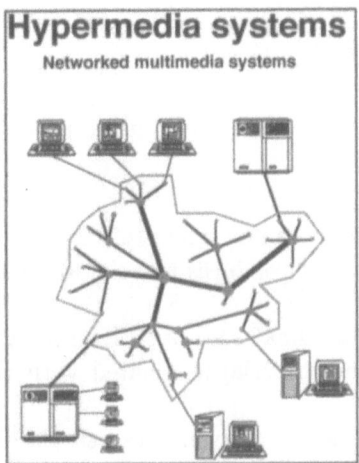

Fig. 1.2. Hypermedia Systems

For further reading on multimedia and hypermedia systems we refer the reader to the surveys by Conklin [Conklin, 1987] and Tomek et al. [Tomek et al., 1991], as well as the texts "Hypertext and Hypermedia" [Nielsen, 1990] and "Multimedia Systems" [Koegel-Buford, 1994].

1.2.4 Nodes in Hypermedia Systems

We shall refer to the various items of data in a hypermedia system as "nodes". A single node may contain just text, a graphic, a single video clip, etc., or any combination of media. Although every additional node normally entails at least one or more links, some designers, for other good reasons, have built applications that do not allow mixed-media nodes.

1.2.5 Links in Hypermedia Systems

The nodes in a hypermedia system are inter-related using sets of pointers, which are commonly called links. A link connects a source anchor to a destination anchor. Either anchor may be a single character, a piece of text, a diagram, video, a section of mixed media, a whole document, or a group of documents. Links are commonly one-to-one mappings and are either unidirectional or, preferably, bidirectional.

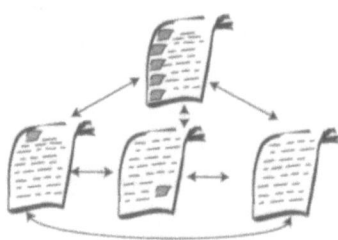

Fig. 1.3. Bidirectional Links

There are also one-to-many and many-to-one mappings which may, along with one-to-one mappings, have *types* associated with them such as "reference" or "index".

Commonly, "following a link" means clicking on a highlighted source anchor which results in the material associated with the destination anchor being displayed.

Both the advantages and disadvantages associated with links are mentioned throughout this book and here we mention only a few.

Advantages:

- The user is given much more control over what appears on the screen at any one time.
- Text is "delinearised", i.e., readers may take any number of alternative pathways through the material.
- Browsing can be associative (analogous to associative human memory where one thing can remind us of something else).
- In many respects links are easier to use than multiple search queries.

Disadvantages:

- Systems all too frequently have "dangling links".
- It is easy to get "lost in hyperspace".
- It is often difficult to retrace one's steps.
- It is easy to go around in circles.
- It is frequently difficult to judge how much material has been covered – or is still left to be covered.

In Chapters 4 and 7 we discuss how modern systems are now being designed to overcome most of these disadvantages.

Fig. 1.4. Dangling Links Left by the Removal of a Document

1.2.6 Structuring Hypermedia Systems

In the early days of hypermedia development designers were excited by the possibilities of free linking between nodes. Unfortunately they had no conception of what would happen when systems really grew!

As elaborated in Chapters 4 and 7 large hypermedia systems need a certain amount of carefully thought out structure to be built into them. Documents can be grouped into logical units which may in turn be assembled in hierarchies.

1.3 New Qualities in Multimedia Entail New Definitions

"Multimedia" means much more than the usual mix of video, animations, still images, sound, and text. Few people appreciate the ramifications of new high-resolution graphics technology. As elaborated further in Chapter 13 it must include the latest advances in panoramic picture viewing techniques, and new forms of *interactive* and *annotated* movies [Jayasinha et al., 1995].

Multimedia must also include *virtual reality* – not to be confused with the form of entertainment that uses the same name along with a lot of expensive gadgetry. The real thrust of virtual reality will come from 3D modelling, including an endless range of simulations and visualisations such as those described in Sections 5.3.4 and 5.3.2. It may indeed revolutionise lifelong learning, as outlined in Chapters 5 and 10.

1.3.1 Interactive Movies

Interactive movies [Jayasinha et al., 1995], as detailed in Chapter 13, have developed far beyond the CD-I type where interaction meant little more than choosing varying places in the movie to skip to. New high-resolution technology is augmenting the lenses in our eyes with zoom, microscopic, and telescopic capabilities, opening the way for movies of television quality that let viewers zoom in and out, and manipulate the image in other ways, without any loss of resolution. We shall also have films where the actual "set" is several times larger than the viewing window, letting the user pan around the scene following visual clues such as clouds of dust (maybe the dinosaurs are coming) or auditory clues such as the sound of drums. Techniques such as these invite us to be virtual participants in multimedia productions of festivals, concerts, and ballet performances.

1.3.2 Annotated Movies

As elaborated in Chapter 13, annotated movies [Jayasinha et al., 1995] expand the definition of multimedia still further. Take, as an example, a training video that describes troubleshooting in a network. If the video of the technician giving step-by-step instructions is shown in just one quarter of the screen, then the remainder of the screen can be used to new effect (see Figure 1.5). The second quadrant may show detailed parts such as connectors, or perhaps a three-dimensional model that can be rotated by the trainee. A third quadrant may show diagrammatic representations of the network. The fourth may give key terms from the film dialogue for which the user can obtain detailed definitions. And still, at any stage in the movie, the user can pause and zoom in for more details using the high resolution technique mentioned in the previous section.

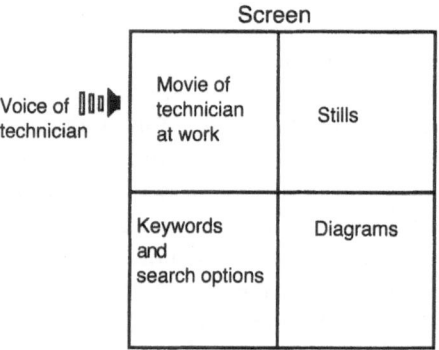

Fig. 1.5. Annotated Movie

1.3.3 Panoramic Pictures

New digital techniques, such as those described in Chapter 13, let viewers look up Mount Everest or down from the Eiffel Tower, or pan through a 360 degree circle. Filming of soccer games is being done with as many as forty different cameras so that users can choose which part of the action they want to watch or replay. Viewers are able to put themselves right in the centre of the action.

1.3.4 Three Dimensional Models

Three-dimensional models and scenes are inevitably associated with virtual reality. We are not, however, thinking of users togged up in helmet, boots, and gloves – data gloves or any other kind. No, we predict that the real thrust of virtual reality will be from 3D, animated data-modelling programs that model the real world on a computer screen and provide total-immersion learning environments. To take the example of the technician given above, with the aid of lightweight shutter or polarising glasses, the viewer will be able to "surf the net" or "fly through" the inside of a faulty computer component using 3D (stereoscopic) viewing. Simulations of this sort have to be included in any definition of multimedia.

1.3.5 A New Definition of Hypermedia

We have computers that can store television movies for later playback. But this is only one facet of multimedia. For example, multimedia includes (besides the usual mix of text, graphics, video, etc., as described above) 3D objects and 3D models of scenes of arbitrary complexity. However, partly because users expect more and more interaction, multimedia is now developing a still broader scope and must be given an even higher-order definition.

It is important to note that any change in the nature of *multimedia* brings about changes in the nature of *hypermedia*. In this book we shall assume that the definition of hypermedia always includes state-of-the-art multimedia.

1.4 Internet: Mess or Messiah?

The uniting of computer users through the introduction of worldwide networks is turning the Internet into the "super-highway" or "infobahn" of the future. True? Obviously not. Internet development has repeated the railway history of several continents – with disparate systems radiating from different centres. Now that unification becomes imperative, the incompatibilities and the proliferation present a mess to work with. Still, we believe that present evolution is following an extremely exciting development curve, as is discussed in Chapter 4.

Few doubt that networked multimedia (i.e., hypermedia) will be an essential part of our future, but there is still too much confusion concerning the Internet.

The Internet is certainly:

- The largest library mankind has ever had
- The messiest library mankind has ever had
- The most amazing communication/cooperation tool
- One of most chaotic structures devised by man.

The information in any network is only as useful as the system that serves it. Chapter 4 introduces the World Wide Web. We suggest that some of the problems that users are currently experiencing are due to first generation systems, but that second generation answers are emerging.

1.5 From Personal Computer to Personal Assistant

Electronic personal assistants are discussed more fully in Chapter 14. Here, a brief introduction to them is given, since they are frequently referred to in following sections.

The idea of having an electronic personal assistant is certainly not new. Computer scientists have long dreamt of having an electronic assistant (i.e., a supervisory program) to help them manage everything from electronic mail to research and teaching commitments. And, of course, science fiction writers have taken the idea of a personal assistant still further by suggesting that it will assist with all our personal problems!

An extensive survey of *intelligent agents* is given in a special issue of *Communications of the ACM* [Communications, 1994b]. The paper "From Personal Computer to Personal Assistant" [Lennon and Maurer, 1994a] also gives an overview of the subject, and we summarise just a few of the more important points here.

Users of today's complex software systems simply do not have the time, or motivation, to browse extensively through printed manuals or on-line help files, so they are frequently unaware of useful features. Many major computer companies are developing what they are now terming *electronic agents*, i.e., prototype versions of systems in which computer programs are capable of learning from repetitive actions. In such a system the agent first of all indicates that the user's actions are being recorded by highlighting selections, menu choices, etc., in a specific colour. Then, if the user decides that all actions have been recorded correctly, there is the option of letting the electronic agent perform the task automatically. Computers carrying out a whole range of voice commands are also no longer fiction: form letters can be written entirely using only voice-activated commands.

We hope that the electronic agent will develop from this rather primitive beginning into a fully fledged electronic personal assistant" (PA); i.e., develop into a general background processor that will help users with their day-to-day work. The widespread problem of information overload will be eased if an electronic personal assistant sets up filters so that all searches can be tailored to the user's requirements. A supervisory program should also help authors cross-reference and check their work. This is becoming critically important as the volume of writing increases the amount of highly questionable data that is being quoted as fact.

1.6 Forecasting: An Impossible Necessity

Although the applications discussed in this book are firmly based on today's technology, the paper "To Forecast Information Technology: An Impossible Necessity" [Maurer and Lennon, 1994], makes some important speculations:

> If you take any arbitrary phenomenon and increase its size greatly, then you do not just get more of the same phenomenon – you get something with completely new properties, a completely new phenomenon. Consider the following analogy. If a Bedouin who has lived in the desert and never seen water in anything but small puddles is told about Lake Taupo or the Tasman Sea[1], at first he will be incredulous. Then even if he does intellectually accept that such large bodies of water really do exist, when you challenge him to speculate on what this implies, even if he has lots of imagination, he will come back with ideas like 'Fabulous: I can water 10,000 camels at the same time.' We believe he has no chance of predicting real implications – such as the development of swimming or boating. Or that if a wind comes up the water will start to undulate in a very strange fashion so that the boat may capsize and people may be drowned. For a Bedouin water has always had only lifesaving qualities, so that the idea that water can kill will be absolutely alien to him. There is no chance that he can make predictions such as these.

In the area of information technology we are going to witness tremendous jumps in quantity. No one can really predict where this jump in technology will take us. For example, when personal computers were first suggested, one of the best proposed uses was for storing recipes.

In ten to fifteen years, many of us may carry small but powerful notebook computers around with us. We may be able to talk into our notebook and have more commands, programs, and facilities available than we can imagine. For example, if we go overseas our notebook may translate words and phrases for us. A global positioning system may display maps and pinpoint our location exactly. A mobile telephone integrated into our notebook may give us access to all the databases in the world, so we can look up theatre programmes and bus and train connections. It may be our digital photo camera, and may replace our wallet and credit cards. Thus, we may well witness a jump in quantity in the computer world, which will then introduce new characteristics and capabilities.

---

[1] Lake Taupo is about 30 km across and the Tasman Sea about 1200 km across.

Computers are turning into the ultimate media machines and in doing so they will change the way we teach and the way we learn. We can store not only text but also graphics, pictures, movies, and audio clips. Interactive movies, currently being researched, involve the user in much more than simple searches and replays from CDs. You can do much more than just zoom into still pictures (see Chapter 13). Movies are available where you are given the control needed to modify the actual plot – to the extent of determining whether or not the hero dies. Or if you prefer you can be Sherlock Holmes and solve intriguing mysteries, or play any one of an increasing number of adventure games with highly sophisticated graphics, such as Myst, Secrets of the Luxor, and Buried in Time.

More exciting for educators, high-resolution virtual reality will offer reluctant learners adventures such as swimming through the body's circulatory system, and becoming totally immersed in informative environments both simulated and imaginary. No one can really predict where this jump in technology will take us. Yet it is part of any computer specialist's responsibility to keep a lookout for new phenomena and to alert the public. Only with this kind of approach will we be able to avoid the worst consequences of the fact that to forecast information technology is an impossible necessity!

1.7 How this Book is Structured

1.7.1 The Parts

Part I (Chapters 1–5) defines the state of the art, sketches its historical context, and discusses the issues engaging most attention at the time of writing.

Part II (Chapters 6–8) focuses on the fundamental technologies which create the Web itself and all the other components of a millennial communication medium.

Part III (Chapters 9–16) extrapolates future applications from current leading-edge initiatives.

1.7.2 The Chapters

2 **Visionaries, Pioneers, and Benchmark Applications.** Chapter 2 gives a brief history of multimedia and hypermedia development over the past thirty years so that later work can be put in context.

3 **The Internet: A First Glance.** The growth of the Internet has been phenomenal. Chapter 3 traces the Internet's development, including pioneer applications such as Gopher and WAIS. We outline a range of widely-used text-based services including email, newsgroups, and bulletin boards.

4 **Hypermedia Systems: Meeting the Challenges.** In Chapter 4 we look at issues facing hypermedia development. We list some of the problems with what we term "first generation" systems, and then suggest some "second generation" solutions. This chapter also contains a review of security issues.

5 **Hypermedia Systems: Their Application to Life, Work, and Learning.** Chapter 5 looks at the applications and impact of hypermedia systems in more depth. It discusses changes which are occurring now in our everyday lives, our work, and in learning environments.

6 **The World Wide Web.** Chapter 6 describes the major software technologies that create the World Wide Web. Since any chapter on the Web can only be a snapshot, we have concentrated on aspects that make it unique.

7 **Hyperwave – An Advanced Hypermedia System.** In Chapter 7 we discuss the powerful World Wide Web system called Hyperwave. Hyperwave solves several of the problems encountered in first generation systems, e.g., dangling, unidirectional links and lack of security.

8 **Hypermedia: Standards and Models.** Chapter 8 gives background information, of a more technical nature, to network access and services, markup languages, compression techniques, and hypermedia data models.

9 **Electronic Presentation, Publishing, and Digital Libraries.** Chapter 9 describes a variety of methods that are emerging for electronic presentation and publishing, including CDs, electronic newspapers and journals, and the Internet. We discuss the important topic of digital libraries. We look at copyright problems and suggest solutions involving novel methods of advertising and sponsorship.

10 **Integrated Learning Environments.** In Chapter 10 we consider formal, informal, and professional education, describing how information technology in general, and the Web in particular, can have significant impact.

11 From Traditional Lectures to CAI. Chapter 11 is a survey of existing lecturing techniques followed by a proposal for a hypermedia-based lecturing system that can generate high quality computer-aided instruction material. The chapter is based on the paper "Lecturing Technology: A Future With Hypermedia" [Lennon and Maurer, 1994b].

12 Hypermedia and Distributed Learning Environments. The survey of distributed learning environments given in Chapter 12 concludes with a description of an exciting "lecturing on the fly" system that is being developed and trialed by two European universities collaborating with a New Zealand university.

13 Interactive and Annotated Movies. Chapter 13 describes how new advances in high resolution graphics may be used to enhance various types of interactive and annotated movies. The chapter is based on the papers "Interactive and Annotated Movies" [Jayasinha et al., 1995], and "New Ways of Using Old Media: Surprising Possibilities" [Lennon and Maurer, 1995].

14 Hypermedia and the Notion of a Personal Assistant. Chapter 14 looks at what we may expect from electronic personal assistants. Since application programs are providing constantly better interfaces, the exact nature of an electronic personal assistant is becoming blurred. Some of its functions may be better controlled by a continuous background process. Others may be delegated to various applications. However, just as there is a move towards "universal documents" that allow text, graphics, spreadsheet and database editing all in the same document, we should also expect a PA to help in activities ranging from simple wordprocessing tasks to scientific research. We believe that a PA should support our work in all areas of computing. The chapter is based on the paper "From Personal Computer to Personal Assistant" [Lennon and Vermeer, 1995].

15 Hypermedia and a New Symbolism for Improved Communication. Chapter 15 considers new symbolism for improved communication. We suggest, as a new and vitally important area of research, the development of multimedia tools that allow more efficient "reading" and "writing" using new types of hypermedia documents. We look beyond traditional hypertext, taking the first steps towards a language of dynamic abstract symbols that will help authors to express precisely and concisely both concrete and abstract ideas. We propose a MUlti-Sensory Language Interface

(MUSLI), an environment where multimedia documents can be written and read more effectively.

The chapter is based on the paper "MUSLI: A MUlti-Sensory Language Interface" [Lennon and Maurer, 1994c].

16 **Hypermedia and a New Multi-Sensory Environment.** Many young people find reading "too slow" and prefer watching a movie to reading a book. They want more control over their communicating media, the level of information they feel motivated to reach and the pace they want to set themselves. In this chapter we look at alternative representations of interactive media. We show how various capabilities of computer environments parallel functions used by our brain's visual system to an amazing degree and discuss implications for education.

The chapter is based on "Mental imagery and visualisation: from the mind's machine to the computer screen" [Lennon, 1995b], and "New ways of using old media in computerised form: surprising new possibilities" [Lennon and Maurer, 1995].

2. Visionaries, Pioneers, and Benchmark Applications

2.1 Introduction

The history of hypermedia development resists reduction to a simple sequence of statements. Developments occurred in complex interrelations, and in many cases ideas cross-fertilised. Brilliant concepts too dependent on hardware that didn't materialise were abandoned – only to be rediscovered by other researchers. It is far from clear even where to start a history. Some of us may prefer to trace developments back from the present to the past. Others may wish to track all the side branches of failed development, seeking all the interesting whys and wherefores. Obviously this book should be hypertext! Even if, as I have chosen, we keep to a more or less traditional view of "developments", it is still not easy to tell what name should be pulled out of the hat and placed on a timeline first – Bush, Engelbart, or Nelson, for example. However, several good surveys of hypermedia systems place Vannevar Bush first on the list [Nyce and Kahn, 1991, Conklin, 1987, Nielsen, 1990, Tomek et al., 1991].

Practical constraints have meant that the list of visionaries and benchmark applications mentioned in this chapter is far from complete. Many have been reluctantly omitted. In fact, the list really consists of only those names that are tripped over again and again when exploring the Net or reading any book on the history of hypermedia. The dates are also necessarily vague. They are meant only as signposts to the events.

2.2 A Brief Timeline

To help give some idea of how the various events described in this chapter interrelate with Internet development (see Chapter 3), here is a brief timeline:

Table 2.1 Time Line

Year			Sect.	Internet Hosts
1945	Vannevar Bush	Memex	2.3	
1964	Marshall McLuhan	Global Village	2.4	
1965	Theodor Nelson	Xanadu	2.5	
1967	Andy van Dam et al.	HES, FRESS	2.6	
1968	Douglas Engelbart	Augment/NLS	2.7	
1969				4
1975	Akscyn	ZOG / KMS	2.8	
1977	Alan Kay	Dynabook	2.9	
1978	Andrew Lippman	Aspen Movie Map	2.10	
1980s	VideoTex		2.11	
1983	Ben Shneiderman	HyperTies	2.12	
1984				1,000
1985	Janet Walker	Document Examiner	2.13	
1985	Norman Meyrowitz	Intermedia	2.14	
1986	Peter Brown	Guide	2.15	
1987				10,000
1987	Frank Halasz	NoteCards	2.16	
1987	Bill Atkinson	Hypercard	2.17	
1989				100,000
1989	Tim Berners-Lee	World Wide Web	4	
1993	Hermann Maurer	HM-Card, Hyperwave	2.18	

2.3 Vannevar Bush: Memex (1945)

The idea of a "memory expander" (Memex) is a fascinating one. Vannevar Bush, director of Roosevelt's Office of Scientific Research and Development, describes, in his famous paper "As We May Think" [Bush, 1945, Nyce and Kahn, 1991], a mechanical device to "extend the human memory":

> A memex is a device in which an individual stores all his books, records, and communications, and which is mechanised so that it may be consulted with exceeding speed and flexibility. It is an enlarged intimate supplement to his memory.

Bush considered the idea of associative memory as being of primary importance. He introduced the concept of *trails* to link documents together, both sequential and branched. Although he was thinking of storage media such as punched cards or microfilm, the analogies to modern hypertext systems are inescapable.

From our present perspective, where we enjoy hypermedia as a tapestry of data captured from every conceivable medium, it is fascinating that Bush foresaw scientists using gadgets such as cordless microphones and head-mounted cameras like an ensemble of instruments to produce related data for his Memex. Bush described his scenario in the 1945 paper:

> One can now picture a future investigator in his laboratory. His hands are free, and he is not anchored. As he moves about and observes, he photographs and comments. Time is automatically recorded to tie the two records together. If he goes into the field, he may be connected by radio to his recorder. As he ponders over his notes in the evening, he again talks his comments into the record. His typed record, as well as his photographs, may both be in miniature, so that he projects them for examination.

We cannot help being impressed that Bush seems to have predicted so much, including:

- The idea of an associative storage and retrieval device (Memex)
- Active voice annotation

Although the Memex was never built, it is certain that many later hypertext developments were inspired by Bush's work.

2.4 Marshall McLuhan: Global Village (1964)

In a hypertext version of this chapter, another detour would be signposted at this point. In the 1960s and 1970s the controversial visionary Marshall McLuhan was writing about popular broadcast media [McLuhan, 1964, McLuhan and Fiore, 1968, McLuhan, 1989].

Although many feel he may have made the right predictions for the wrong reasons ("in spite of all these objections one is left with the disturbing suspicion that McLuhan is 'on to something'" [Miller, 1971]), McLuhan's vision of a "global village" is now being very widely quoted in the context of global networks.

- Popularised the idea of a "global village"

2.5 Theodor Nelson: Xanadu (1965)

Ted Nelson, who coined both the terms "hypertext" and "hypermedia", is a visionary whose whole life has been a crusade for hypertext [Nelson, 1965]. Again, in a hypertext document there would certainly be a link here to Bush since Nelson starts his article entitled "As We Will Think" [Nelson, 1972,

Nyce and Kahn, 1991] with the words "BUSH WAS RIGHT". There would also be a link to Engelbart (see Section 2.7), since in a footnote in *Literary Machines* [Nelson, 1987] Nelson writes, "This is the first hypertext system to be so called (though Engelbart's NLS system... was *really* the first hypertext system)."

In 1960 Nelson had started a Master's level project that "has taken over 25 years to complete" – his Xanadu project. He says, "This book [Literary Machines] describes a new electronic form of the memex, and offers it to the world." He is, of course, convinced that "it was the *right* problem. It just took longer, and led further, than I expected."

He built on Bush's ideas, dreaming of a system that "would have every feature a novelist or absent-minded professor would want" [Nelson, 1965].

Xanadu, based on library and publishing paradigms, supports backtracking as well as versioning for the comparison of documents. Nelson hopes it will become a "distributed repository scheme for worldwide electronic publishing", where there is a small "royalty on every byte transmitted".

The term *transclusion* has recently been coined to describe the function of including chunks of text from a linked source into the body of a document in much the same way as we include inline graphics. Nelson called this *"windowing"*. He considered the function to be of primary importance, anticipating a global *"docuverse"* where documents owned by one author can be included in another author's work.

- Nelson coined both the terms "hypertext" and "hypermedia".
- Xanadu, which is based on a library paradigm, includes the following features:
  - Lists which are cross-linked
  - Transclusion
  - Persistent Versioning
  - Copyright
  - Accounting
  - Royalties

2.6 van Dam: Hypertext Editing System (HES) (1967)

Credit for developing the first hypertext system goes to Engelbart. But the first fully functional hypertext application was built at Brown University by a team that included Andries van Dam and Ted Nelson [Carmody et al., 1969]. Their system was simply called a Hypertext Editing System, later abbreviated to HES.

By 1969 the team had developed procedures that let users browse and edit using a special function keyboard and lightpen (besides an alphanumeric keyboard for data entry). A prompt area is displayed on the screen to help users keep track of system options.

The system supports two types of links as well as annotations (called tags). The HES screen consists of a scrollable text area followed by the tag and prompt areas.

In contrast to Engelbart's design principles, HES does not impose hierarchies. Instead data "segments" are freely connected in two ways:

- In-text links
- Branches

The position of the in-text source anchors are indicated by asterisks. Users may jump within the current segment, or to another segment, which then replaces the previous one in the window area. Branches to other segments may be selected from a menu situated at the end of the current segment.

HES was sold to NASA's Manned Space Program to produce documentation for the Apollo program. It was later distributed in commercial form as FRESS, a File Retrieval and Editing System. FRESS was followed by the Electronic Document System, which included colour raster graphics as well as additional navigational aids. Later still, researchers at Brown University furthered their outstanding efforts by developing Intermedia (see Section 2.14).

In a keynote address at the Hypertext'87 conference van Dam stated, "One of the most important things [Nelson] taught me was that this is a new medium and you really can't be constrained to thinking about it in the old ways" [van Dam, 1988]. Nelson, on the other hand, felt that Van Dam's group over-emphasised "paper output". In hindsight it is interesting to note that, with the advent of PostScript files, hypertext documents are once again returning to a paper-oriented format!

- HES was the first fully functional hypertext system

2.7 Douglas Engelbart: Augment: NLS (1968)

Engelbart, a prolifically inventive scientist working at the Stanford Research Institute, laid the groundwork for many features of modern personal computers. But here we are concerned only with his hypertext pioneering. An intriguing glimpse into the history of hypertext is provided by a letter he wrote to Bush in 1962, describing his ideas: "I might add that this article of yours has probably influenced me quite basically. I remember finding it and avidly reading it in a Red Cross library on the edge of the jungle on Leyte" [Engelbart, 1962].

Engelbart had a vision of a conceptual framework that could "augment" and structure cognitive processes, concepts, symbols, processes, and physical artefacts [Engelbart, 1963].

He was also concerned with improving human effectiveness by providing more efficient tools. For example, he is thought of as the father of word processing. In the 1962 letter to Bush, Engelbart wrote:

> We plan a sequence of tasks, initially involving primitive but essential symbol-manipulation capabilities such as composing and modifying different forms of information portrayal (text, diagrams, etc.). This will lead progressively through developments for intermediate capabilities of personal 'bookkeeping', composing or modifying computer-service designations (programming), calculating, planning, etc. Upon an integrated base of such human-controlled, machine-aided capabilities, we plan finally to develop the highest-ordered processes that real-world problem solvers can utilise [Engelbart and English, 1968].

In the field of hypermedia, Engelbart's most important achievement was NLS (oN-Line System). Developed as part of his Augment project, this was probably the first implementation of a simple hypertext system. Over 100,000 pieces of information were stored and users could navigate between them by following links instead of relying on more traditional techniques.

An important feature of NLS was that information was both structured and cross-referenced.

Engelbart is thought of as the father of:

- The mouse
- Word processing
- Windows
- Shared document spaces
- Email
- Hypertext

A truly awe-inspiring list of achievements.

2.8 Akscyn: ZOG: Knowledge Management System (KMS) (1975)

Another early forerunner of modern hypermedia models is the Knowledge Management System (KMS) – which in turn evolved from ZOG.

ZOG [Akscyn et al., 1988] was developed at Carnegie-Mellon University as a "distributed hypermedia system for managing knowledge in organisations". It is a "frame" based system, with only one or two frames showing at a time (see Figure 2.1). Since there is "no mode boundary between navigation and editing operations", users "directly manipulate the contents of a frame at any time". The model supports multiple hierarchies with cross-links between them.

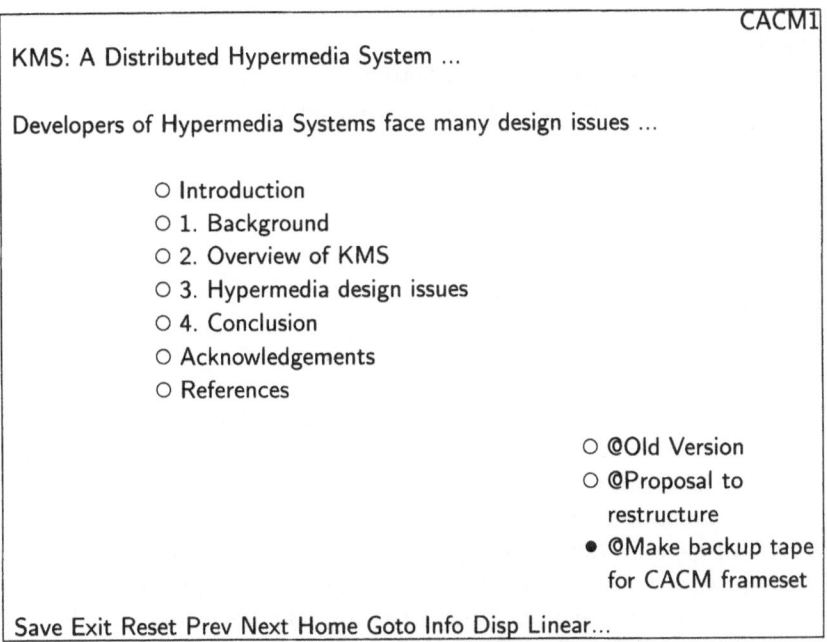

Fig. 2.1. ZOG/KMS Frame (Redrawn from [Akscyn et al., 1988])

While aiming to provide fast response times, KMS supports:

– Multiple users
– Versioning
– Annotation

2.9 Alan Kay: Dynabook (1977)

The Learning Research Group at Xerox Palo Alto Research Center (PARC) designed a portable hypermedia system called Dynabook that included many visionary ideas [Kay and Goldberg, 1977]. It consisted of a flat screen display with graphical interface, a complete read/write environment, and communication links (via phone lines and wireless) to other Dynabooks and networked resources.

The team implemented a non-portable version that includes fascinating features such as:

– User-created fonts that could include pictograms.
– Interfaces designed for use by children.
– Interfaces designed and implemented by children.

- Frame animation that could be edited during playback.
- Support for creating simulations.
- A system for audio "animation" where music can be drawn using a mouse or captured directly from a keyboard using the OPUS tool. The music can then be edited at the user's whim.

However, the idea of the Dynabook was far ahead of its time, a vision that technology is just catching up with now.

- The idea of a portable digital assistant

2.10 Andrew Lippman: Aspen Movie Map (1978)

In the 1970s and 1980s a number of researchers incorporated other media such as graphics, animations, and video into their hypertext systems – signalling the arrival of genuine (according to our definition) hypermedia. The Aspen Media Map was probably the first such system to be implemented. It was developed at the Massachusetts Institute of Technology Media Laboratory under the direction of Andrew Lippman.

It used two displays, one for a map and one for videodisk clips of streets and buildings in Aspen, Colorado. Users could navigate through the map (moving forward, backward, left or right) or point directly at a location on the map and jump straight to the corresponding section of video.

The number of projects that have since been undertaken at the Media Lab is legendary, one notable example being the Athena Project. As part of this project there is a language learning unit for the learning of French by immersion [Murray and Malone, 1992].

- First linked multimedia system implemented

2.11 VideoTex (1980s)

Although the above projects were moderately successful in educational settings, they still did not bring about the widespread acceptance of hypermedia that was predicted by the visionaries – despite the fact that, also in the 1980s, VideoTex services for the general public were started by several European national telecommunication corporations.

VideoTex is based on a nationwide network of computers, accessible to the general public via ordinary phone lines and somewhat modified TV sets or similar terminals. VideoTex systems offer, albeit on modest technical platforms, most of the features of hypermedia including delivery of non-textual data, the integration of communication and cooperation features, and access to terabytes of information (telephone directories, land property registers, dozens of encyclopedias, and so on). Their development, however, was less rapid than predicted, mostly because their archaic user-interfaces and functionality could not convince a sufficiently wide audience to participate [Schneider, 1995].

In Austria, in a unique development, a special Z80-based colour-graphics computer, MUPID (see Section 2.18), was designed and marketed as a Video-Tex terminal. It was a net computer (NC) in the sense that it could download software (then called "telesoftware" – a forerunner of today's Java) to be executed immediately. Although tens of thousands of MUPID were installed the emergence of the IBM PC caused the demise of this computer as with all other Z80-based machines.

2.12 Ben Shneiderman: HyperTies (1983)

Ben Shneiderman is internationally renowned for his work in visualisation and dynamic queries (see Section 5.3.2). While working at the University of Maryland he also developed The Interactive Encyclopedia System (TIES) [Nielsen, 1990]. This was later commercially distributed under the name HyperTies. The HyperTies interface was deliberately kept simple with museum applications in mind.

Unique to HyperTies is a check for the user on the relevance of a document before the link to it is traversed: when the HyperTies pointer is placed over an anchor, a brief description of the destination document is displayed at the bottom of the screen. When a link is activated the document is presented at the first page. Another interesting design feature is the control over links achieved by the system insisting that links with the same name should reference the same source document.

- Easy-to-use interface for library and museum users
- Brief descriptions of source documents displayed before the links are traversed.

2.13 Janet Walker: Document Examiner (1985)

1985 saw the first commercial hypertext system in production, Document Examiner. The system was created as a front-end help system for Symbolic's moderately large database of technical documentation. It is based on a book paradigm but, in contrast to Xanadu and NoteCards, has its user function kept separate from author function [Walker, 1987].

Document chunks (called records) are uniquely named within a certain type. A considerable amount of meta-data is held such as version numbers, keywords, record type, and descriptions both short and long.

Links provide access to destination records, precis, cross references, and lists of names.

Source anchors are text (indicated by bold lettering) and the destination is a record. When a link is traversed, the text of the source document is included in the active page.

- A real world application
- A simple-to-use book metaphor interface
- Built-in keyword search capabilities
- Bookmarks

Implemented on Symbolic's relatively expensive workstations, Document Examiner remained a privilege for the few.

2.14 Norman Meyrowitz: Intermedia: IRIS (1985)

Another truly innovative system was "Intermedia" [Yankelovich et al., 1988], and its successors "Internote" [Catlin et al., 1989], and "IRIS Hypermedia Services" [Haan et al., 1992].

Intermedia, developed at Brown University's Institute for Research in Information Scholarship (IRIS), was built on the experience of 20 years' work with three prior systems HES, FRESS, and the Electronic Document System (Section 2.6). It was one of the first systems to address the problems of large networked systems.

Users welcomed the support of interfaces such as graphical user interface where the contents of each type of document appear in multiple windows that may be scrolled and overlapped. Links are bidirectional. Source anchors may be single letters, words, sentences, paragraphs, or special link icons. Destination anchors are not restricted to the whole document but may be strings within the document. Anchors can be queried to display multiple links.

To help users keep their orientation within the document space, Intermedia supports dynamic "tracking maps" that display the user's current position in relation to its predecessor and successor links.

Operations, as described in "Intermedia: The Concept and the Construction of a Seamless Information Environment" [Yankelovich et al., 1988] and "IRIS Hypermedia Services" [Haan et al., 1992], "behave identically across all applications" (just one feature of beautiful design).

In contrast to systems such as Document Examiner, Intermedia makes no distinction between authors and users. Designed to run on networked Unix-based workstations, it supplies a range of tools such as:

- InterText (a style sheet based editor)
- InterDraw (a line drawing program with a tools palette)
- InterPix (a program to clip, copy and paste scanned images)
- InterSpect (for manipulation of 3D models)
- InterVal (for creating and viewing data along timelines)

The interfaces for each of these tools are designed for easy to use consistency.

- An easy to use graphical system encourages academics to use a wider range of linked media.
- Operations behave identically in all sub-systems.

2.15 Peter Brown: Guide (1986)

The first version of Guide was developed by Peter Brown at the University of Kent [Nielsen, 1990]. Marketed by a series of companies, it was the first hypertext system to be commercially distributed for a range of personal computers. Files could be interchanged between Macintosh and IBM PC.

Links are associated with text areas and in-text links are supported. An interesting feature is that different cursor shapes indicate the several different classes of links: an arrow for the usual hypertext link, a star for pop-up notes, and a circled cross for inline replacement.

Guide is both an authoring and a browsing tool. It is comparatively easy to use, e.g., links can be created without scripting.

- First commercial hypertext system for a range of personal computers.

2.16 Frank Halasz: NoteCards: Seven Issues (1987)

Frank Halasz was important for his part in developing the commercial application NoteCards, and then became famous among the Hypertext community for his landmark "Seven Issues" papers, which identified fundamental problems that would soon become urgent for all large hypertext systems.

2.16.1 NoteCards

NoteCards, developed at Xerox PARC, first publicised at the CHI 87 conference and published in 1988 [Halasz, 1988], has been widely used commercially. It was designed to help researchers and designers organise and develop their ideas.

As its name suggests, NoteCards is based on the paradigm of rectangular NoteCards that contain individual data chunks (ideas). Since ideas are con-

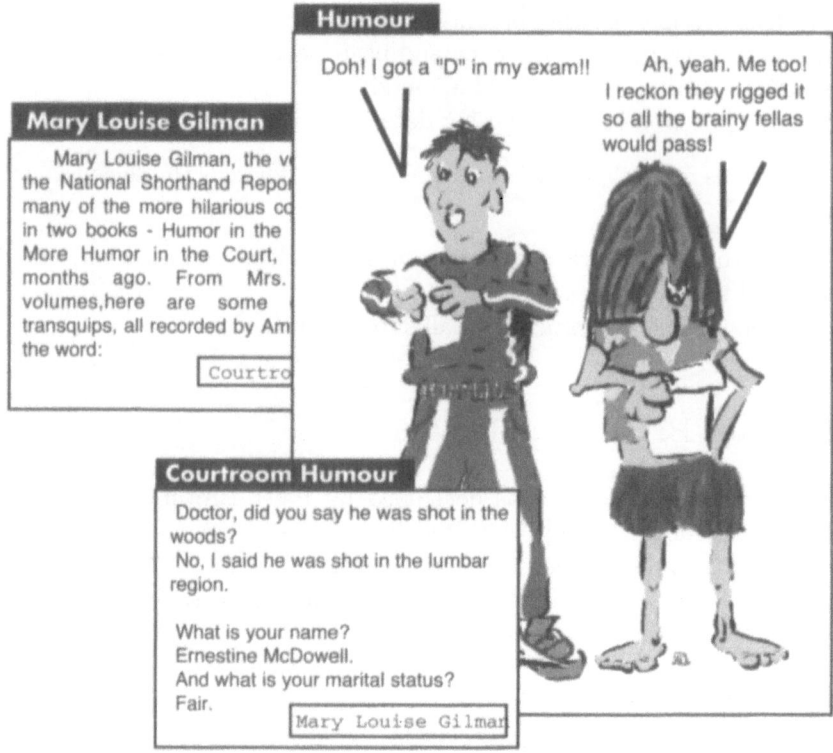

Fig. 2.2. NoteCards

ceptually small, complete cards are displayed when links, indicated by boxed text, are activated. Browser cards provide a clickable map of the underlying structures. One-to-many links are also supported. In contrast with KMS, NoteCards can display multiple cards stacked in a window (see Figure 2.2). In keeping with the notecard paradigm, cards can be organised in "fileboxes" (in analogy to shoeboxes!). A limited search facility is also included.

2.16.2 Halasz's "Seven Issues"

The historic 1988 paper "Reflections on NoteCards: Seven Issues for the Next Generation of Hypermedia Systems" [Halasz, 1988], is such a definitive analysis that it provides the focus of our study of both problems overcome and the issues still facing hypermedia system development (see Chapter 4).

2.17 Bill Atkinson: Hypercard (1987)

Bill Atkinson designed Hypercard to be deceptively simple. It is certainly more than just a toy system that constrains users to a card paradigm. In fact a great many Hypercard applications have been written that are full-screen interactive multimedia productions.

Although Hypercard is not really a hypermedia system according to our definition, since it is for stand-alone machines, it does provide many of hypermedia's functionalities. Hypercard [Hypercard, 1989] and its many followers such as Toolbook [Toolbook, 1994], Authorware Professional [Authorware, 1991], and HM-Card [Maurer et al., 1995], provide authors with easy to use facilities for creating links, buttons, and hot spots.

Bill Atkinson exhibited both genius and philanthropy with the design, development, and distribution of Hypercard. He says in an interview with Goodman [Goodman, 1988] that although Hypercard was designed primarily as an authoring tool, it is "all about sharing information". And it was he who insisted that Apple should bundle Hypercard with every new Macintosh sold from 1987 until 1992, which at last opened interactive multimedia authoring to the general public.

- An extremely simple graphical user interface that first-time computer users could identify with, to handle graphics, video, sound, and interactive links (buttons) to other cards.
- A scripting language for more advanced users.
- Open script for incorporating buttons, sounds, etc., that users could modify for their own use.

2.18 Hermann Maurer: HM-Card and Hyperwave (1993)

Hermann Maurer is a noted mathematician and computer scientist with an extraordinary amount of foresight. In the late 1970s/early 1980s he directed the development of the microcomputer MUPID in Graz, Austria. It was the first colour-graphic Network Computer (for VideoTex, see Section 2.11) with a particularly easy to use graphical interface. MUPID was also the first attempt to use a nation-wide network for teleteaching, culminating in over 500 lectures worth of courseware useable on a variety of LANs and WANs as part of the COSTOC (COmputer Supported Teaching Of Computer science) project [Huber et al., 1989], in which over 50 universities participated in the late 1980s!

Later, foreseeing the results of uncontrolled growth on the Internet, and the need for organisation of files in large distributed databases, he developed the Hyperwave system that is described in Chapter 7. In addition, he master-minded HM-Card [Maurer et al., 1995], and also the HM-Data Model, which is introduced here and described more fully in Section 8.5.6.

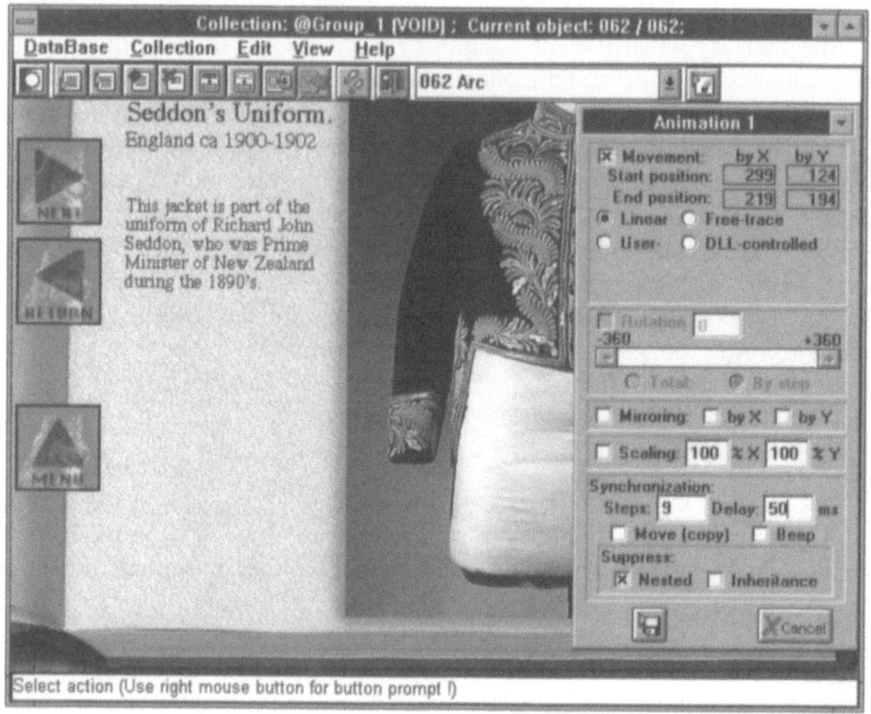

Fig. 2.3. HM-Card

HM-Card is an easy-to-use authoring tool for creating, linking, and view-ing linked multimedia [Maurer and Scherbakov, 1996], [URL13]. It has, for example, particularly user-friendly tools for the creation of animations. Also, since all internally created pictures consist of vector graphics, the resulting files are surprisingly small.

As we have mentioned, HM-Card is based on the HM-Data Model [Maurer et al., 1993a] (see Section 8.5.6). The HM-Data Model addresses each of the following problems usually associated with any large volume of linked documents:

– Disorientation suffered by users.
– Tedious editing of links where, as we have mentioned in Section 1.2.5, deleting documents can result in dangling links.

– Loss of visible semantic structure when sets of nodes are combined with other sets [Andrews et al., 1995].

Information in HM-Card is stored in a secure database. The database items consist of three types: Media Objects, pages (groups of Media Objects) and S_collections (navigable hierarchies) [Maurer and Scherbakov, 1996]. In particular, documents can be organised as navigable structures such as menus, maps, and ordered lists.

Links are encapsulated within S_collections. In practical terms the advantages of providing structures such as these outweigh any disadvantages associated with the absence of global links. Users are provided with a manageable environment, link maintenance is minimised, and semantic meaning among nodes is preserved. Also, because links are not embedded, it is easier to provide maps and tours to aid user navigation. The HM-Data Model is described more fully in Section 8.5.6.

Most important, since the HM-Card application manages all linking functions, link integrity is always maintained.

– Implementation of structured collections within an authoring environment.

End Point

At this point we conclude our brief history – but not because there have been no more great innovators! There have been, more than ever, but their work is inextricably entangled with the Internet developments described in the next chapter.

3. The Internet: A First Glance

3.1 Introduction

As the timeline in the last chapter illustrates, fast-moving events were also taking place in the development of the Internet. But before we can discuss these advances we need to determine just what we mean by the "Internet" – or the "Net", as many people call it. Is it:

- A great way of sending personal messages via electronic mail?
- A means of logging into remote machines?
- A collaborative tool supporting a wide range of multimedia?
- Or, as for increasing millions of users worldwide, is it something to be mined (or "surfed") for a wealth of information, commercial opportunities, relaxation, and addictive fun?

In following chapters we shall explore each of these different aspects of the Internet, but here we shall start with a definition that is much more prosaic:

The Internet is a network of networks.

However, the simplicity of this definition is exceedingly deceptive since it hides multiple layers of complexity.

3.2 The Fundamental Interconnections

First of all, just what is meant by a "network"? Historically it referred to the wires (usually copper) that connected two or more computers. Nowadays, particularly with the advent of routers and virtual connections, the definition has to be broadened to include the computers as well. We have also long since broadened the concept of "wires". Today, two computers may be connected via a variety of metal cable, optical fibre, microwave (including via satellite), or infrared links.

The next important factor to consider is the enormous range of hardware that is interconnected on the Internet. Powerful Unix servers have to talk the same language as lowly PCs. Today's Internet incorporates countless different subnets all using a range of different *protocols* (communication specifications).

To unravel the tangled web and appreciate the complexity behind today's Internet it is necessary to have a brief look at its early development.

3.2.1 The Early Internet Pioneers

The history of the Internet is every bit as convoluted as today's Web itself. Even though the "early days" were less than forty years ago, the various reports by participants (e.g., on the Web) expose unanswerable questions about influences, motives, and vision. For example, the various perspectives on the development of ARPANET make fascinating reading.

ARPANET. In the very early 1960s, when timesharing was a novel idea in a world of batch processing, Dr J. C. R. Licklider headed research at the Advanced Research Projects Agency (ARPA). He saw computers as a communication tool and referred to an "Intergalactic network".

ARPANET was a direct predecessor of the Internet. To several Internet historians the birth of ARPANET is solely tied to military projects where, because of the rise of the Soviet space programme and a particularly serious missile scare, the military wanted a decentralised distributed system that could remain in service despite widespread destruction. In contrast, many of the computer scientists working on the early projects pursued the concept of distributed computing primarily as a means for scientific collaboration.

The requirements, as envisioned by men such as Paul Baran [URLd2], were for a system with no central control where information could be routed over alternate paths, which included radio and satellite links besides wire and cable. A key concept was the packet switching network (see Sections 3.2.2 and 8.2.1).

In 1969 the fledgling network, appropriately named ARPANET, consisted of just four connected host computers at separated locations in the West of the USA.

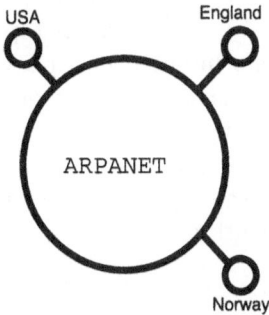

Fig. 3.1. ARPANET Goes International

By 1971 there were 23 hosts connecting university and government centres throughout the USA. In 1972 Bob Kahn organised the first public demonstration of ARPANET where the public were allowed to run distributed applications. Also about this time, researchers were discovering the richness and efficiency of email correspondence.

In 1973 the first international connection of ARPANET linked the USA, England, and Norway. Several groups worked on the early systems but one really remarkable demonstration of using ARPANET in combination with satellite communication and packet radio, in 1977, is described in an interview with Vinton Cerf [Aboba, 1993]. Packets were routed from a mobile vehicle in San Francisco through ARPANET to SATNET to Norway and England, before completing the round trip "without losing a bit!"

By 1981 ARPANET had over two hundred hosts with a new one being added every couple of weeks. Also around the year 1981 several other networks were built, including BITNET (Because Its Time NETwork), CSNET (Computer and Science NETwork), and Usenet.

Birth of the Internet (1983). Now the challenge was to make all these different networks talk to each other. They needed a common communication language. Around 1974 the ARPANET team, led by Vinton Cerf and Robert Kahn, worked on the set of TCP/IP protocols (see Sections 3.2.2 and 8.2.1). Since the new protocols provided a "network of networks" the term Internet was used.

In 1983 when ARPANET began to use TCP/IP, and MILNET split off to form its own subnet, the Internet was deemed to have been born [URLd2].

3.2.2 TCP/IP (Transmission Control Protocol/ Internetwork Protocol)

In 1974 Vinton Cerf and Robert Kahn published a paper entitled "A Protocol for Packet Network Intercommunication" [Cerf and Kahn, 1974], describing TCP in detail.

IP is the main transport protocol that carries packets across the Internet (see Section 8.2.1). TCP is the layer on top that ensures a "reliable" service. TCP splits the user's message into packets, each with a sequence number, full destination address, and some error correction data. The packets are then routed along possibly different paths to be finally reassembled, in the correct order, by TCP at the destination. The routing algorithms are extremely complex but one thing you can be sure of is that rarely is the shortest path the most efficient!

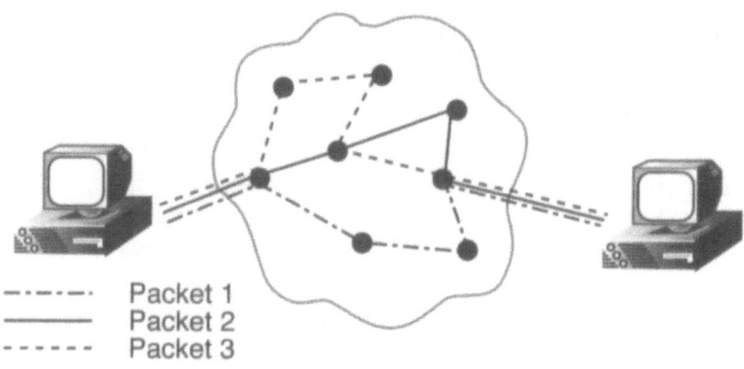

- - · - - - ·   Packet 1
————————   Packet 2
- - - - - -   Packet 3

Fig. 3.2. Packet Switching

3.2.3 Area Networks (LANs, WANs, MANs, RANs, and GANs)

The smallest functional units of the Internet are Local Area Networks (LANs), which are used by many companies and institutions to connect their machines. LANs make use of packet broadcasting where a packet transmitted from one machine is received by several other machines. There are a variety of different topologies: ring, tree, or bus [Stallings and van Slyke, 1990].

While most LANs today operate on any one of a number of communications protocols, as we saw above, the Internet is reliant on the single set of TCP/IP protocols. This introduces problems when trying to get pre-existing LANs to communicate on the Internet, since they speak different languages. A common solution to this problem is to attach a gateway computer to the LAN, which acts as a link between the LAN itself and the rest of the Internet. The gateway handles the differences between the protocols, resulting in a seamless interaction between the two networks.

Wide Area Networks (WANs) use packet switching to distribute packets between component LANs.

As networks have evolved they have been grouped into various functional categories. Businesses, for example, may protect their confidential data behind firewalls, in Intranets (see next section).

Cities are introducing Metropolitan Area Networks (MANs). And in the United States, for example, Regional Area Networks (RANs) include:

- HealthNet
- InformationNet
- ArtsNet
- BusinessNet
- LearnNet
- CollegeNet
- JobNet
- GovernmentNet
- TelecommunicationsNet

Now there are plans for Global Area Networks (GANs) . To provide an adequate service to users, each of these area networks has to be supported by a suitable infrastructure that includes a very high bandwidth "backbone". The complexity of all these interrelated networks is such that we are left with a feeling of stunned surprise, coupled with more than a hint of trepidation, that they work as well as they do.

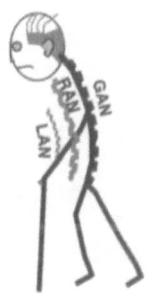

3.2.4 Intranets

An Intranet may be thought of as a self-contained mini-Internet. It may be a single LAN or WAN, or separate WANs may be connected via the Internet through servers which have a special relationship with each other. Web technology, including browsers, has been designed specifically for use within Intranets by developers such as Oracle [URLq2] and Netscape [Andreessen, 1996].

Since these systems are usually commercial, they are often isolated from the rest of the world by firewalls.

3.2.5 Firewalls

It is an unfortunate fact of life on the Internet that, as in any large community of people, there will inevitably be a proportion of miscreants. System break-ins and computer viruses are prevalent (see Section 4.6). One solution to the problem, embraced by the business community, who arguably have the most to lose, is to isolate each at-risk LAN with a *firewall*. Usually this does not completely isolate the LAN from the Internet at large; instead all communication between the two is screened by special computer programs (the firewall), usually running on a stand-alone computer, before being passed on.

There are two distinct types of firewall protection, each with varying degrees of security. Small systems may choose to let the router filter packets using header information. Unfortunately hackers can attack router protocols. Moreover, since access rules (governing who can access what from where) can become very complex, larger systems may need to install a dedicated firewall system. In this case all incoming information is monitored by firewall programs and all requests are translated before being passed along to the protected system.

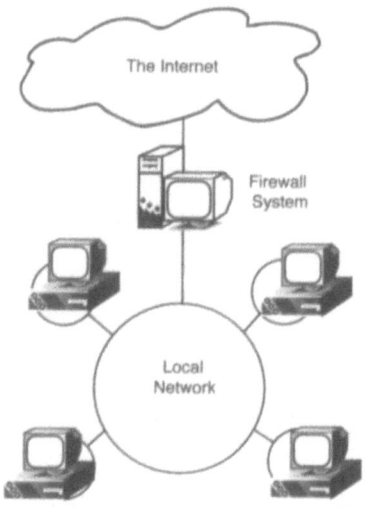

Fig. 3.3. Protecting LANs with a Firewall Computer

3.3 Client/Server Architectures

Servers, as their name suggests, provide databases of files and services that other machines (clients) can access via network connections.

For example, users can make requests for particular files to be downloaded from a remote server onto their own local PC. To achieve this, the client program running on the PC must first initiate a "conversation" with a program running on the remote server. The server program then has to authorise the user and respond to the request. Once the files have been downloaded, they can be accessed using applications that reside on the local machine.

It is important to note that servers can talk to many different types of client machine (Unix, PC, Macintosh, etc.), although the different types of client will, of course, run different versions of the client programs.

Useful client and server programs have been developed which have vastly increased the functionality of the Internet (see Sections 3.4 and 3.6).

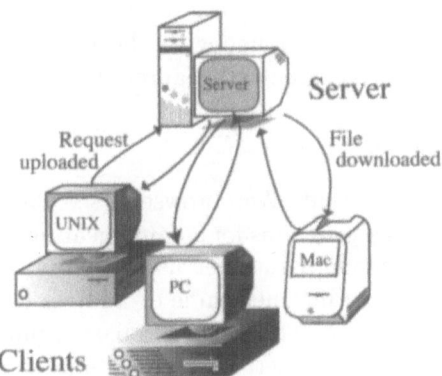

Fig. 3.4. Client/Server Architectures

3.4 Internet Services

3.4.1 Electronic Mail (Email)

It seems appropriate to consider electronic mail (email) before we look at more sophisticated systems, because so much communication is conducted by email across the world – as well as between people in adjacent offices.

Although email correspondence is usually text-based, the Multi-purpose Internet Mail Extension (MIME) is a standard for sending various document types, such as PostScript files and images, via conventional electronic mail. Each of the four MIME categories – text, multimedia, application, and structured types – is comprised of a main type and a subtype. Two examples of this main-type/subtype pairing for the multimedia category are image/gif and video/mpeg. When a document attached to an email message contains data which is not conventional ASCII then it is converted to pure ASCII before being sent, so as not to confuse the mail system. The conversion back from ASCII to the original document is performed when the email message is received.

Although email is indeed an invaluable service, most users still experience problems associated with receiving large quantities of unsorted and frequently unsolicited mail [Denning, 1982]. Unfortunately, we know of managers, enthusiastic email correspondents, who now have completely given up reading any email. Their secretaries now act as human filters, processing email along with the standard mail. Some is forwarded, some is printed out and filed, together with relevant documents, for personal attention. And of course much is simply discarded.

We believe that the problem needs an entirely different approach from those we are currently seeing in practice – system oriented approaches such as that described in Section 4.5.1 under the heading "Active Communication/Information Systems" [Kappe and Maurer, 1994].

3.4.2 Telnet

Before the advent of World Wide Web browsers (see Chapter 6), Telnet was one of the most widely used programs for communicating with remote servers. The problem that most modern Internet users face is that in order to use Telnet you have to know the Internet name or address of the computer that you wish to communicate with. There are also basic commands that have to be learnt, e.g., open, close, quit, set. However, Telnet is a great workhorse, particularly for the Unix buff [Hahn and Stout, 1994].

3.4.3 File Transport Protocol (FTP)

Using File Transport Protocols (FTP), users can login to remote servers and download files. Many thousands of servers using these have been set up all around the world. Collaboration, particularly among university researchers, has seen the widespread use of shareware sites where users are able to login and download files using an anonymous userid.

3.5 Pioneering User-Oriented Support

3.5.1 Archie

The "Archie group", Peter Deutsch, Alan Emtage, and Bill Heelan, were a team of volunteers at McGill University's Computing Center [Deutsch, 1992].

They were among the first to help users discover resources on the increasingly complex Internet. In particular, they developed an index and search system for FTP servers.

Once they had successfully set up their local site, word of their achievements spread rapidly. Archie sites were set up that systematically updated their indexes of other registered anonymous FTP servers. It is easy to imagine the delight of the group on heady days when Archie traffic reached 50% of McGill's total network traffic!

Archie searches, which are supported by a range of options for setting preferences (including search patterns with wildcard characters), provide a list of hosts and directory paths where files matching the search criteria can be found.

Archie servers can be accessed via:

- Telnet. Sites around the world (including McGill's) let users login as "archie" with no password. And of course many Unix users still find this the most desirable option.
- Local client programs. Special client programs were developed to help users and to minimise loadings on the servers.
- Email. The term archie@ is prefixed to the server address.
- Internet browsers. Sites such as ArchiPlex [URLf2] (developed by the NASA Lewis Research Center in Cleveland, Ohio [URLe2]) provide an HTML form interface for searching Archie sites.

For further information about Archie the reader is referred to [Gilster, 1994, Hahn and Stout, 1994].

3.5.2 Gopher

Another group of pioneers on the Internet was a team headed by Mark McCahill and based at the University of Minnesota [URLb1]. There was tremendous interest among the Internet community when their Gopher[1] system solved some very basic problems. For example, up to this point in time many users of network systems (particularly novices) were daunted by cryptic commands and hard to remember machine addresses. The Gopher system provides graphical lists of menus where users can browse up and down the hierarchies, without even being aware of changes in server addresses. Cross-hierarchical jumps are supported by bookmarks (in the form of personalised menus).

---

[1] A gopher:

(a) small North American burrowing rodent.
(b) [also gofer] someone who runs messages (American term "go for").
(c) name of the University of Minnesota football team.

Gopher Menu

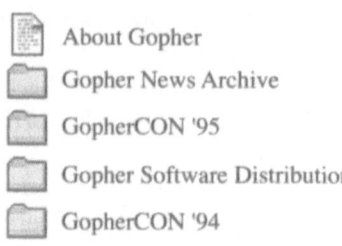

About Gopher

Gopher News Archive

GopherCON '95

Gopher Software Distribution

GopherCON '94

Fig. 3.5. Gopher Menu [URLb1]

Gopher is both a protocol and an application and was developed primarily as a "distributed document delivery system" [Alberti et al., 1994]. Like Archie, Gopher files can be accessed in several different ways:

- Telnet
- Local Gopher client program
- Web browser

Although Gopher was a great step forward as a system for obtaining information by browsing, it lacked fundamental support for searches. Veronica[2], developed at the University of Nevada, lets users make keyword searches in databases of Gopher titles. However, before long WAIS full-text searches were incorporated.

3.5.3 WAIS (Wide Area Information System)

The WAIS (Wide Area Information System) project, initiated in 1989 by Thinking Machines, Cambridge, Massachusetts, provided important functionality that was missing in Gopher: full text searches. A landmark article on WAIS appeared in Byte magazine in 1991, and was entitled "Browsing through terabytes: wide-area information servers open a new frontier in personal and corporate information services" [Stein, 1991].

Like Gopher, WAIS is based on a client/server model with the client programs providing (comparatively) simple user interfaces on a wide variety of platforms.

WAIS employs "powerful full-text search routines based on natural language requests" [Fenn and Maurer, 1994]. The searching algorithms are based

---

[2] Very Easy Rodent-Oriented Net-wide Index to Computerized Archives; note that Archie and Veronica are characters in a popular comic strip.

on the Z39.50 protocol – an ANSI standard – originally designed for networking library catalogues [Lynch, 1992].

A user initiates a search session by first selecting one or more servers from a menu list. WAIS then performs its search and the resulting documents are selected and ranked – not only ranked in order, but graded out of a score of 1000 for relevance. Users can also refine their searches [Gilster, 1994].

The fact that WAIS was accessible from other systems such as Telnet and Gopher, made it widely used in the early 1990s.

3.6 Group Communication Services on the Internet (Text Based)

The services we have discussed up to this point have all been one-to-one. Now we shall look at some of the programs that are available for letting whole groups of users communicate among themselves. The services described here are all primarily text based, since we are leaving the forms of collaboration that need higher bandwidth for later chapters. Also, in the following summaries we are diverging to a form of "news speak". For lists of the emoticons used see [Sanderson, 1993].

3.6.1 Newsgroups

Newsgroups took off very early in the evolution of the Internet, first among Unix users, and then among the general public as easy to use news readers became widely available, such as NewsWatcher (for the Macintosh [URLa3]), Free Agent (for the PC [URLz2]) and the news readers built into Internet browsers. Nowadays there are thousands of newsgroups to choose from, both local and international.

Advantages:

- They are frequented by a large number of people – some of whom actually know what they're talking about ;-)
- They don't require full Internet access (i.e., they are more accessible than FTP, the Web, etc.).
- They are a good place for major (or minor) announcements, since most people have access to them.

Disadvantages:

- There is a poor signal-to-noise ratio, i.e., there is a high ratio of irrelevant banter :-(
- There can be delays of up to several days before a post is fully propagated around the world.
- It is often the first Internet-based technology to be censored (:-x

- Many sites don't receive a full newsfeed due to the bandwidth required to stay up to date.
- You have to be careful when you post since you're telling the world (including spammers) how to get in touch with you via email.
- It can be difficult to find particular newsgroups that you're interested in (although the hierarchies, like soc and rec, facilitate searching to a limited extent).
- It is a text-only medium (although binary distribution is supported via uuencode/uudecode).

3.6.2 List Servers

List servers, as their name suggests, broadcast email messages to users on subscriber lists.

Advantages:

- They often discuss niche topics which don't warrant their own newsgroup.
- Discussion tends to keep to the topic at hand.
- Lists are often subscribed to by people who know a lot about the particular topic, so conversation is often more useful than that found on newsgroups.
- Mail can often be provided in digest form, where a number of messages are sent as a single block rather than individually (which aids in reading, archiving, etc.).
- They provide efficient distribution of specialised information, such as bug reports or software upgrades, to interested parties.

Disadvantages:

- Some mailing lists can have a high throughput, which clutters the subscriber's mailbox. For example, the BMW enthusiasts mailing list generates, on average, about 75 KB per day (this arrives in digest form, each digest being about 25 KB).
- Some people pay for email, whereas news access is usually free.
- It can be difficult to find out what mailing lists exist, and how to subscribe to them.

3.6.3 Bulletin Board Services (BBS)

Bulletin boards provide an automatic answer service for users' calls and thus facilitate the sending and receiving of files, as well as both public and private messages. Although some services allow only one caller at a time, others provide real-time (text-based) conferencing [Aboba, 1993].

Advantages:

- They provide a community facility since the people on the BBS are often from the same town/city.
- They often provide online games/chatting (usually text or ANSI-based).
- They often provide a more "hometown" atmosphere :-)
- They can be quite specific in content, with some BBS providing only clipart files, others being devoted to programming, etc.
- Access is often cheap, since the calls are usually local and the subscriber fees (if any) aren't intimidating.
- They can be set up and run on relatively inexpensive equipment.

Disadvantages:

- Access can sometimes be difficult, especially on popular boards with few phone lines :-(
- They are often only of parochial interest (although national and international message nets such as FIDOnet are also common).

3.6.4 Internet Relay Chat (IRC)

Based on a client/server model, Internet Relay Chat (IRC) provides real-time conversation with anyone around the world – anyone, that is, who has Internet access and an IRC client.

Advantages:

- There are hundreds of "channels" for talking about specific topics.
- Clients exist for all major platforms.
- There are multiple servers to choose from, as well as multiple networks (such as EFFNet and UnderNet).
- IRC provides a good way to meet people (although you probably wouldn't want to meet some of them in the first place).
- It is a good cheap place to hold meetings, interviews, etc., especially since most networks provide locked channels which are accessible through invitation only.

Disadvantages:

- It is one of the seedier parts of town :->
- It is text only (which isn't necessarily a disadvantage).
- IRC is prone to "Net-splits", where the servers temporarily lose contact with one another, leaving participants unable to talk.

3.6.5 Multi User Dungeons (MUDs)

Without a doubt, Multi User Dungeons (or Multi User Dimensions, or MUDs for short) can be either a relaxation or a downright addiction [Herz, 1995]. They evolved early in the life of the Net when Unix programmers needed a break in their lonely all-night vigils.

Advantages:

- They support simultaneous users.
- They support real-time conversation and interaction amongst participants, as well as allowing users to manipulate their virtual environment.
- They often allows users to program their own "synthetic beings" or "bots".

Disadvantages:

- The steep learning curve is a barrier to access although but the complexity is often seen as a good way to keep out the "plebs".
- They can be addictive. This is more serious than it sounds. We know of people who almost lost their jobs from repeatedly turning up late after long nights on the computer, and many universities have had to ban their students from all participation.

3.7 Summary

The Internet is such a highly complex interrelation of software and hardware that we are left with a feeling of respect that it works as well as it does! In this chapter we illustrated the complexity of the Internet by briefly reviewing its history and the fundamental hardware and software. We then discussed Internet services and applications ranging in scope from email to MUDs, and in time from the pioneering days to the present.

4. Hypermedia Systems:
Meeting the Challenges of the Web

4.1 Introduction

The World Wide Web (WWW or simply the Web for short) is an Internet-wide distributed hypermedia information retrieval system [Liu et al., 1994] which provides access to a large universe of documents. The Web is certainly the most widely talked about networked information system existing today, and is definitely the largest hypermedia system in existence. Based on a typical client/server model, several widely used browsers are available (see Section 4.2.1).

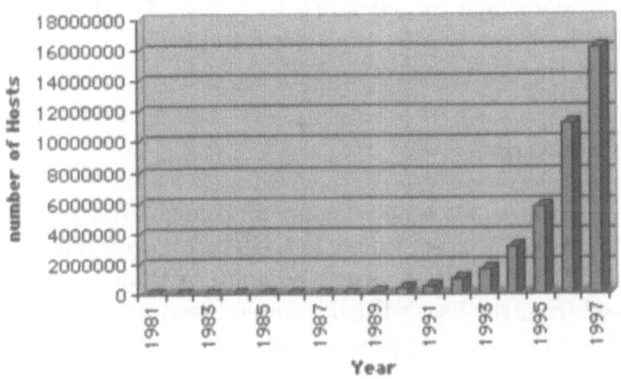

Fig. 4.1. World Wide Web Growth

The Web was originally developed at CERN in Geneva, Switzerland, by T. Berners-Lee, R. Cailliau, J-F.Groff and B. Pollermann [Berners-Lee et al., 1992, 1994a]. It obtained a major boost from the National Center for Super Computer Applications (NCSA) in Illinois which developed MOSAIC (see Section 4.2.1), the first widely used Web browser, to run on a variety of hardware platforms such as PC, Mac, and Unix.

4.2 The Weaving of the Web

The number of Web servers on the Internet has grown phenomenally – as is graphically shown in Figure 4.1 (data obtained from WWW Domain Survey, Jan 1997).

So, why has the World Wide Web evolved so fast? After all, by the end of the 1980s linked multimedia were still primarily standalone applications (see Chapter 2), while the Internet was mainly a text-based communication tool (see Chapter 3).

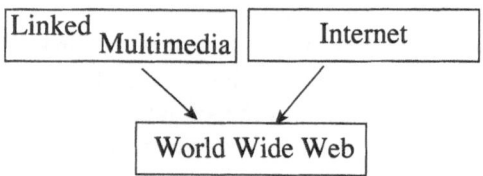

The fast growth of the Web was dependent upon five major developments which are described in detail in Chapter 6:

1. A consistent addressing system (URL) (see Section 6.2)
2. A fast transfer protocol (HTTP) (see Section 6.3)
3. A hypertext document format (HTML) (see Section 6.4)
4. Easy-to-use browsers (see Sections 4.2.1 and 6.7)
5. Good search engines (see Section 6.8)

4.2.1 Web Browsers

Browsers allow a user to fetch and display multimedia documents from local or distributed servers, by either typing in a URL, following a link, or accessing a *bookmark* (a URL stored on the user's computer). Bookmarks can be added to and retrieved from the user's list by simple menu or command options. It is the job of the browser to request a particular document from the server and display it in a form determined by the HTML specification. Note that if the document being displayed contains images or other non-text based information, then the browser will request those objects separately.

Mosaic. Much of the early success of the World Wide Web was undoubtably due to the success of the Mosaic browser. Mosaic, developed by the National Center for Supercomputing Applications (NCSA) at the University of Illinois at Urbana-Champaign [URLe1], was the first really easy-to-use graphical browser [Andreessen, 1993] (see Figure 4.2). Versions of Mosaic were developed in rapid succession to run on a variety of hardware platforms such as PC, Macintosh, and Unix.

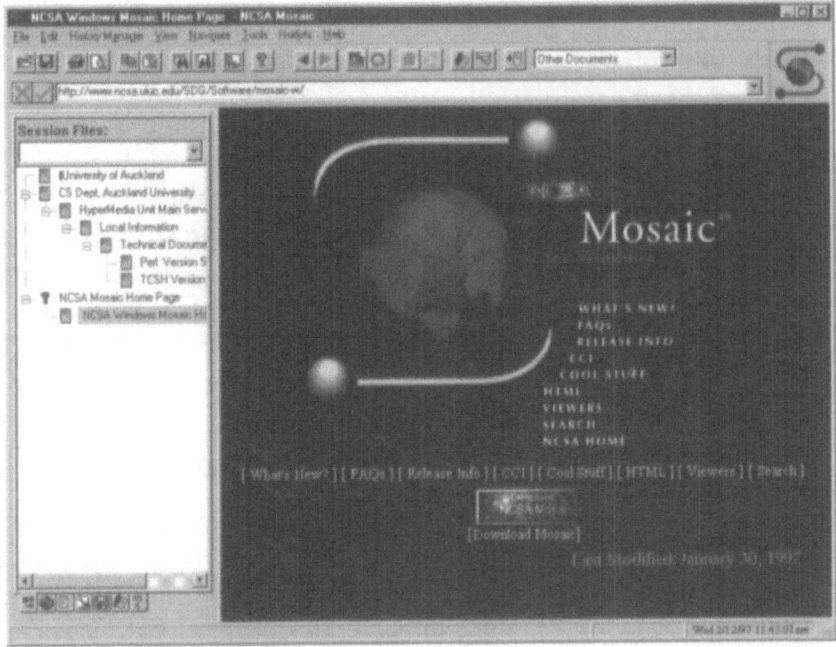

Fig. 4.2. Mosaic Home Page [URLe1]

4.2.2 The Future of the Web

As discussed in Section 4.3, it has become apparent that a number of dramatic changes are necessary if the Web is to continue to grow and be used for larger and larger projects.

Halasz, in his 1988 paper entitled "Reflections on NoteCards: Seven Issues for the Next Generation of Hypermedia Systems" [Halasz, 1988], saw the following challenges for Hypermedia systems:

– Search and query in a hypermedia network
– Composites – augmenting the basic node and link model
– Virtual structures for dealing with changing information
– Computation in (over) hypermedia networks
– Versioning
– Support for collaborative work
– Extensibility and tailorability

Three years later in the closing plenary address of the Hypertext'91 conference, Halasz renewed and revised his seven issues. Once again the talk was extremely timely and created considerable interest.

Now, several years later, most of the issues are still open. For example, in the 1991 address Halasz grouped the first three issues (search and query, composites, and virtual structures) into one issue which he entitled "Ending the Tyranny of the Link" [Halasz, 1991]. In Section 4.3 we list the issues as we now see them before discussing possible solutions.

4.3 First-Generation Problems

Many hypermedia systems have serious limitations, and we suggest that they should be seen as typical instances of "first-generation" hypermedia systems [Lennon and Maurer, 1994d].

Here we give a partial list of problems encountered using Web systems – problems with which readers will be all too familiar.

1. Poor search hit rates: How do you know where to look? What search terms should you choose? How can you search across index boundaries? How do you know it is the best document available?
2. Dangling links: Halasz's reference to the "tyranny of links" [Halasz, 1991] is still valid. The problem of dangling links is one of the most fundamental problems of large systems. Nearly everyone will have experienced the frustration of encountering links left dangling when documents were moved or removed.
3. Getting lost: Take one "side track" to follow something interesting and you can't get back to where you were in the first place.
4. Delays: Information retrieval at the speed of light? For hypermedia documents? How many people who make these assumptions have actually tried to transmit a single large picture over the Web, let alone a whole movie?
5. Poor support for collaborative work: Email on its own does not allow structured discussions or systematic collaboration (particularly between more than two persons), and most information systems still provide information only in text form.
6. Censorship: Unrestricted access for everyone? To everything? It certainly doesn't take children long to find the newsgroups that their parents disapprove of!
7. Advertising: Just how much flashy advertising are users prepared to put up with – let alone pay for?
8. Junk mail: 100, 500, or 1000 pieces of mail per day?
9. Internet charging and billing: Many people believe that the Web will remain a toy until "real", and secure, costing and billing systems are in place. Extravagant claims are made by people who may have successfully transmitted a few kilobytes of text over the Net, but are quite unaware of the cost to transmit one movie.
10. Security. How can I be sure that you have access to this bit, and not that byte, of my data? How can we ensure that my credit card number is accessed only where and when it should be?

How can you really be sure that a particular piece of information down-loaded from the Web is accurate? If, for example, you retrieve an article from Stanford University's database, can you really be sure that it was written by an authority on the subject? Was it perhaps written by a student, or, even worse, was it a particularly clever hoax?

The murky depths of the Internet are reminiscent of old BASIC programs with their spaghetti-style messes of GOTOs. Unfortunately, first-generation hypermedia systems were heralded with as much hype as the FORTRAN language was back in the early 1960s. Nevertheless, the second-generation systems that are emerging can certainly be compared with high-level pro-gramming languages. And third-generation systems are already in the wings!

4.4 Second-Generation Answers

Recently, several systems have been developed that significantly advance the science of information retrieval as applied to very large databases [Maurer et al., 1994a]. Hyperwave [Kappe et al., 1993, Kappe et al., 1994], discussed in detail in Chapter 7 system.

We look to second-generation systems to provide the following answers to the problems listed in Section 4.3.

4.4.1 Improving Search Hit Rates

As discussed in Section 6.8, increasingly sophisticated search requirements have led to growth in search programs. The filtering and searching algorithms used by modern systems are improving search hit rates almost daily. For example, in early 1995, Infoseek, one of the more popular search engines on the Web, provided only a one-line keyword entry form. By mid-1996 it boasted a hierarchical index of categories, searchable by keyword and other attributes such as date, title, author, and physical location.

Since so much highly questionable data is being quoted as fact it is becom-ing critically important to be able to check documents efficiently. We need still more assistance in searching documents – our own and other people's. Unfortunately, in practice it is still difficult to avoid having either too many or too few hits – assuming we do avoid the "run out of time processing your search" messages.

There are many important requirements to be met by search programs, and here we list just a few:

– Appropriate use must be made of filters. In a Hyperwave system, for exam-ple, users can restrict the scope of searches to particular sets of collections. The focus "may be to one or more collections on one or more servers or may be as wide as all collections on all Hyperwave servers worldwide." [Andrews et al., 1994b].

– We look to better hit rates in searches. An intelligent search program will tailor its algorithms to fit the type of document being searched, deducing probable error types. For example, when text is entered from the keyboard it will look for transposed characters. Scanned documents on the other hand commonly produce different types of errors. Since scanning produces only a simple bit map, an Optical Character Recognition (OCR) program must be used to convert the bit map into text. This is required so that the text can be (1) compressed and (2) searched. Even the best OCR programs introduce new errors into the scanned text such as "g"s being confused with "q"s [Cushman et al., 1990]. Here again we look to increasingly intelligent search algorithms to improve translations. We also look forward to a much better hit rate for finding words, even with several errors, by using improvements that fuzzy[1] search techniques seem likely to achieve [Baeza-Yates and Gonnet, 1992, Wu and Manber, 1992].

– The system should be able to make fuzzy searches based on semantic nets instead of just lists of synonyms. A search for "air" could lead on to "gas", "oxygen", etc. These are of particular importance in areas such as Computer Courseware (see Section 10.2.2) where we wish to avoid categoric true/false answers and instead give graded responses. For example, if the answer to a question is "Oxygen", then answers like "gas" or "air" do not warrant an unqualified "no" response. The response could be "Yes, but what type of gas?" or "Please be more specific."

– If a search is not successful then the system should be capable of making alternative suggestions – it is frustrating when unsuccessful searches leave us no better off.

– The system should help the user by prompting for alternatives. For example, a search for "kiwi" could well generate the prompt, "Bird, person, or fruit?"

– Certainly we would like to have phonetic searches, as well as the option of searching dictionaries that include inflected forms of words, abbreviations, accents – and entire foreign languages.

– The search should cope with abbreviations and synonyms.

– Intelligent fuzzy searches should not be restricted to just text files. We should be able to efficiently search file names, directory lists, program names, and so on.

– Above all, such a system must be easy to use. To take a trivial example, if I read that the Sun is 20% helium and 80% hydrogen I will check the figures if and only if it can be done quickly – perhaps on just the click of a mouse.

However, an average user may be hopeless at picking effective keywords but know the general subject area in which their target of interest lies. They may prefer to browse down the broad list of categories provided, for example,

---

[1] We use the word "fuzzy" to mean "not fully constrained".

by Yahoo [URLw2]. This has led to search engines dividing their database into finer and finer categories, and allowing searches within a category.

Unfortunately, even the best search engines cannot determine the quality of the retrieved content, so we watch with interest the development of electronic publishing houses (see Section 9.5).

4.4.2 Maintaining Link Integrity

Although in many respects link management is the crux of hypermedia system design, it is, unfortunately, the weakest aspect of many modern systems. Indiscriminate use of links, particularly in large distributed systems, has led to tangled and mismanaged webs, which is frustrating for system managers and users alike. In Section 4.5.2 we discuss the structuring of data in ways that can minimise the use of links with no loss of functionality.

Since in large hypermedia systems it is impossible to maintain all anchors manually, at least some computer support must be provided. For example, if the source anchors reside in a local database then they may be made inactive, and un-highlighted, automatically as is done in the Hyperwave system (see Chapter 7). In a distributed database the link engine can at least send a message (possibly by email) to the system administrator of the originating document. Once the administrator has assessed possible implications of removing the source anchor, one click of a mouse should make it inactive.

4.4.3 Orientation

Applications such as Netscape Navigator provide easy-to-use graphical interfaces that let users retrace their steps, jump back home, and place "bookmarks". Several graphical browsers are providing history trails in the form of two-dimensional and three-dimensional maps of hyperspace [Andrews et al., 1994b]. A tremendous amount of work has also been done on electronic guided tours such as those in the Hyperwave system [Kappe et al., 1993]. Systems can provide users with guided tours, both two- and three-dimensional, as well as paths to help them navigate through the hierarchies [Andrews et al., 1994b].

4.4.4 Avoiding Data Download Delays

New compression techniques such as JPEG and MPEG (see Chapter 8) are helping reduce data transmission speeds, while other methods are being explored. For example, preloading data is one solution for LANs. In this case, since most hypermedia documents have a basically linear structure, data can be downloaded from the Net before it is actually needed for display. This is not such a good solution for WANs, especially where significant costs are involved. One suggestion is that supervisory programs should be developed that keep usage statistics, and by assigning weights to various links, can make intelligent guesses on what should be downloaded when.

4.4.5 More Support for Collaborative Work

Computer Supported Collaborative Work (CSCW) is discussed more fully in Section 10.2.3. Tools for supporting collaborative work range from simple email to high tech computer conferencing systems (see Section 10.2.4). In efforts to control costs, many firms are now investing in CSCW. However, it is becoming increasingly apparent that the issues are highly complex, and solutions that work in one context may not work in another. Nonetheless, in a world of decreasing resources, electronic support is felt to be so important that many large firms and institutions are devoting part of their research budget to its development.

4.4.6 Censorship

Since to many people the Internet is a symbol for freedom of speech, censorship is an exceedingly complex problem – particularly since so much new material is being added to the Web daily. We believe that where censorship is a sensitive issue, such as in schools, one solution may be to have specialised servers, i.e., censorship by source.

School administrators will have the responsibility of setting filters to define which servers may freely be viewed by students, and what is open only to staff. There may be "green" servers suitable for children and "red-hot" ones that are out of bounds.

On a wider scale, some governments are very concerned about what is available on the Web; this is hampering the global spread of the Internet.

4.4.7 Advertising

Certainly advertising is an integral part of the Web. However, it may be that advertising, as we know it, will become outdated. For example, on commercial nets, particularly those controlled by small businesses, buyers may prefer to let their electronic agents [Communications, 1994b] rove the Web and supply all pertinent information.

As described more fully in Section 6.10.8, we may also see new forms of sponsorship. For example, electronic journals could be distributed for a low price with advertisements or for a higher price without advertisements. Since it will be possible to target potential purchasers more accurately, advertisements may not be as aggravating as at present.

4.4.8 Electronic Mail (Email)

Second-generation systems should actively support users in coping with their email (see Section 4.5.1). As multimedia mail becomes more widely used, (and misused) additional levels of management will be needed to avoid further degradation of an essential service.

In an active system it is the system itself that filters incoming information, getting rid of "spammed" mail, and notifying the recipient in appropriate ways. It helps users organise, manage and archive all types of electronic communication in well structured directories or folders where messages can be categorised by author, subject, date, etc., as well as by keywords. Messages thus saved in an orderly manner are amenable to semi-automated retrieval and purging systems. Messages stored with recall dates will be automatically displayed at appropriate times. Out-of-date messages such as seminar notices can be automatically deleted (with safeguards) once the date for the event has passed. In this case, the user can provide a default date for purges – which, of course, can still be overridden.

4.5 Second-Generation Extensions

Applications that were previously considered to be outside the hypermedia domain are now being generalised to include various aspects of hypermedia. For example, Oracle [URLr1] is a multimedia relational database with embedded links. This, of course, means that we as consumers are now expecting more and more functionality from our hypermedia systems, i.e., we want a system that combines all the best features of databases, authoring tools, video conferencing, etc. (see Figure 4.3).

4.5.1 Active Information Systems

An *Active* system is one that can notify users when changes, such as the addition or deletion of documents, take place. In the paper "From Hypertext to Active Information Systems" [Kappe and Maurer, 1994] the authors identify the following list of requirements that an active information system should support:

- Both synchronous and asynchronous communication.
- Group aliases.
- Multimedia mail.
- Inclusion of linked material.
- Reference links for reply mail.
- User-definable archive spaces and user-definable keyword attributes for all incoming messages.
- User-definable archive spaces and user-definable keyword attributes for all outgoing messages.
- User-defined timing attributes for both incoming and outgoing mail. For example, the user can request that mail be sent at specific times and that incoming mail be re-sent at specific times, thus forming a reminder system.
- Search facilities by author, subject and date, as well as full text search capabilities.

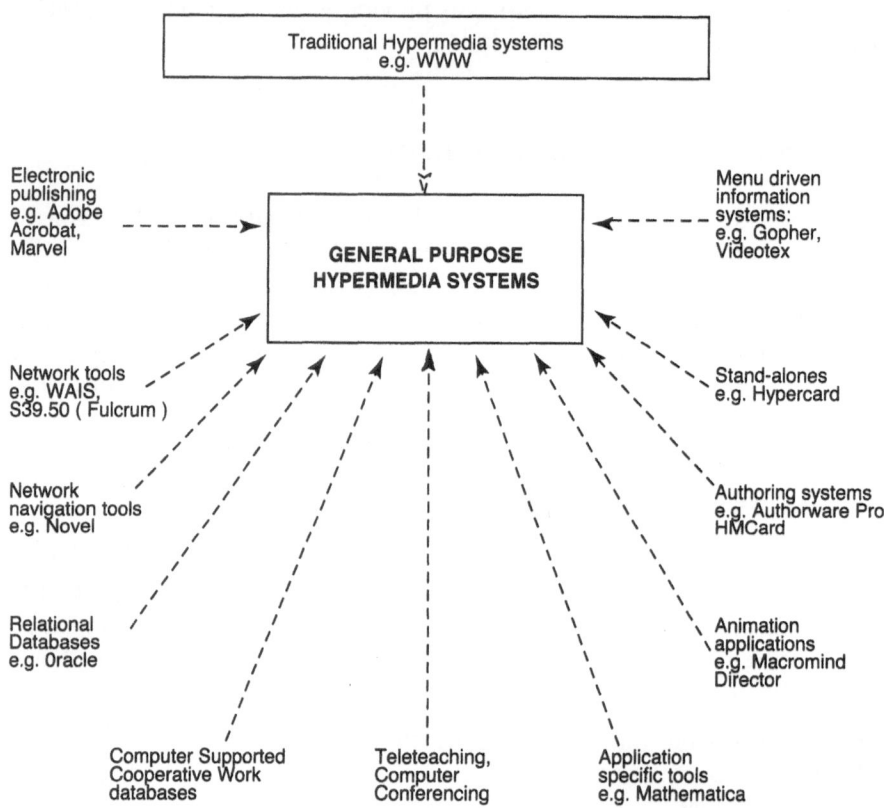

Fig. 4.3. General Purpose Hypermedia Systems

- Discussion groups.
- Sending messages among members of a discussion group.
- Easy overview of threads of a discussion – if possible a graphical representation of questions, answers, arguments, etc., similar to gIBIS (see Figure 4.4). The gIBIS project aims to help teams solve large "wicked" problems. Fundamentally it is "a conversation among the stakeholders (e.g., designers, customers, implementers) in which they bring their respective expertise and viewpoints to the resolution of design issues" [Conklin and Begeman, 1988].
- Users "subscribing" to discussion groups where discussion mail is automatically sent to the members' own specific mailboxes.
- Comprehensive boolean filtering for all incoming messages.

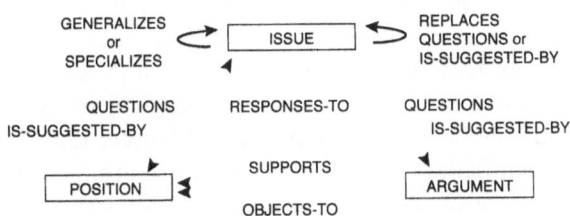

Fig. 4.4. The Set of Legal Rhetorical Moves in IBIS [Conklin and Begeman, 1988]

Certainly important progress on many of these requirements has been made at MIT with the Information Lens and Object Lens projects [Malone et al., 1987, Lai et al., 1988, Robinson, 1991] .

Another system addressing these issues is Hyperwave, described by Kappe in the paper cited above. For example, all electronic notices will be "time-stamped" when the notice is first entered. The system will generate a default expiry date, from the date of the event, but this may be over-ridden by the user. In addition to this the user will be asked to say what is to be done with the notice once the date has expired: delete the notice, or place it in a Past Events list to be maintained by the system. This list will be invaluable for compiling not only end-of-year reports but usage histories as well. Decisions must be made on how to maintain the Past Events list. After two years in the list, certain items may be archived – for fifteen years, or one hundred years?

4.5.2 Link Management

One solution to the problem of link management (see Section 4.4.2), which has been incorporated into Hyperwave (see Chapter 7), is to separate all links into a separate link database – there are no *embedded links*. This, together with the fact that links can be bi-directional, gives the following advantages:

- Data can be dynamically linked.
- There are no dangling links.
- Links can be maintained automatically.
- Overviews and navigation histories can be easily produced.

Yet another advantage is the provision of cross server-boundary links. This helps avoid the fragmenting of servers – or "Balkanization", to use the term coined by Ted Nelson [Nelson, 1987].

4.5.3 Imposing Structure

The unstructured and tangled nature of links in many Web systems is a source of frustration to users and administrators alike. As van Dam said, people "got linkitis" [van Dam, 1988]. There is certainly no significant data model for the Web, and in many ways first-generation systems may rightly be likened to novice programs that used too many GO TO statements. A case for developing hypermedia systems without links is made in [Maurer et al., 1994c].

System administrators should be able to implement systems which reflect the data's inherent structure. Hyperwave [Maurer, 1995b] organises data objects into clusters [Kappe et al., 1993], that are grouped into collections, which in turn may be grouped together in a pseudo-hierarchical manner. This gives us overlapping hierarchies as shown in a trivial example in Figure 4.5.

Hyperwave thus imposes structure on top of a flat file database. Most significantly, it provides users with an alternative to link browsing. Users navigate up and down hierarchies and thus can follow the inherent structures [Flohr, 1995].

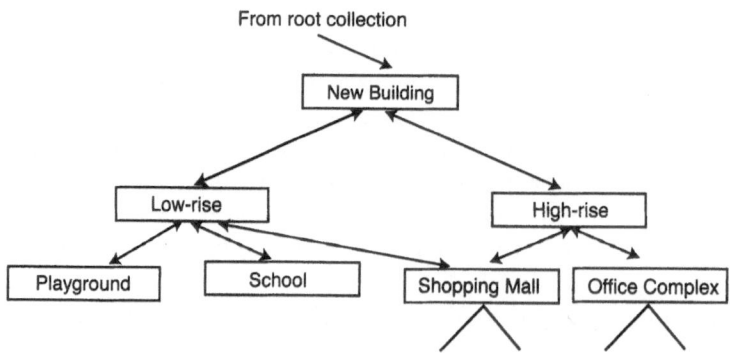

Fig. 4.5. Hyperwave Structure Showing Overlapping Hierarchies

4.5.4 Levels of Access

First and foremost in any system containing confidential data there must be certain tight levels of security – integrated with flexible access and update facilities. Several levels of user access have been recognised [Maurer and Flinn, 1994], and the four available in Hyperwave [Kappe et al., 1993] are as follows:

1. Identified mode where, subject to strict password control, the user has read and write access to data.
2. Semi-identified mode, which differs from 1 in that the users' names are known to the system but they may log on with a pseudonym and password. This allows a certain level of anonymity on mail items, etc.
3. Anonymously identified mode, giving read access but restricting write access to the user's private files.
4. Anonymous mode, giving read-only access.

Systems should monitor all types of user access, and the importance of the statistics obtained is difficult to overstate. For each type of user, programs must keep track of just what was done, when, and how often. This information can provide valuable feedback to database authors. If an author has little feedback on just how much their work is being referred to they will not be motivated to either contribute more to the system or to keep the existing work up to date. Feedback statistics are also important for helping maintain an error-free database. If, for example, statistics show that only the first fifteen pages of a sixteen-page report are ever read then something is wrong!

4.5.5 Java

Java [URLa2], developed by Sun Microsystems, is a language designed:

– To run on any type of computer,
– To have code that can be transferred electronically between computers,
– To support full graphics including animation.

The dominant use of Java so far is in the writing of *applets* which run when a Web page is accessed. A Java-enhanced browser downloads the applets as they are needed.

The applets can, among other things, animate images and receive input from users, thus adding a degree of interactivity to the formerly static Web.

Java itself is a fully Object Oriented language, similar to C++ but disallowing any direct pointer manipulation. This and other built-in security features are heavily promoted. However, it is a hotly debated point just how strong the security is – and only time will tell.

4.6 Aspects of Web Security

4.6.1 Motivation

Why the worry about security? Surely one aim of the Web is to unite the world into a global village, with shared interests and open communication? Only people with guilty or valuable secrets, like criminals, politicians and large corporations, want security on the Web! The complications of security processes would kill the pleasures of direct communication the Web has made possible.

The above paragraph probably represents the sentiments of many Web users. Really now, why should security be an issue on the Web, for the vast majority of users? There are four important reasons:

- Prevention of fraud. The Web is already being used as a medium of commerce. Fraud is a well-known risk; the pages of Risks Digest [URLq3] are full of fraudulent schemes on the Internet.
- Privacy is very important for some people, so there will always be a demand for the use of message secrecy in personal messages. It is becoming common for a public key (see below) to be included in an email signature (although one of the author's friends who does this admits that the key has only been used twice in five years). Apart from personal communications, there are some areas where everyone must agree that confidentiality is essential. For example, it would be very convenient if everyone's medical records were available on the Web so that immediate access, from anywhere in the world, was available for a doctor in an emergency. But this wider availability will not occur until a solution is reached to the problem of preserving privacy while allowing access to approved users.
- Protection from malice. Unfortunately there are people who write virus and worm programs (see [Hoffman, 1990] for a review of this field). Everyone is at risk from this activity, and it is becoming more common to exercise security precautions against this, just as home security increases as cities grow.
- Anonymity of access. At first sight, knowledge that an ordinary Web site is visited by an ordinary user would seem to be of little interest to anyone. But by tracking the sites visited by a user, it is possible to build up a profile of their interests and then exploit this information for marketing or other purposes. Tracing people who make payments electronically gives even more information. Is this an invasion of privacy or not? People who feel exploited by this use of information are interested in schemes for anonymous connections and anonymous payments (like electronic cash). Perhaps one day Web firms will have to offer incentives to get users to pay or access traceably, thereby paying the users themselves for their profile.

The rest of this section will discuss the issues of encryption (the only practical way of ensuring privacy on a large scale) and authentication (proving electronically that you really are who you claim to be). Authentication includes techniques for digital signatures, which provide ways of legally signing electronic documents. Anonymity and electronic cash require more exotic techniques such as blind signatures. All these issues are defined and discussed briefly below; there are many books devoted entirely to this subject, for example [Salomaa, 1990].

Finally, extra trouble for the user is not the only problem posed by security measures. Governments become concerned when their citizens communicate in ways which make it impossible for them to listen in, because then they cannot be sure that their laws are being obeyed. Tension between privacy on the one hand, and censorship and law enforcement on the other, has led to some interesting developments in the USA, which are discussed in Section 4.6.6.

4.6.2 Definitions

Encryption is the process of changing a message into an entirely different message (usually unintelligible), so that the original message can only be recovered by someone who has some special knowledge.

An *encryption algorithm* is a technique for encryption. It is customary to assume that the algorithm used for any encryption is public knowledge. In practice, secret algorithms have not remained secret for long.

Ciphertext is an encrypted message. Usually it is in the same alphabet and of the same size as the original, but appears to consist of random letters (or bits).

Decryption is the process of changing a ciphertext back into the original message. Sometimes the decryption algorithm is the same as the encryption algorithm.

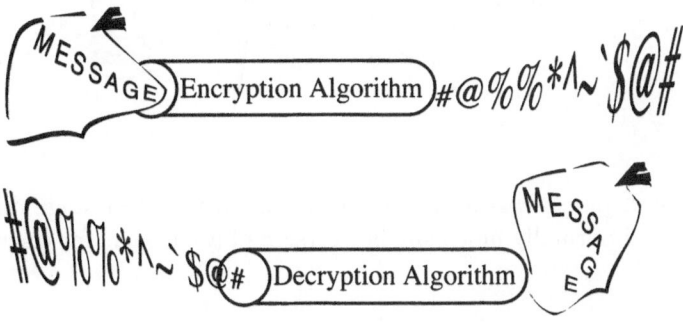

A *cryptosystem* is a combination of an encryption algorithm and its matching decryption algorithm.

A *key* is a variable item of data used in an encryption algorithm. The key used for messages exchanged between two people is normally constant for several exchanges. Any useful encryption algorithm must allow for sufficient variability in the key so that it is infeasible for an eavesdropper to conduct a computer search over all possible keys in order to find the right one (a *brute force attack*).

A *symmetric-key cryptosystem* is one which uses the same key for encryption and decryption. Usually this means that the decryption algorithm is the same as the encryption algorithm.

A *public-key cryptosystem* is one that is secure even when the encryption key is made public; only the decryption key needs to be kept secret. This is possible if it is computationally infeasible to deduce the decryption key from the encryption key (ie it would take many years on a large collection of the most powerful computers likely to be built in the near future).

A *secure hash function* is an algorithm for creating a "message digest", an encrypted and normally much smaller version of a message, for checking purposes.

A *MAC* (Message Authentication Code) is a "message digest" created by a secure hash function. Any changes in the message during transmission can be detected because the hash computed from the message by the receiver will not agree with the MAC sent with the message.

A *digital signature* is an attachment to a message which can be verified (by anyone) as being uniquely connected with that message, and having a unique signer; often the signature is an encryption of a MAC (see Figure 4.8). The signer must publicise the fact that they have some knowledge (e.g., that they possess the decryption key for a certain public-key cryptosystem), and it must be computationally infeasible for anyone other than the possessor of this knowledge to produce the signature. Copies of a signed message cannot be changed because this would invalidate the connection between the message and signature. Digital signatures are stronger than ordinary signatures (which can be forged and transferred from one message to another), but they have never been tested legally.

Digital authentication is a technique used by someone to prove electronically that they are the person they claim to be. Anyone wishing to use such a technique must first publicise widely their name and the fact that they have some secret knowledge. Digital signatures can be used for digital authentication; other techniques are sometimes used because digital signatures are computationally expensive to produce.

Blind signing is the process of attaching a signature to a document without knowing its contents (rather like a notary public). Usually the intention of the document's originator is to "unblind" the document after it is blind signed, in such a way that the signature is still valid but the document can be read.

Digital cash is an electronic message which can be passed from one person to another and which, if sent to a bank, will result in the bank transferring money into the sender's account. The bank must have withdrawn money from some other account when the digital cash was created, but there is no (computationally feasible) way of finding out the original account.

4.6.3 Overview of Cryptology

Cryptology has a fascinating history in the pre-computer era, full of spy and counter-spy stories (see, for example, [Kahn, 1967, Bauer, 1997]). It has been claimed that the British machine called Colossus, which was built to crack encrypted messages during the Second World War [Winterbotham, 1974], was the first computer.

The use of computers for cryptology for non-military, non-political purposes started in the late 1960s, when researchers at IBM used some proposals of Shannon [Shannon, 1949] to develop a cryptosystem for electronic data called Lucifer [Feistel, 1970, Feistel, 1973]. In 1973, the US National Bureau of Standards (NBS) became sufficiently convinced of the importance of encryption for the commercial traffic that it saw developing on the emerging networks, to call for proposals for the development of a standard encryption algorithm. The initial lack of interest showed that the Bureau was somewhat ahead of its time, but eventually the Lucifer system was developed into a symmetric-key cryptosystem known as the Digital Encryption Standard, or DES (see Section 4.6.4 for a description).

DES is widely used commercially by banks and for network security; however, it took some time to gain acceptance with the general public, partly because of the controversy surrounding the role of the US National Security Agency in the choice of the standard (for many years it was widely, and mistakenly, believed that DES had deliberate hidden weaknesses). However, wide use of standard (non-public-key) encryption methods such as DES is really only be feasible if there are a small number of organisations involved, and a large number of messages between any two of them, for two reasons:

- A key needs to be exchanged via a totally secure channel between the parties communicating, and it will have to be updated from time to time in case it is compromised. If the number of messages is small, it is simpler just to exchange the messages via the totally secure channel.
- If encrypted messages become the norm, then it will be impossible to communicate with anyone until a key is exchanged. Furthermore, if N people are communicating then in order to ensure secrecy for everyone, $N(N-1)/2$ keys will need to be exchanged. The business of rapid secret key generation and carrying could become very profitable! ("Brand-new keys made and delivered across the US in 10 hours! No proven security leaks in the last 2 years!")

Public-key Cryptosystems. The first step towards the public-key idea was taken in 1975 when Merkle proposed a method of publicising keys which gave a large computing advantage to the two parties involved in a particular exchange (unfortunately his paper [Merkle, 1978] was not published until 1978).

The idea of true public-key encryption was first developed in the much-quoted paper by Diffie and Hellman [Diffie and Hellman, 1977], in which they introduced the concept of a "trap-door one-way" function. A function is "one-way" if it is easy to compute but its inverse can be found only by solving a computationally hard problem; it is "trap-door" if its inverse can be found easily provided certain information is known. The secret key is this information, and it is known only to the inventor of the function.

Diffie and Hellman did not propose a specific trap-door one-way function in their paper, although they did demonstrate a way, based on their ideas, of secretly exchanging a standard symmetric encryption key over a public channel. The first working public-key encryption method was based on the knapsack problem [Merkle and Hellman, 1978]; it was cumbersome and was broken in [Brickell, 1984]. The next suggestion was made by Rivest, Shamir

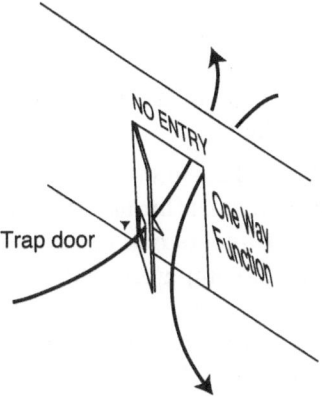

Fig. 4.6. One-way Trap-Door Function

and Adleman [Rivest et al., 1978]. Their method, now labelled RSA, is simple and looked extremely secure because it was closely related to the factorisation problem; an easy solution to this problem has not been found, despite the efforts of some of the best mathematicians during the last 350 years. While breaking RSA has never been proved to be the same problem as factorisation, no-one has found any way of attacking RSA more easily than by factorisation (despite much work over the last 20 years). In this paper [Rivest et al., 1978] the first working digital signature was also described.

The public-key idea, and the RSA algorithm, were patented in the USA, and a firm RSA Data Security Inc (RSADS) was set up to cope with the expected flood of applications of this new cryptosystem. Another expectation, in those days, was that many different public-key cryptosystems would soon be discovered. Neither expectation was realised; RSADS initially struggled for many years, as the general public proved to be just as uninterested in public-key cryptography as in traditional symmetric-key cryptography (note that RSA does involve much more computation than DES). However, success eventually arrived for RSADS; RSA is now used in a large number of applications, and is especially popular for digital signatures. On the other hand, the flood of public-key systems never eventuated; while a few more public-key systems were eventually proposed (many have been published in the proceedings of the annual Crypto conference, which have appeared in the Springer-Verlag Lecture Notes in Computer Science series since 1984), some of these have been broken and the remainder definitely involve more computation than RSA.

"Ordinary" encryption, using symmetric-key cryptosystems, has not been replaced by public-key encryption. Because even RSA does involve a lot of computation, message transfer using a public-key cryptosystem is too slow. It is now usual to use a person's public key to send them a key for a symmetric-key cryptosystem. Messages can then be exchange in secrecy using the fast symmetric-key algorithm. If the original message containing the symmetric key is signed, using the sender's private key, then both sides can be sure of the identity of the other (or at least, be sure that the other person holds the private key for a certain public key).

Encryption and the Web. The Internet was not designed initially to be secure; breaking into secure systems through the Internet became so common that the verb "to hack" is now understood to have this meaning even by those who know nothing else about computers. Even supposedly secure Defence sites have been "hacked" (see, for instance, what briefly replaced the US Central Intelligence Agency (CIA) web site in 1996 at [URLt3]). One security break, the Internet worm of 1988 [Hoffman, 1990] became world news and is still remembered by many people who have little to do with computers. This incident led to the formation of the CIAC (Computer Incident Advisory Capability), which provides security information free of charge within the USA.

The wish for privacy and freedom for the individual in the USA led to the creation of Web freeware called PGP (Pretty Good Privacy), which in 1991 made encryption tools available for everyone on the Web (see Section 4.6.6 for the resulting legal problems). Now cryptology is being used to make the basic Web software itself secure, with the addition of the SSL (Secure Sockets Layer) to Web clients and servers, and secure methods for electronic payments using cryptology tools are becoming commonplace [URLr3].

4.6.4 Encryption Algorithm Details

Mathematically, encryption is a one-to-one function from the set of possible messages to the set of ciphertexts, and decryption is the inverse of this function. Essentially all methods are based on the idea of breaking the message into components of the same size and encrypting each component. For example, a simple letter substitution cipher replaces each letter in the message by a different letter, determined by a "shuffled" alphabet as shown below, where the key is "thequickbrownfxjmpsvlazydg". Note that there are 26! ($> 10^{26}$) possible keys.

$$\text{attackatdawn} \quad \xrightarrow{\text{thequickbrownfxjmpsvlazydg}} \quad \text{tvvteotvqtzf}$$

Letter substitution ciphers are easy to break using the known frequency of occurrence of the components (although they may be safe in a situation where the component frequencies are unknown, such as computer data). The Playfair code, which was a simple-to-use extension of this idea using pairs of letters as the components, was somewhat safer, but still susceptible to frequency analysis. Better security was obtained by making the particular substitution used vary from component to component. For example, the Enigma machine used by the German armed forces during the Second World War effectively used up to 10 successive substitutions, and the shuffled alphabets changed with each letter being encrypted. The process was done in a machine, by wheels which contained the (fixed) shuffled alphabets; the key was the particular wheels used, their order and their initial settings.

Stream encryption. The Vernam cipher, which is (potentially) the most secure method possible, uses the same substitution idea. A message is turned into bits (e.g., the ASCII codes of its letters) and XORed with another stream of bits (the key). The decryption algorithm is the same as the encryption algorithm – the ciphertext is XORed with the same key (this works because (A XOR B) XOR B = A). This is the simplest possible substitution cipher; in this case the message components are single bits, and only two substitutions are possible:

$$0 \to 0, 1 \to 1 \quad \text{(identity)}$$

$$0 \to 1, 1 \to 0 \quad \text{(swap)}$$

The particular substitution which is used on any bit in the message depends on the corresponding bit in the key ($0 \Rightarrow$ identity, $1 \Rightarrow$ swap). If the key is a random stream of bits used only once (a *one-time pad*) this encryption method is provably unbreakable. In applications, often the key used is a repetition of a short key, or is the message itself offset by a short key. Frequency analysis will eventually break this weakened form, given large enough quantities of ciphertext and the relevant frequency knowledge.

The Vernam cipher is the most useful form of encryption for stream encrypting, i.e., for encrypting data arriving as a continuous stream of high volume; other methods would mean the stream would have to be batched, so a large amount of storage could be needed. For security, a continuous stream of random bits is needed, but the same stream must also be available at the receiving end. This requirement is becoming possible with the development of cryptographically strong random bit generators (for example, [Blum et al., 1986]). These are algorithms which will produce a stream of bits with the property that it is computationally infeasible to predict the next bit, no matter how many previous bits have been observed. However, the algorithm is deterministic, so if both sites start with the same initial data (the key) then they will both produce the same stream of bits. It appears that the RC4 algorithm (invented by Ron Rivest and a proprietary secret of RSADS – but see Section 4.6.6) is of this type, with a key size of up to 2048 bits.

DES Encryption. DES encryption uses both permutation and substitution repeatedly to thoroughly mix the message and the key. The message is broken into blocks of 64 bits, and the key is 64 bits long (but eight of these are parity bits). Each block first has its bits permuted according to a published table, then goes through 16 processes in each of which half of it is expanded (by duplicating some bits) and XORed with the expanded, permuted key, to give a 48-bit block. This is split into eight chunks of six bits each, then each chunk

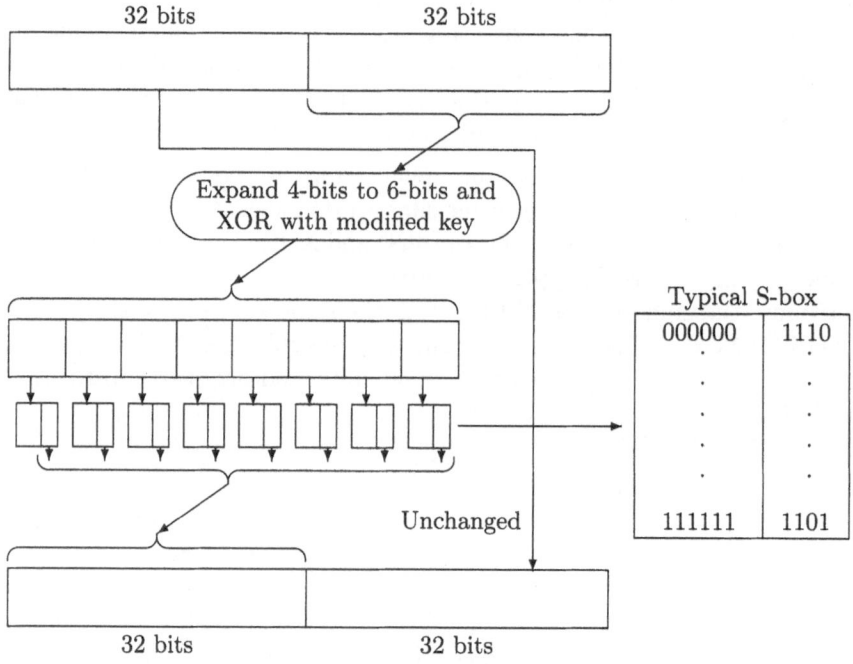

Fig. 4.7. Single DES Round

is substituted by a four-bit chunk defined by a published set of eight tables (the S-boxes). One of these 16 processes is illustrated in Figure 4.7; this does not show the process of key permutation and expansion, which involves more public tables and is different for each of the 16 steps. At the end of the process the reverse of the initial permutation is applied. The decryption process is exactly the same as encryption, except that the 16 key modifications are done in exactly the reverse order. The system is so non-linear and involves the key so intrinsically that there does not appear to be any quicker way of breaking this algorithm other than the brute-force searching of all possible keys (2^{56} – actually a bit less, by using symmetries in the algorithm).

The cost of a brute-force search was first estimated in [Diffie and Hellman, 1977]; the current cost must now be affordable to a number of large organisations, and double- and triple-encrypting is now common. Several other similar encryption algorithms have been proposed; one of the most successful is IDEA (International Data Encryption Algorithm), developed in Switzerland by Lai and Massey [Lai et al., 1991]. Like DES this works on 64 bits of the message at a time, but has a 128-bit key. It has been adopted as part of the PGP system (see Section 4.6.6).

RSA Encryption. Of the public-key encryption methods and signature schemes, only RSA will be described here. This system is based on the fact that, for any number N, there is a number $\varphi(N)$ (the Euler totient function for N), such that for every number B, relatively prime to N,

$$B^{\varphi(N)} \bmod N = 1 \qquad (4.1)$$

A person who wants to create an RSA key first finds two large (100+ digits) prime numbers p and q (there are fast ways of verifying if a number is a prime), and multiplies these together to form a number N. This is the public key, together with some small number e which is often set at 65537 (to avoid possible weaknesses, p, q, and e need to be chosen carefully). Note that finding p and q from N is computationally infeasible for N greater than 200 digits (and probably will remain so for many years).

A message M to be sent to the key creator is turned into binary, and divided into blocks B each of which has fewer bits than N. Each of these blocks is then raised to the e power mod N:

$$B' = B^e \bmod N \qquad (4.2)$$

The ciphertext is then the string of blocks B'.

Because the key creator knows p and q, he or she can find the Euler totient function $\varphi(N)$ which in this case is $lcm((p-1),(q-1))$ (where lcm is the least common multiple of the two numbers). Using this, they can calculate the (unique) number $d < N$ such that $ed \bmod \varphi(N) = 1$. The number d is the secret key. For every number $B < N$, if B is not divisible by p or q (the chance of this happening is astronomically small), we have $B^{ed} \bmod N = B$ since:

$$
\begin{aligned}
B^{ed} \bmod N &= B^{k\varphi(N)+1} \bmod N \quad \text{for some k} \\
&= (B^{\varphi(N)} \bmod N)^k (B \bmod N) \\
&= (1)^k (B) \quad \text{by equation 4.1 and } B < N \\
&= B \qquad\qquad\qquad\qquad (4.3)
\end{aligned}
$$

Hence if B' is one of the encrypted blocks then the original block B can be found because

$$B'^d \bmod N = B^{ed} \bmod N = B, \text{ by equations 4.2 and 4.3.}$$

A signature of a message is the encryption formed by using the number d instead of e in the normal encryption algorithm. Anyone can recover the original message by using e instead of d in the decryption algorithm. This works because:

$$B^{de} \bmod N = B^{ed} \bmod N = B, \text{ by equation 4.3.}$$

In practice, a publicly-known hash function is usually applied to the message first, to reduce its size to a single block (a message digest). A satisfactory hash function will ensure that if even a single bit of the message is changed, the

message digest will be entirely different. The signature is the message digest
encrypted with the sender's private key. The message is sent, together with
the signature. The receiver decrypts the signature and compares the result
with the message digest which they create from the received message (see
Figure 4.8). If these are identical, the receiver can be sure that the message
is unaltered and was sent by the possessor of the secret key matching the
public key used in decryption.

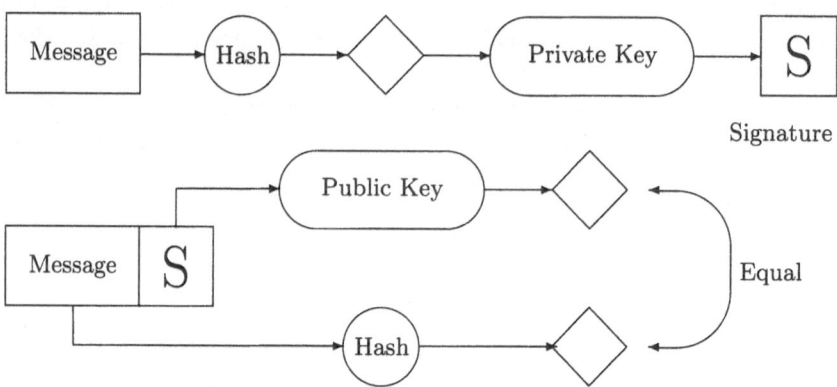

Fig. 4.8. Digital Signature

4.6.5 Protocols for Security

Security is not guaranteed by using a particular cryptosystem; the "security
protocol", i.e., the way in which it is used, is an essential ingredient. Some protocols, in fact, ensure security without any cryptographic components at all.
New protocols are being designed all the time (for example, [Lennon, 1993]),
but very few are actually adopted. The book by Schneier [Schneier, 1994] is
an excellent compendium of a large number of protocols. We now describe
some of the more important ones used or suggested for use with the Web.

Secure Sockets layer. This is a "low-level" security arrangement for communication, which is incorporated into recent versions of browser programs;
it interacts with both the TCP/IP protocol and the user interface program.
When a connection between two servers is first established, the SSL layers
agree on which cryptographic and compression algorithms to use and (optionally) use authentication algorithms to establish each others bona fides;
each server must have first been certified by a "certificate authority" (there
are now many of these available in the US). Then the servers use public-key
encryption techniques to exchange a key for a symmetric-key cryptosystem.
The messages between the servers (which are compressed) are secured against

tampering by a (cryptographically strong) MAC being sent with each message, or (if more security is needed) by being encrypted by the symmetric-key algorithm.

HTTP	Telnet	NNTP	FTP	SMTP	SHTTP	$\cdots$
SSL							
TCP/IP							

RIPEM (Privacy Enhanced Mail) and PGP (Pretty Good Privacy).
Both of these are protocols which allow encrypted email to be exchanged.
RIPEM was developed by Mark Riordan and uses RSA public-key encryption in order to exchange DES keys between the participants; the mail is then encrypted using these DES keys. PGP was developed by Philip Zimmermann, and uses RSA in order to exchange IDEA keys. People who wish to use these services include information in their email signature, including their public key, so that those who also use the service can set up a session. For more information on RIPEM, see [URLw3]. PGP appears to be considerably more popular than RIPEM, possibly because of the controversy stirred up by the fact that its legality was unclear for a long time (see Section 4.6.6). There are currently two sources for PGP: [URLx3] within the US and Canada, and [URLy3] outside.

Electronic Payment. The current system of credit and debit cards make electronic transfer of money over the Web easy. However, security issues such as authentication and privacy need to be looked at very carefully. In the past, no security was in place and credit card numbers were transmitted "in clear", with no attempt at authentication. Numerous protocols have now been set up for security purposes, using encryption for the concealment of numbers and, in a few places, signature schemes for authentication. The situation is evolving rapidly and, at the time of writing, it is unclear what methods will become widely accepted; for a list of current payment protocols, see [URLz3].

Digital Cash. One disadvantage which credit card charges have is that they are not anonymous; buyers must identify themselves to the bank, at least, in order to make purchases. A method for obtaining electronically the anonymity provided by cash has been proposed by Chaum [Chaum et al., 1988]. In essence the protocol goes as follows:

– By negotiation with a bank, the buyer obtains a message called an "electronic coin", which states the bank and the value of the coin, and is signed by the bank, making it unforgeable and unalterable. The coin will have a number hidden in it, using a one-way function, which the buyer knows but the bank does not, and the bank blind-signs this part of the coin. The amount of the coin's value will be withdrawn from the buyer's account.

– When making a purchase, the buyer sends the coin and the number to the seller. The seller can check that the bank's signature is valid and that the number given really is hidden in the coin by the one-way function (so the coin must have originated with the buyer – this makes digital cash difficult to steal).

– The seller then sends the details to the bank, which checks to see if that number has been presented before (the bank must keep a list of all numbers presented – this will mean that electronic coins must have expiry dates). If not, then the bank will credit the seller with the value of the coin.

Note that, because the bank blind-signed the number hidden in the coin, it cannot determine who originally purchased the coin; the buyer is completely anonymous. Note too that if the buyer uses the same electronic coin twice, the bank will not honour it the second time. Sellers need to check with the bank before completing the transaction, or risk finding themselves with the electronic equivalent of a dishonoured cheque.

Extensions of this protocol have been proposed in which the seller also remains anonymous, the coin can be subdivided, and any attempt to use a coin more than once will identify the coin purchaser. The firm DigiCash [URLb3] has developed a system for the Web – the first bank to make use of this appears to be the Mark Twain Bank in St Louis, Missouri [URLc3].

Remailers. Remailers are used to enable untraceable message sending. A remailer receives messages which are encrypted in its public key. It decrypts these messages and follows the instructions inside, which are typically "Delay for time <delay> then forward the attached message to <somewhere>", and the attached message is encrypted in the requested destination's public key. This will mean the messages bounce around from one remailer to another until eventually the "real" message is sent to its final destination. If there are enough remailers and enough messages, then traffic analysis will be impossible and no-one will be able to find who is sending messages to whom. Many of these remailers are operating currently; see the Web for current information (which seems to be changing constantly).

This protocol has a major drawback in that it increases the traffic on the Web as a message is bounced between remailers – each message would, in effect, be sent many times. If it becomes commonplace, the extra load on the Web will become significant. Perhaps this protocol may be acceptable when we have unlimited network capacity (predictions that this will occur Real Soon Now have been made for some years), but for the present the gain in individual privacy seems contrary to public interest.

Childproof Digital Containers. It has been proposed that "adults only" sites on Web be made accessible only to those who are certified as adults.

Unfortunately a method for identifying adults electronically has not yet been found, so the certification process would have to be by personal (or at least voice) contact. This non-electronic component takes the protocol outside what is normally regarded as electronic security. The only electronic solutions which have been proposed for this problem are outlined in Section 4.4.6.

4.6.6 Legal Issues

Banks use encryption techniques widely in EFTPOS terminals and Automated Teller Machines. The international bank network for funds transfer, SWIFT, which routinely handles single transactions of hundreds of millions of dollars, uses RSA encryption. However, many governments have restrictions on the use of cryptography by individuals or firms other than banks; in fact it is illegal to use encryption for non-banking purposes within a number of countries (in 1996 this included France, Russia, Iran, and Iraq). The situation is changing all the time; for example, it is rumoured that at one time Germany had a law stating that any communication over the phone lines had to be in one of 100 approved languages (getting fax machines to convert pictures to verbal descriptions would be a real challenge). Exporting, or importing, cryptographic material, such as software, is illegal in a number of countries, including electronic transfer of the software to or from a site in another country. There are two important reasons for these restrictions, even in countries regarded as "free":

- Cryptography is defined as a "dual-use" technology; it can be used either for commerce or for acts of war and terrorism (dual-use goods include some types of fertiliser).
- Wire-tapping is a major weapon against crime in some countries.

In 1995, an agreement (the "Wassenaar Arrangement on Export Controls for Conventional Arms and Dual-Use Goods and Technologies") between 31 countries (most major Western countries plus Russia and some developed Asian countries) was reached, which allowed the export of mass-market cryptographic software to some countries, but maintained restrictions on its export to countries regarded as "terrorist-friendly". However, some of the parties to this agreement maintained their existing, more restrictive, export controls. In particular, the relevant Unites States regulations, called ITAR (International Traffic in Arms Regulations) [Hoffman, 1995], forbid the export of cryptographic software (except to banks and US enterprises) with strong keys. Until late 1996 the allowed key-length limit was 40 bits, but currently the limit is 64 bits for DES and 768 bits for RSA, with the proviso that the key will be held by an "escrow agent" when these are set up. Control over the export of cryptographic software has now been removed from the State department and given to the Commerce department; future developments will be watched with interest.

Another difficulty is that RSA is patented within the US (but not outside it) so cannot be used legally without a licence from RSA Data Security Inc. Furthermore, IDEA is patented in a number of countries (including the US and much of Europe) and also needs a licence in these countries. As PGP software was developed and distributed as freeware without the benefit of any licences, and quickly became widely used outside the USA (with full-strength RSA keys), its legal status was definitely dubious. For more than two years, its chief originator, Philip Zimmermann, was under investigation for breaching the ITAR. The case was dropped in early 1996 without any charges being laid. Also, an arrangement was reached with RSADS and Ascom Systec (the licensors of IDEA) whereby use of PGP freeware for personal, non-commercial purposes is now totally legal, provided those within the US and Canada use the USA version [URLx3] and those outside use the International version [URLy3]. Both versions are completely compatible with each other and both allow the use of keys of up to 2048 bits. In 1996, a company called PGP Inc. was formed by Philip Zimmermann; the impact of this development on the Web remains to be seen.

In a parallel development, software (source code in C) claiming to be the proprietary stream cipher RC4 appeared in a newsgroup in early 1995. Tests against a valid copy of RC4 indicate that it acts identically. RSADS have not stated whether it really is RC4 or not. Study of the code shows that a stream of random bits is generated rapidly in a cryptographically strong way, and the stream is used in a Vernam cipher. The publication was anonymous; it will be interesting to know what the full story is, if it ever appears.

The difficulties for legal wiretapping, resulting from the possible use of encryption on telephones have caused various governments to attempt to restrict the free use of encryption. Internationally, there appears to be widespread government interest in the mandatory use of "trusted third parties", or escrow agents, to hold encryption keys. In 1995, for example, Belgium passed a law which appears to prohibit the use of encryption over the telephone line unless the keys are held by an approved agency, although the law was not being enforced at the time of writing. The moves within the US in this direction can best be described as the "Clipper Saga".

The Clipper Chip In 1993, a US government-approved computer chip (the Clipper chip), incorporating an encryption algorithm called SKIPJACK, was proposed in the United States. The chip could be used for encrypting telephone conversations. The full specification of the SKIPJACK algorithm has never been revealed, but every transmitted message contained a LEAF (Law Enforcement Access Field) which identified the chip used. The key for each chip would be split into two parts and each would be held by a government agency, NIST (National Institute of Standards and Technology – the successor to the NBS) and a branch of the Treasury. A court could order the agencies to reveal their key parts and a law enforcement agency could use these to decrypt recordings of messages (or possibly messages as they were being transmitted). No restriction was proposed on other forms of encryption; whether it was intended to eventually bring restrictions in, or whether it was believed market forces would ensure that only Clipper chips would be used (the cost was going to be very small), was not clear. The majority of security professionals in the US opposed the scheme as being unworkable, and in 1995 a revised proposal was announced in which the use of commercial escrow agencies was allowed. In 1996 another proposal was made in which a Key Management Infrastructure (KMI) would be set up, in conjunction with overseas countries, incorporating key escrow. Participation in the KMI would be voluntary (except that it would be mandatory for exported encryption software), and there would be a free choice of encryption algorithms. Law enforcement agencies could order escrow agencies to surrender keys. At present only proposals have been made; again, future developments will be watched with interest.

4.7 Afterword

The widespread use of fully-fledged hypermedia systems is revolutionising life, work, and learning. We hope to see the computer continue its evolution from a simple-minded tool to a cooperative agent that can help us manage the mega-quantities of data already available on the Internet.

5. Hypermedia Systems: Their Application to Life, Work, and Learning

5.1 Introduction

In Chapter 4 we discussed how the merging of multimedia and networking technologies has led to the spread of global hypermedia systems. In this chapter we discuss how the convergence of computer-based digital technology, analog technology (such as film, video, etc.), and networking could revolutionise our:

- Everyday lives (see Section 5.4)
- Work (see Section 5.5)
- Lifelong learning (see Section 5.6)

The boundaries of these rather arbitrarily defined aspects of life, already blurred, will overlap increasingly as hypermedia systems expand. One thing is certain: the impact will be tremendous and probably irresistible.

5.2 Converging Technology

Analog and digital technology is converging at a tremendous rate, and we cannot predict what the long term result will be if it all comes under a networking umbrella. As an example of the difficulty of predicting future trends, consider the conflicting growth in the marketplace of CD-I (interactive CD) and CD-ROM (computer disc) technology. Since CD-I was standardised back in 1986, it is of lower resolution and its access time was at least four times

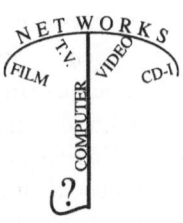

slower. CD-ROM also supports more diversity. However, because CD-I technology was "packaged" together with existing, easy-to-use, home-consumer items (including music CDs), it initially gained a significant proportion of the consumer market.

Certainly, much important material is already available today only on CD-ROM. Currently, one CD-ROM disk can contain about 600 million bytes of data – as much as 300,000 pages of text. Drawings and colour photos can of course also be included, and all this information can then be accessed in a wide variety of ways. We note with interest that IBM has demonstrated optical disk technology that could produce disks with about 6.5 billion bytes of data by storing up to ten layers on a single disk. And if this is coupled with new "blue laser" technology it is theoretically possible to put several thousand 200-page books on one CD.

As Maurer states, "Due to the speed/cost limitations of the Internet some of the more advanced multimedia applications will first be available on a CD basis, rather than via Internet (publications such as 'From Alice to Ocean' or sophisticated games like 'Myst', 'The 7th Guest' or 'Space Quest V' are typical examples)." [Maurer, 1994b].

5.3 Computer Animation and Simulation

Instead of static pictures, or recorded views of moving objects, it is now possible to generate and animate complex graphical objects in real time. In this section we discuss the related applications of animation, modelling, simulation, and *virtual reality* so that we can refer to them in later sections.

5.3.1 Virtual Reality

The real thrust of virtual reality research is not really in the gimmicks like space helmets and data gloves (exciting as they may be to use), but is in modelling. As we will see in Section 5.3.2, we already have both two and three dimensional animated data-modelling programs. Virtual reality enables investigators to interactively explore three-dimensional models. Whether we model a human heart, a museum, a city, or a planet (either actual or imaginary) this involves basic virtual reality research. We are also very close to being able to model complete interactive environments.

Some of the most challenging research in this area is undoubtedly the work on modelling human figures, such as that achieved at the University of Geneva's MIRALab [Magnenat-Thalmann and Thalmann, 1991b, Magnenat-Thalmann and Thalmann, 1991a, Paouri et al., 1991]. The human eye is certainly amazing at noting even minuscule imperfections in human anatomy! But we are close to succeeding even here. It is interesting to note that this work was, to a considerable extent, encouraged by funding from the textile industry. Many of the problems associated with producing lifelike movements of human figures arise from the complex movement of the clothing covering the models, and this in turn depends on the type of cloth. All this is, of course, of great interest to the textile industry since the way that garments move needs to be discovered before, not after, costly mistakes are made.

One outstanding project is worth mentioning here: the Athena project developed at Massachusetts Institute of Technology [Murray and Malone, 1992]. This includes a total immersion learning environment for teaching French – a virtual French world. Students can walk through the streets and buildings of Paris with full-scale video on one screen while they interact with the plot via a computer display of maps and dialogue boxes. They have the options of dictionary searches, phrase by phrase replay, and even sterile Language Lab French if they require it.

As an indication of the scope of current virtual reality research we conclude this section with a quotation by Nadia Magnenat-Thalmann: "What researchers try to do is recreate autonomous life by giving the computer all the know-how, or appropriate physical and behavioural models. In this case, we, as real humans, will be able to speak to virtual actors. With them, we will be able to interact and exchange information. They will learn from us as we will learn from them. This is the research's challenge for the coming years" [Magnenat-Thalmann, 1994].

5.3.2 Data Visualisation Tools

Physical scientists and mathematicians have traditionally made considerable use of graphs and diagrams, but now with computer support the field can be further extended [Domik, 1993]. Programs are now available enabling scientists to visualise: the "greenhouse effect", quantum tunnelling, brain tumours [Computer, 1989], the dynamics of the atmosphere, bioelectric fields, stresses and strains, 3-D fluid flow fields, and robotic surgery [IEEE, 1993] – to name just a few. A great deal of work has already been done to enable hyper-dimensional problems to be visualised [Maurer, 1992b], [Hanson and Heng, 1992].

The Human-Computer Interaction Laboratory at the University of Maryland has developed many innovative projects involving data visualisation – projects ranging from the visualisation of nested directories [Johnson and Shneiderman, 1993] to interactive programs that enable users to select their own ideal piece of real estate [Williamson and Shneiderman, 1993]. In the introduction to "Information Visualisation: Dynamic Queries, Treemaps, and the Filter/flow metaphor" [Shneiderman, 1993c], the author states: "Our eyes can carry a hundred times more information to the brain than our ears. Adding user-controlled animation can further increase comprehension. The world of the future will be more like driving or flying a plane through colourful three (or four) dimensional information spaces. Users will rapidly select, combine, eliminate and construct new displays."

Dynamic queries enable a user to control animated displays and filter the data by using graphical sliders as well as menu options, graphical buttons, text, etc. Programs such as these provide a powerful medium for showing trends – as exemplified by the dramatic animation of an influenza virus spreading across Europe. Of particular note is the project "Dynamic Queries on a Health Statistics Atlas" or "Dynamaps". Pages and pages of indigestible numeric medical data form the database for the program, which displays the information graphically by:

– Geographic region
– Year
– Sex
– Education level
– Smoker/non-smoker

Startling correlations can be demonstrated, such as between education levels and deaths by cervical cancer. Shneiderman concludes that exploring data interactively lets researchers see correlations by looking at patterns, and find scientific insights that can be demonstrated in a convincing manner.

5.3.3 Process Visualisation Tools

Animated diagrams provide a most effective way of showing many processes, whether in commerce, medicine or the physical sciences. New authoring tools can be used to good effect. In the field of computer algorithm visualisation, there are systems such as Balsa [Brown, 1988], Tango [Stasko, 1990], and XTango [Badre et al., 1992] that use graphical facilities to show how a program works. There has been doubt cast on just how much these aids really do enhance a student's understanding of any particular process, but it is certain that the tools can be of considerable help in debugging and optimising programs.

5.3.4 Simulation

Simulation is a widely used tool for exploring scenarios whose evolution is too complex to model in other ways. Data visualisation techniques can be used in conjunction with simulations to aid immensely in understanding the processes which are occurring. For example, watching simulated traffic patterns can help in locating bottlenecks, and in finding solutions. Powerful simulations with visualisation have also been developed for attempting to predict tornadoes and fire paths.

Visualised simulations can be an extremely helpful teaching and learning tool. With Apple Macintosh's Cocoa application, a program designed specifically for use by children, learners can readily create simulations ranging from ant feeding patterns to fish breeding [URLp3].

Because there is usually no second chance in the field of operative medicine, much research is directed at obtaining good medical simulations. Many sophisticated modelling programs already exist. We have seen one that simulates brain slices, in any direction, using high-quality scans. The fact that even surgical computer "games" exist must give us pause for thought.

5.4 The Impact of Hypermedia on the Way We Live

In technologically sophisticated societies, information on the Web assists many people in their day to day activities: choice of restaurant (taking into account parking), purchase of music, books, clothes, and so on. In this section we look at a few of the more novel uses of hypermedia systems.

5.4.1 Virtual Experiences as Preparation for the Real Thing

There is little doubt that hypermedia at its best can provide very valuable services when it is used as preparation for real experience. Already training applications for pilots and doctors are widely used. However, there are also other exciting options:

- Training for recreation, including parachuting or even bungee jumping
- Previews of art and museum exhibitions
- Films and shows
- Tours of cities, buildings, and wineries
- Travel (see Section 5.4.4)
- Practice in driving on the other side of the road – to be available to airline passengers on international flights.
- Universal driver training in the handling of emergencies such as skids and impending collisions. The need for this is so great that it might well become compulsory as soon as it is developed!

5.4.2 Electronic Market Places

Networks such as the Web are already providing fascinating worldwide marketplaces. Books [URLj1], music, software, and flowers can all be ordered using credit cards, although security concerns still remain a barrier to many prospective customers (see Section 4.6). However, an enormous range of shareware is available, particularly software. Also, a number of sites provide pictures, even if frequently in low resolution, for viewers to use as they wish free of charge [URLk1, URLl1, URLm1]. Providing such information on the Web, often referred to as electronic publishing, is discussed in more detail in Chapter 9.

5.4.3 Teleshopping

Many teleshopping projects, small and large, already exist. They range from simple extensions to the local supermarket, to large trials by Time-Warner and NTT in Japan.

Shopping via videophones is certain to be a growth area. Besides conversing with remote shop assistants, buyers will be able to obtain a wealth of valuable background information about items they are interested in from the computer database.

Casino complexes may pioneer this application. Once hotel rooms are linked with video connections to stores, and supported by multimedia databases, the possibilities are endless [Maurer, 1995a]. If, for example, you are interested in purchasing a model of a Maori war canoe, you can discuss the options with the salesperson while viewing them in 3D on your screen. A selected carving will appear to be much more valuable, in both monetary and aesthetic terms, once you have accessed information on the name of the carver, the type of wood, historical information of the tribe that used such canoes, and so on. Also, for fine workmanship you may appreciate being able to zoom in to high-resolution photographs of the work – and perhaps purchase high-quality colour printouts of various views of the 3D model.

5.4.4 Public Information Systems

Although we still occasionally see public information systems of the shake-the-fist-and-walk-away type, we are also seeing many more highly successful ones. Information displays, widely used at airports and on street corners, give users touch screen options for locating a wide variety of services such as hotels, taxis, and rental car firms. At railway stations wall-sized maps of train connections let the traveller, using touch screen options, build up and print out their own itineraries – complete with connection times and costs.

Information displays can be made available at public kiosks, in entrance halls, and information centres such as those provided by any large institution, such as a National Tourist Board.

It would be possible for information bureaus to act as servers for whole networks of kiosks. Besides supplying a wealth of publicity, information bureaus will be able to provide specialist information as diverse as sports therapy programs and regionally specific horticultural material.

Personal querying of databases, leading to making one's own decisions, are spreading into fields now normally in the hands of professionals. As airline flight information becomes more widely accessible via the Web, increasing numbers of travellers are compiling their own itineraries, making decisions such as how early is "too early" and how much risk to take in shortening connection times. Of course, we would prefer to also do the actual bookings ourselves, not to speak of bypassing all the red tape at the airport with a simple swipe of a general purpose chip-controlled credit card.

Some facilities becoming available are of science fiction character and quality. Interactive maps based on Global Positioning Systems data are being developed by several major car companies. All new Porsches, for example, have them installed. A "back seat driver" system using local radio transmission stations, developed at MIT, give voice commands such as "Turn left" or "Oops, you missed" as well as driver education hints such as "Isn't it time you changed back to the cruising lane!" Once a significant proportion of cars have such displays, information from traffic control vehicles can be directly integrated into traffic flow diagrams and drivers can have alternative routes automatically displayed.

The Images of Austria project [Maurer et al., 1994e] and the A.E.I.O.U. [Maurer, 1994a], [URLk3] projects are noteworthy examples of large public information systems. Many aspects of Austria (stored in a 50 GB database) are available as a series of CD-ROMs, public kiosk applications, and a multi-platform presentation via the Internet [Maurer, 1994a]. It includes a database of Austrian culture, a collection of maps, a world atlas with over 2000 pictures, an Archive of Scientific Movies, a collection of Special Topics, a presentation of the National Library, and a collection of 400 video clips [Maurer, 1994a]. The *Handbook of Austrian Music* contains excerpts of most famous Austrian composers up to the present day and includes music, scores, and descriptions.

5.4.5 Disseminating Topical Information

Audio clips of new tape and CD releases are already available on the Web. Once previews of films, shows and concerts are widely available in the form of multimedia clips, people will look back on the ways we currently choose our entertainment as like buying a pig in a poke.

5.4.6 Help Lines

Virtual communities on the Web first evolved from Unix, PC, Macintosh, and other computer-based user groups. We are now seeing valuable networks for people involved in other fields, ranging from health issues to victim support. Once groups such as these are integrated with existing medical systems, we foresee radical changes in all areas of community health care. For example, pacemaker signals may be directly routed to emergency care facilities in the event of an emergency.

Once a significant proportion of personal computers have microphones, or better still video input, we shall see further improvements. Emergency calls can be sorted and routed directly to police, fire, civil defence, or medical departments. Since all time and place details will be automatically included, the problem of human error in emergency situations can be greatly reduced. In addition, with video surveillance a human may not even need to initiate the call!

As an example, consider the benefits of having an integrated hypermedia system in a civil emergency. Army, air force, police, fire, and civil defence may all be involved, and for coordinated efforts they need interactive access to all relevant and up-to-date data.

Once we start thinking globally about help information systems we can look forward to their support in all areas of life, from critical repair work on space or atomic power stations, to helping a new user discover a useful shortcut in a word-processing package.

The effectiveness, and use, of all types of help systems will undoubtedly be greatly enhanced once they are integrated with electronic personal assistants such as those we describe in Chapter 14.

5.4.7 Leisure Activities

Hypermedia has been used for leisure activities many years now, at least if you count computer games such as Myst. Another hotly pursued development, video-on-demand, also belongs in this category. Virtual reality games in your own home are being touted as "coming real soon now". A survey of current hypermedia development for leisure activities would thus be voluminous and out of date immediately.

A wealth of interesting possibilities for future interactive hypermedia developments is described in "Hypermedia in a Gambling Casino Setting" [Maurer, 1995a]. Although the paper is, as the title suggests, directed towards gambling applications, most of the examples given are applicable to any LAN supporting high-end graphical workstations. The paper discusses, among other topics:

- Video-on-demand services
- Video telephony
- Interactive telewatching [Qualtrough and Schneider, 1994]. Clients will be able to view live video of certain areas, such as swimming pools or bars, to help them decide whether it is a good time to participate in leisure activities. In the gambling scenario, clients will be able to view actual gambling tables and make off-table bets from their own rooms.

Like it or not, the entertainment industry is the driving force behind many of the changes we are describing. In Chapter 13 we describe techniques that significantly extend the usual definition of an "interactive movie", and to illustrate the wide applicability of the new technology the paper gives examples for the ballet and orchestra enthusiast, the reader of great literature, the surgeon, and students of medicine, geography, and history.

The impact of commercial interactive movie technology should not be underestimated – it will invade work, leisure, and learning.

5.5 The Impact of Hypermedia on the Way We Work

The impact of email and the Internet, as discussed in Sections 3.4.1 and 4.5.1, is already changing the way a great deal of business is transacted. Hypermedia systems with well designed graphical user interfaces can enhance many aspects of work, including:

- Computer supported collaborative work (CSCW) (see Section 10.2.4)
- Electronic publishing (see Sections 5.5.1 and 9.3)
- Electronic commerce (see Sections 5.5.2 and 5.4.3)
- Business administration (see Section 5.5.3)
- Contract preparation (see Section 10.2.7)
- Computer conferencing (see Section 10.2.5)
- Meeting organisation (see Sections 10.2.8 and 10.2.6)
- Publicity (see Section 5.5.5)

Should the interface consist of pages and pages of numbers or just a few well chosen graphical representations? What about static pictures or dynamic graphs that reflect changes? Should the interface be two dimensional or three dimensional? The choices are many. Reports, sales catalogues, schedules, and timetables, can all be produced, checked, annotated, and distributed electronically.

5.5.1 Electronic Publishing

The important topic of electronic publishing on the Web is covered in Chapter 9. There are, however, other options for electronic publishing besides the Web. Consider the possibilities that may be created if material is transmitted in digital form using radio bandwidths – possibly in the "dead" hours of the night. PCs, with only the addition of inexpensive capture boards, will be able to download material much more cheaply, quickly, and reliably than is currently possible on the Internet. They will also be free of the tie to physical networks. This option is one that must be considered seriously for distance learning programs.

Other options gaining popularity are "broadcasting" and "multicasting", either over LANs or the Internet. Although Internet traffic is usually on a one-to-one basis, material can alternatively be transmitted on a one to many basis (broadcasting) or, as with MBone [Eriksson, 1994], on a one-to-select-group basis (multicasting). MBone is currently a very popular method for distributing multimedia on topical subjects such as space flights, natural disasters (e.g., volcanic eruptions), conferences, or software demonstrations.

5.5.2 Electronic Commerce

Electronic Document Interchange (EDI) is being used for a growing number of national and international business transactions. Although it is really just formalised email, legally binding electronic documents can be created by using digital signatures as discussed in Section 4.6.

Provision of Web services is becoming a major market. Some firms can provide services such as complete support for EDI and Electronic Funds Transfer (EFT) [URLg2]. They also provide Web presence and data management for large and small firms. They can manage parcel distribution and custom clearance. There may be no set-up charge but a small percentage is taken from all transactions.

New techniques are being developed to enable complex business interrelations to be comprehended. One successful application produces a simulation of the state of the stock market. In a virtual reality setting the viewer can navigate through landscapes reflecting the state of stock by using geometrical representations. While the user is investigating areas of personal interest the system will note other relevant changes.

5.5.3 Business Administration

Many operations are characteristic of any large corporation: maintenance of personnel files, payroll systems, stock control, and forecasting. A well designed database system with a good human interface can today be regarded as essential.

Traditionally, offices have tended to simply computerise existing processes. However, there is a broader view of workflow as more than mere process automation [McQueen, 1993]. New workflow tools are being developed that include such important aspects of administration as negotiation techniques and customer satisfaction [Medina-Mora et al., 1992]. Since students can be regarded as customers, universities should benefit from these new programs as much as businesses will.

As businesses amalgamate, nationally and internationally, networks are being used increasingly to coordinate operations. For example, the International Maritime Satellite Organisation is a cooperative involving about seventy nations. Their satellites, built by an international consortium, are launched by US and French companies using Russian rockets.

5.5.4 Supporting the "Culture" of Organisations

In this vital area of any organisation the problem is not so much how to distribute and collect such things as forms and notices, but how to keep control over them. All too often in today's systems, expired notices are littered amongst the current ones. However, using techniques described in Section 4.5.1, information can be accessed and managed more intelligently. Notices, for example, will be arranged by certain criteria and keywords such as training programs, conferences, public lectures, open days, and block bookings for theatrical events (both music and drama), to name but a few.

Company esprit de corps will be enhanced when "virtual common rooms" contain information such as bulletin boards, photos, best performance awards, and names of past innovators.

In university and school settings, graduation events will take on a new dimension when photos of the graduands in their regalia are archived along with statistical information. They can be presented to each graduate immediately after the ceremony as a memento!

Besides accessing information on the Web, employees will use LANs to run all types of bulletin boards, displaying club information, accommodation listings, sporting calendars, and virtual "flea markets" of second-hand goods including books (both physical and electronic). In all these areas there will be the question of whether or not outside commercial interests should be allowed to place paid advertisements, and if so what control there should be to prevent abuse. As discussed in Section 9.5.1, new forms of advertising may emerge. Advertisements can be targeted much more readily within WANs; and local sponsors, such as those described for sponsoring journals in Section 9.10, can be provided for a wide variety of local services.

As to interpersonal life, workers will be able to keep in contact with friends across the world. Telepresence may be the next best thing to telepathy!

5.5.5 Publicity

Good publicity, both local and international, is obviously critical for the success of any enterprise. Every time a new media channel (billboards, radio, TV) has opened this century, firms have competed vigorously for attention in it. Advertising on the Web is in its infancy and it is not yet clear how publicity is best obtained on it. Whatever the Web equivalent of billboards, home pages are well established, and some businesses have discovered that an outstanding home page can be a significant lure for customers. Even non-commercial organisations like universities and government departments are finding that an attractive home page can have benefits outweighing any cost of creating it. Like exotic flowers, colourful home pages with clever animated displays are sprouting in all sorts of unlikely places.

Many highly sophisticated mail ordering systems, with attractive graphical interfaces, already exist. Countless small businesses have their own Web sites with reply forms included. As suppliers, we shall be able to finely target small markets. Consumers, by simply sending their own electronic "intelligent agents" [Communications, 1994b] through the Net, will command and receive personalised service – possibly to the level of receiving individualised products such as designer jeans with the wearer's own emblem emblazoned on them!

For organisations with large sites, such as universities, orientation displays such as the one produced by the University of Auckland, New Zealand [Hypermedia Unit, 1994], provide information about the site in a form easily understood by all visitors. For the benefit of overseas users, a world map picturing New Zealand can be "opened up" to show Auckland and the location of the University. When users select the University icon they are presented with a large-scale map of the campus that they can "walk through" or "fly through" and zoom into any part of. Here they can orient themselves and then locate any facility, whether a carpark, a lecture theatre or an individual office. Selecting any feature will bring up more detail. Experienced users can bypass any of the above steps and, by using powerful query options, directly access specific information such as lecture times, room numbers, and telephone numbers.

5.5.6 User Management of Data

Keeping accurate lists of addresses or telephone numbers is a notoriously difficult task even for small organisations. Imagine the headache for universities, which must be able to send letters to students, some of whom seem to change their address every week of the academic year! Also, many firms depend, for their livelihood, on having accurate addresses and risk losing a valued customer if they get one of the hundreds of daily address changes wrong.

One solution to this problem which has emerged recently is the principle of having customers put their own address changes into the system. Each customer has on-line access to their own data (using a private PIN), and they can inspect it at any time, and change parts of it (such as their address) if necessary. Several universities have installed a system like this, available through the university computer system or through special terminals in the administration building (for greater security). Of course in this case the client base is largely computer-literate and is totally dependent (for career purposes) on the university's stored addresses being correct, but the approach will also work for very Web-oriented firms and, we predict, will become very much more common.

5.6 The Impact of Hypermedia on Lifelong Learning

Is hypermedia an art or a science? Artists are collaborating with computer scientists in all manner of fields, ranging from high tech CAI to movie making. It is a trend that we hope will extend to all areas of education, and hypermedia networks can facilitate this collaboration. Although at school students interact with friends of varied interests, later in life many specialise early and lose contact with other disciplines – to the detriment of more than just the students' interests. Staff and students need to hear other problems being discussed to realise that their own work may hold solutions. Fundamental theory, advanced technology, wider perspectives, ethical, social, legal considerations and can unexpectedly revolutionise the way an undertaking is viewed. Hypermedia networks can provide the needed communication channels. Also, as it becomes more and more difficult to separate education and entertainment, we shall see students controlling their own education in new and probably unpredictable ways.

5.6.1 Computer Supported Learning

The classical "chalk and talk" lecture has certainly stood the test of time. It is cheap, and coupled with a good duster it allows the teacher a great deal of flexibility. The last few years have seen the increased use of overhead projection slides, which allow the lecturer to prepare beautiful, detailed colour diagrams in advance. However, in an OHP presentation, spontaneity and audience participation may both be sacrificed because they may suddenly demand a change in either the content or the order of the prepared slides. The whole effect may be spoilt if a teacher has to illustrate points by trying to draw, with an inadequate pen, in corners of the transparencies. There is an additional problem with making references back to points on previous slides, since it can be difficult to find a particular slide amongst a pile of used ones. However, since both chalk and OHPs are so widely used, any serious alternative must combine the flexibility of the classical blackboard method with the ability to show prepared material. The use of electronic media with a projector or multiple screens can provide this combination, and much more besides.

Since tools such as word processors, spreadsheet packages, database management systems and CAD packages became widely used, we have seen a revolution in the quantity and quality of the documents produced by teachers. Graphs can be printed directly from spreadsheets, and output from computer simulations can be captured in pictorial form and included in reports. Many publishing houses accept electronic versions of papers and books for in-house editing or as final copy for directly incorporating into edited books.

In 1989 Dartmouth College was the first university to require every student to either purchase a computer or arrange the loan of one. It is becoming such a widespread practice that before long all staff and students at universities may find the possession of a personal computer as essential as a slide rule was for engineers back in the 1950s.

5.6.2 Electronic Classrooms

Electronic classrooms, [Shneiderman, 1993b], [Lennon and Maurer, 1994b] and electronic campuses [Press, 1994] are evolving into interactive remote teaching environments [Maly et al., 1994] and distributed learning environments [Davies, 1994]. Several systems, such as the virtual classes held at the New Jersey Institute of Technology, [Hiltz, 1986] and [Hiltz and Turoff, 1994], offer complete on-line courses. We elaborate on this topic much further in Chapters 10 and 11.

5.6.3 Digital Libraries

Digital libraries on the Web are discussed in Section 9.8 and in a special issue of *Communications of the ACM* [Communications, 1995]. We believe that the next few years will see dramatic changes in traditional library systems. As more members of the public have access to networked computers, more browsing of catalogues will be done away from the library than ever before. Physical library space is a particularly expensive commodity when you take into account such factors as security and construction problems (such as floors having to be designed to withstand the weight of books). Many libraries in educational institutes allocate this space to students as study areas. However, it is our observation that students often simply work on assignments, making no use of the library's resources except for the convenient sitting spaces. A better and more cost-effective solution is to provide students with alternative study areas where they can not only work but sip coffee and get involved in important group collaborative exercises. We discuss electronic libraries further in Chapter 9.

Part II

Web Technologies

6. The World Wide Web

6.1 Introduction

This chapter could have been subtitled "Grappling with Medusa" – except that would give a wrong impression. We enjoy the Web. It can be enormous fun. Nevertheless, the analogy is apt since it is huge, multi-faceted, and writhing.

Based on a typical client/server model, the World Wide Web is an Internet-wide distributed hypermedia information retrieval system [Liu et al., 1994].

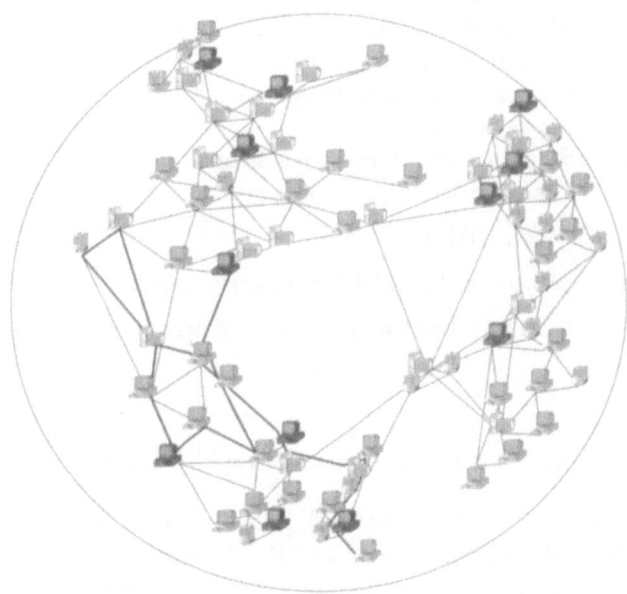

Fig. 6.1. The World Wide Web: A View From the Pacific

As mentioned in Chapter 4, the fast growth of the Web was dependent upon five major developments:

1. A consistent addressing system (URL) (see Section 6.2)
2. A fast transfer protocol (HTTP) (see Section 6.3)
3. A hypertext document format (HTML) (see Section 6.4)
4. Easy to use browsers (see Section 6.7)
5. Better search engines (see Section 6.8)

6.2 Uniform Resource Locators (URL)

One of the key components for the success of the Web is its use of Uniform Resource Locators (URLs), [Berners-Lee et al., 1994a, Berners-Lee et al., 1994b]. These are the "addresses" of the objects on the Web. A URL consists of the name of the particular locator scheme (http, ftp etc.,) followed by a colon, then some scheme-dependent code that starts (usually) with // and includes path information:

```
<scheme>:<scheme-specific part>
```

The following schemes are widely used:
http	Hypertext Transfer Protocol
ftp	File Transfer Protocol
gopher	The Gopher protocol
mailto	Electronic mail address
cid	Content identifiers for MIME
news	Usenet news
telnet	Reference to interactive sessions
WAIS	Wide Area Information Servers

An example of a Web URL is:

```
http://www.ncsa.uiuc.edu/SDG/Software/Mosaic/
```

The part between the // and the first / (www.ncsa.uiuc.edu) is the *Internet domain name*.

6.3 Hypertext Transfer Protocol (HTTP)

HTTP (Hypertext Transfer Protocol) [Berners-Lee et al., 1994a] is a file transport protocol (running over TCP/IP) to transport World Wide Web documents. It also initiates certain actions within a browser, such as displaying files.

On the Internet, the communication takes place over a TCP/IP connection. It could, however, be implemented over some other protocol on the Internet or other networks.

The protocol is basically a stateless transaction consisting of:

1. A connection. The establishment of a connection by the client to the server.
2. A request. The sending, by the client, of a request message to the server.
3. A response. The sending, by the server, of a response to the client.
4. A closure. The closing of the connection by either party.

The format of the request and response parts is defined in the specification; a standard (ISO Latin-1) character set with CR/LF terminated lines is used. It may take several HTTP connections to transfer a single document because, for instance, the retrieval of an image is a single operation.

An HTTP request gives the URL of the the object requested and possibly additional data. A response provides the object or an error message such as "404 Not Found" (which is all too common). When an object is sent, it has a header attached giving information which a browser can interpret to correctly display it. This makes the protocol browser-independent, and, since browsers simply ignore header information they do not understand, also means that extensions can be added easily.

6.4 HyperText Markup Language (HTML)

HTML (HyperText Markup Language) was designed primarily as a way of embedding formatting and link information into text documents, so that hypermedia documents can be sent across the Internet. For example, a formatted document may use a variety of text styles such as bold and italics, and embed both graphics and links. HTML defines a set of "tags" to describe and delimit the required formatting.

We discuss tags more fully in Chapter 8, but basically they are keywords, such as HTML, TITLE, ADDRESS, that are identified by using special characters < and >, i.e., < HTML>, <TITLE>, <ADDRESS>. We can delimit words that need formatting by using a tag which includes the / character. For example, if we need to make the words "very important" appear in boldface, perhaps in the middle of a sentence, we can mark them up as follows:

<B> very important </B>

In this case the <B> is the start tag indicating the beginning of the boldface text, and </B> is the end tag.

It is important to note that Web servers are just document servers and do no formatting. HTTP is used to transfer the raw HTML between clients and servers; the client then parses and displays the result. HTML is defined in terms of SGML (see Chapter 8). Several very easy to use tutorials are available on the Web [URLh2, URLi2, URLj2]. To give a brief idea of how formatting is achieved by the use of tags we include a small example here:

Fig. 6.2. Home Page of the Ruritanian Folkdance Club

```
<HTML>
<HEAD>
    <TITLE>RURITANIAN INTERNATIONAL FOLK DANCE CLUB</TITLE>
</HEAD>

<BODY>
<IMG SRC="BannerRIFDC.jpg" ALT="Banner" BORDER="0" WIDTH="408"
HEIGHT="98" NATURALSIZEFLAG="3" ALIGN=bottom>
<BR>

The Ruritanian International Folkdance Club promotes folkdancing
in Auckland, New Zealand, and beyond. Dancers can choose amongst
a wide range of activities: classes, performing groups, socials,
workshops, weekend camps, and shared-interest get-togethers
including nature walks.
<BR>
<BR>

<A HREF="Social.jpg"><IMG SRC="SocialTN.jpg" ALT="Dancers1"
BORDER="0" HSPACE="20" HEIGHT="70" WIDTH="102"
NATURALSIZEFLAG="3" ALIGN=bottom></A>
```

```
<A HREF="LMA.jpg"><IMG SRC="LMAtn.jpg" ALT="Dancers2"
BORDER="0" HSPACE="20" HEIGHT="70" WIDTH="103"
NATURALSIZEFLAG="3" ALIGN=bottom></A>

<A HREF="Greek.jpg"><IMG SRC="GreekTN.jpg"
ALT="Dancers3" BORDER="0" HSPACE="20" HEIGHT="70" WIDTH="105"
NATURALSIZEFLAG="3" ALIGN=bottom></A><BR>
<BR>
<EM>RURITANIAN CLUB NIGHT / PUBLIC SOCIAL</EM><BR>
<BR>

Last Friday of every month, 8pm<BR>
St George's Hall, Ranfurly Rd, Epsom, Auckland<BR>
CONTACT: Michele<BR>
<BR>

<TABLE BORDER>
        <CAPTION>INTERNATIONAL FOLKDANCE CLASSES</CAPTION>
        <TH>
        <TH>
        <TH>TIME
        <TH>CONTACT
        <TR>
                <TD>Monday
                <TD>International Folk Dancing
...
```

In addition to providing text styles, inline graphics, and links to other documents, HTML can be used to represent:

– Tables
– Forms such as questionnaires (see Section 6.6)
– Menus of options
– Hypertext news, mail, online documentation, and collaborative hypermedia
– Database query results
– Simple structured documents with inline graphics
– Hypertext views of existing bodies of information
– Frames for displaying information in multiple windows

In addition, Common Gateway Interfaces (see Section 6.5) and Java applets (see Section 4.5.5) allow interaction with other applications.

6.5 Common Gateway Interfaces (CGI)

The very basic HTML code shown in the previous section produced a static
document, i.e., one which allowed no user interaction. CGI (Common Gateway Interface) is a standard for interfacing HTTP documents with applications running on other (non-Web) servers. These applications may range from
simple scripts to process forms (see Section 6.6), to more complex programs
that give access to other types of databases.

The CGI programs, or scripts, must be placed in a specific directory on
the server machine. Since CGI programs let users from all over the world
access the local server, security issues suggest that CGI development is best
left to the expertise of the local Webmaster.

A significant factor in the rapid acceptance of Web technology has been
the ability to access other existing servers. CGI is also a standard for interfacing external applications with information servers, such as Gopher, Oracle,
Sun, or Hyperwave servers.

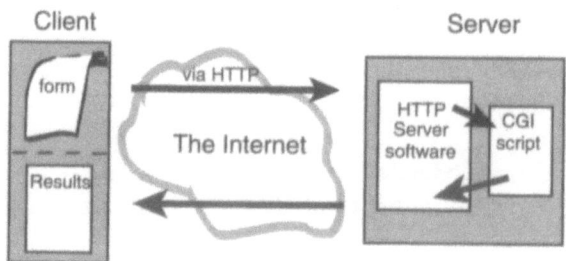

Fig. 6.3. CGI

6.5.1 Oracle

An Oracle Webserver [URLr1] consists of a Listener, an Agent, and an Oracle
server. The Listener is a server-end process which listens to the network. It
supports cached file handling, HTTP, CGI, and security. An Agent is a procedural gateway to an Oracle server. When an Agent first calls, the Listener
spawns a dedicated process to look after all requests for service. "Hypertext
links in any HTML document can point directly to a stored procedure, allowing the Oracle Server to build a dynamic HTML document on the fly using
PL/SQL, Oracle's procedural extension to SQL".

The Oracle Media server provides multimedia library services, on a variety
of platforms, supporting a large number of simultaneous users.

6.5.2 Hot Java

Java [URLa2], a language designed to facilitate development of secure Internet applications, and HotJava [URLb2], a Web browser written in Java and supporting the viewing of Java programs (see Section 4.5.5), are recent developments by Sun Microsystems.

6.6 Providing Interaction With Forms

One common application of CGI scripting is to provide forms for user interaction [URLg1]. For example, whenever a home page has a text box and a "SUBMIT" button, there has to be a CGI script on a server somewhere to process the submission. Here is a trivial example of some HTML markup for a form that will send one line of text to the CGI script when the Submit button is pressed:

```
<FORM METHOD = "POST"
    ACTION = "http://a.web.server/cgi-bin/myform">
<INPUT TYPE = "text" NAME = "the_string"
    SIZE = "1" MAXLENGTH = 20>
<INPUT TYPE = "reset" VALUE = "Clear fields">
<INPUT TYPE = "submit" VALUE = "Send string">
</FORM>
```

The CGI script on the server reads the text and actions it, after performing a certain amount of error checking. Since CGI scripts can create HTML on the fly it is good practice for them to notify the user how their submission has been actioned.

6.7 Internet and Intranet Browsers

Browsers are the main tool with which users access the multimedia aspects of the Web (see Section 4.2.1).

When companies like Netscape Communications began to develop commercial versions of Web browsers, along with variants of the original HTML code, the need for standardisation became apparent. The World Wide Web Consortium (W3C) was founded for this purpose [URLu2]. It is an industry consortium, jointly hosted by the Massachusetts Institute of Technology Laboratory for Computer Science (MIT/LCS) in the United States, the Institut National de Recherche en Informatique et en Automatique (INRIA) in Europe, and Keio University's Shonan Fujisawa Campus in Asia [URLv2].

6.7.1 Netscape

Shortly after Mosaic (see Section 4.2.1) was released, Netscape Communications Corporation distributed their upmarket product called Netscape Navigator [URLf1] (see Figure 6.4). Although Netscape Navigator is primarily a

Fig. 6.4. The Netscape Navigator [URLf1]

browser, third party plug-ins provide a wide range of third party capabilities. Interactivity was heightened by the introduction of forms (see Section 6.6). Now, with the advent of CGI scripts (see Section 6.5) and Java applets (see Section 4.5.5), browsers can run an endless number of different applications on remote servers.

A further significant development was Netscape's security system, based on SSL (see Section 4.6.5).

6.7.2 Microsoft Internet Explorer

The Microsoft Internet Explorer is Microsoft's entry into the competitive Web browser market [URLj3]. Whilst supporting most of the features of Netscape's Navigator, Internet Explorer includes additional capabilities such as support for VBScript (a subset of Visual Basic) and ActiveX controls, which allow OLE (Object Linking and Embedding) objects to be inserted into Web pages.

One problem with having two major Web browsers in the market is that they both render HTML slightly differently, which means that Web pages can differ in appearance depending on which browser is being used. In addition to this, both browsers support their own extensions to HTML which are not understood by competing products. These differences mean that HTML authors have to be careful, when designing their Web pages, to ensure that all common browsers are supported.

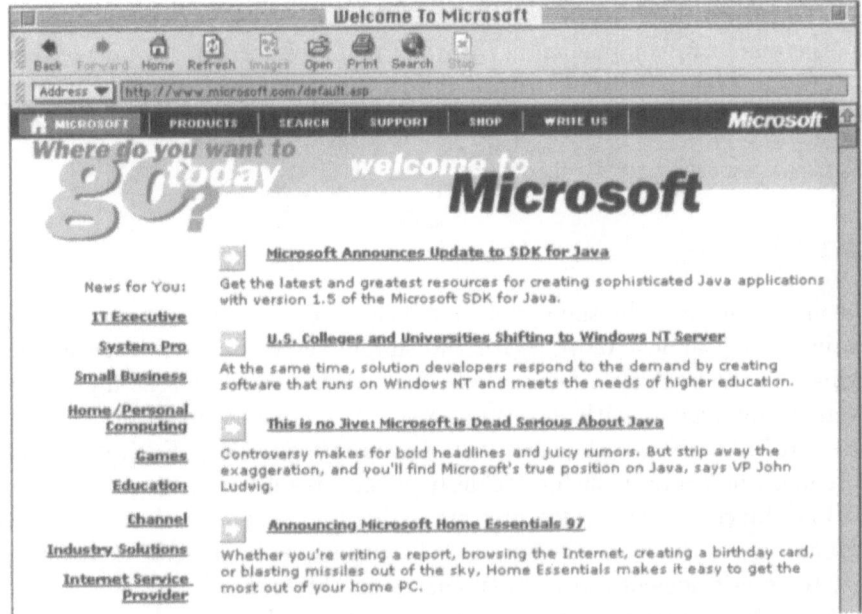

Fig. 6.5. Microsoft Internet Explorer [URLj3]

6.8 Search Engines

It is no exaggeration to say that the success or otherwise of any large electronic information system is dependent on the quality of its search engines. The Web is no exception. Increasingly sophisticated search requirements have resulted in phenomenal growth in Web-based search engines.

Search engines consist of two main components: a gatherer which automatically searches the Web for new and updated information (see Section 6.9), and an inference engine that interprets users' requests (see Section 6.8.1). The gatherer creates an index of the document space and the inference engine translates the user's queries, finds suitable matches, and displays the resultant list.

The various search engines currently being used are constantly competing with each other to have the largest indexes and the best features. Popular search engines include:

- AltaVista [URLk2]
- Excite [URLt2]
- Infoseek [URLx2]
- Lycos [URLy2]
- Yahoo [URLw2]

Most are supported by commercial sponsors and come complete with flashy advertisements.

There are two complementary ways of finding information on the Web:

1. Searching, using one or more of the available search engines (see Section 6.8.1).
2. Browsing (see Section 6.8.3).

6.8.1 Searching

The algorithms used by the various inference engines to query a search index are improving almost daily. With the simple keyword searches users were doomed to the frustration of overkill – or underkill. Modern search programs are more intelligent, with most supporting the boolean operators of AND, OR, and NOT. Many other features are supported such as Excite's concept searching where a term such as "elderly people" is related to "senior citizens" [URLr1]. Since the various features are so diverse, we suggest that users make frequent use of the help pages provided by each engine, where the most up-to-date descriptions of the various options can be found.

As an illustrative example we have chosen Infoseek, one of the older search engines. Infoseek, for example, introduced:

- The prefix + to indicate terms that must be included, e.g., folk +music will return results which contain both words.
- The prefix - to indicate that a term must be omitted, e.g., folk -music will return results which contain the word "folk" but not the word "music".
- Double quotes to indicate a phrase or title, e.g., "Cajun Folk Dance Club".
- Capital letters to denote proper names, e.g., Cajun.
- Square brackets to give a proximity delimiter for words that should appear near each other, e.g., [Cajun jitterbug].

Sites such as Infoseek can also provide options for searching in Web pages tiles, URLs, and embedded hypertext links.

6.8.2 Relevance Scores

Most search engines return a list of links (each link often accompanied by a scattering of sample text) sorted by "relevance". It is difficult to determine just how the relevance values have been calculated but Infoseek states that the following factors "influence" the score:

- The query terms are found near the start of the document or in the title.
- The document contains query terms which have a high weight (words which are relatively uncommon in the database will have a high weight).
- The document contains more of the query terms.

6.8.3 Browsing

There are two orthogonal ways of browsing. Users may determine their own paths by choosing likely-looking links, or authors may create hierarchies that users can browse up and down. There is no "best" method since the choice depends heavily on user preference and on the document space. For example, users with time to spare may wish to spend their time surfing the Web following associations (as dreamt of by Bush [Bush, 1945]). However, particularly in educational settings, users may prefer to use hierarchical structures so that they can cover material more efficiently.

Several search engines, such as Yahoo [URLw2], also link to an increasing list of general categories (see Figure 6.6).

Fig. 6.6. Yahoo [URLw2]

6.9 Web Gatherers (Crawlers, Spiders, Robots, and Bots)

Information contained in the various search sites is gathered in two ways: by users submitting their own URLs and by computer programs called gatherers (or crawlers, spiders, robots, or bots) [URLs2]. These gatherers regularly link to a succession of globally distributed servers and collect new information to add to their databases. Traditionally, since each of the search engines such as Lycos, Excite, Infoseek, and Yahoo have maintained separate indexes, users

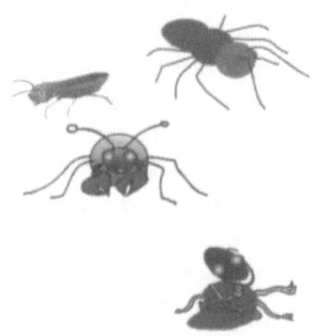

Fig. 6.7. Some Graphical Icons Representing Crawlers

have never quite known which search engine would return the best hit list for any particular query. Now programs such as MetaCrawler [URLp2] can query a whole range of engines, collate the results, and present the user with a unified hit list sorted by a combined relevance number.

6.10 The World Wide Web of the 90s: A Snapshot[1]

As we have seen, the introduction of simple, machine-independent protocols and standards allowed the World Wide Web to become immensely successful. The Web has now grown far beyond its beginnings as an academic network for collaborative research, and has entered many other areas of our lives such as commerce, entertainment, politics, and information dissemination. This section looks at some of the consequences of the Web's recent growth and describes new features, such as sophisticated editing tools, the divergence of standards, plug-ins, and security issues.

6.10.1 Is it Really a World Wide Web?

The Web has developed largely as an English-language medium, based in Western culture. The implications of this, while not immediately obvious, are important. Much of the world is marginalised by the use of English-only documents, especially the developing world which could stand to benefit the most from the Web's transparency of location. It requires much effort to provide multiple translations of each document, and can also require a clumsy introductory page where the user is asked to choose a language. Much worse, many written languages (Chinese, Japanese, Hindi) are difficult to represent within the limitations of the ISO-Latin1 character set defined in the HTML specification.

---

[1] This section was written by Carolyn Sanders, HMU, University of Auckland.

A difficulty experienced by commercial Web sites offering goods for sale is the global distribution of their customers. Even when details of payment are resolved, the delivery of goods is problematic. In practice, many sites request only State and Zip code on the order form, and have no space for Country!

Also affected by this lack of a global mindset are contact information, keywords and titles. There are many sites on the Web entitled "national something or other" without any mention of which nation they belong to. A more sophisticated mindset, and a more sophisticated Web server standard, may be required so that country-specific information is presented in an appropriate way.

6.10.2 The Need for Refereed Publishing

Web traffic accounts for more Internet usage than anything else – FTP, Telnet, Gopher, WAIS, or video conferencing. One consequence of this huge popularity is the increasing presence of redundant, inaccurate, and uninteresting data. Searching for a specific piece of information becomes more and more difficult as each search creates thousands of possible avenues to explore. Unfortunately, although search engines and directory services have been forced to become more sophisticated, refereed publishing is still in its infancy (see Chapter 9).

6.10.3 HTML Web Publishing Tools

The comparative simplicity of HTML and the graphical, aesthetic nature of the modern Web has attracted many users previously reluctant to use the Internet, including private users unwilling to master the intricacies of FTP and News, companies without Unix personnel, and publishers of traditional material with no Web experience. Demand from such sources has led to the supply of more and more sophisticated Web publishing tools.

Early Web documents were written in raw HTML (see Section 6.4). The authors used ordinary text editors and word processors, and typed in the HTML tags by hand. Many Web authors still work this way, claiming a greater control over the finished product.

An increasingly important issue in Web site design is that of images and loading speed. As sites become more graphics oriented, users are less than happy with the amount of time and money spent receiving and displaying images that turn out to be large in both screen and file size – and often worthless. A tool which shrinks image file sizes (using JPEG compression or reducing the GIF palette) is a necessity for every site designer.

Currently such work is done by hand, either in sophisticated graphics programs such as Adobe Photoshop or in specially designed programs like DeBabelizer (a Macintosh application), both of which are enormously expensive and complex.

HTML Text Editors. The first advance in Web page editing came as an add-on to existing text editing tools. BBEdit, a popular Macintosh text editor, supplied macros allowing an area of text to be selected and the appropriate tags to be automatically inserted. This saved much laborious typing and eliminated annoying typing errors, but the user was still left with no immediate view of how the document would appear in a browser.

HTML WYSIWYG Editors. WYSIWYG (What You See Is What You Get) HTML editors were the next major advance. Applications such as Adobe Page Mill, Netscape Navigator Gold, HotDog, and Hot Metal, allow users to place text, images, and links where needed, creating the necessary HTML invisibly and automatically.

This made it easy for new Web authors to quickly create home pages without having to learn HTML, and it also aided experienced Web publishers to prototype pages and select images, colours, etc., and then tweak the resultant machine-generated HTML at their leisure.

The latest advance is the addition of HTML WYSIWYG editors into common applications. Anyone who has handcrafted a large table in HTML will appreciate the ability to automatically create a table from a complex spreadsheet, or attach a search front-end to an existing database.

HTML Checkers. An addition to the plethora of HTML editors now available, there are tools such as HTML Checker and WebLint. These programs check HTML documents (hand or machine-generated) for compliance with HTML standards. This sort of checking has become increasingly necessary with the growth of browser-specific HTML tags (see Section 9.4).

6.10.4 Web Sites, Their Care and Nurture

As the number and variety of Web pages grows, so does the size and complexity of Web sites. A Web site is a logical collection of Web pages, with a structure, linked together so as to provide ease of navigation and information retrieval. Maintaining the integrity of links within a site, updating necessary pages, testing that all parts of the site are available, and doing all these reliably and quickly, has become the province of the "Webmaster", a new breed of person whose responsibility is the maintenance of Web servers and sites.

As with Web page development, in the early days Web site creation and maintenance was done by hand. This function was performed by people with good Unix skills, since the first Web servers ran only on Unix machines (although later ones run on Macintosh, Windows NT, and other platforms). As sites grew, and the number of non-Unix people wanting to develop sites also grew, maintenance tools emerged. Unfortunately such tools are still not nearly as advanced as HTML editors, mostly because site maintenance is a much more complicated task, and one with more scope for personal preference. There is no standard for the logical or physical structure of a Web site, and each Webmaster is left to reinvent the wheel in this respect.

As implied in the previous paragraph there are two sides to a Web site – the logical structure and the physical structure. The logical structure includes the links between documents, navigational tools, searches, and so on. The physical side is concerned with such matters as the placement of HTML and other files (such as images and movies) within a directory structure on the server's file system, and the access permissions granted to users.

When, for example, a new document is added to a Web site, it must first be put into the physical structure, and then linked into the logical structure. The average HTML document has many links to it and from it, and each one must be checked and updated when the document is added, moved, renamed or deleted.

With the advent of Web site maintenance tools such as Adobe Site Mill and O'Reilly's WebSite, maintaining links and page consistency became much less laborious.

6.10.5 Web Publishing Companies

Another effect of the complexity of site design and maintenance is the arrival of Web publishing companies, institutions which create and maintain Web sites for clients who do not wish to do the work themselves. This is directly analogous to the traditional publishing company or advertising company, and in fact some of those traditional companies are expanding into the Web. This is a good example of how the boundaries are blurring between the electronic world and the physical "real" world.

6.10.6 User Access Statistics

With the rise of separate Web publishing entities, the issue of user access statistics arises. How can a company know if their Web presence is effective? The success of traditional forms of advertising is measured in sales and in customer recognition level surveys. The most common way of assessing a site's effectiveness is to count its visitors. Because of the statelessness of the HTTP protocol, it is impossible to keep track of actual users, and one can only count file retrievals ('hits') instead of single sessions by individual users. This doesn't generate a true figure of a site's popularity, since some hits may be generated internally (Web masters checking links), some by automated agents gathering data, and some inadvertently or even maliciously by users repeatedly reloading a page.

Other sites require a user to register upon arrival and then identify themselves upon re-entry. This gains significantly more user data, but may be off-putting for some users who wish to remain anonymous.

6.10.7 Commerce on the Web

Late 1995 and early 1996 saw the migration of "real world" interests onto the Web. The most important of these interests, in terms of the effect it had on the Web, was business. Advertisements, formerly rare and reviled, suddenly poured onto the Net in the form of commercial sites offering goods for sale or trial, and sponsorship of non-commercial sites.

This has caused problems (and the search for solutions) in three major areas:

- Transaction security (payment over the Internet)
- User accounting (just who is visiting my site)
- Social and moral issues (the effect of advertising and sponsorship on free speech)

Transactions on the Web. Ever since people started transmitting financial information such as credit card numbers over the Web, security has been a critically important issue. An Internet packet passes through many computers en route to its destination, and any one of those computers can read that packet. Efforts to encrypt the information have often met with reluctance, from the US Government in particular (see Section 4.6.6).

Digital banks offering virtual cash have sprung up. Browsers and servers are being sold on the merits of their security features, notably Netscape's secure socket layer (see Section 4.6.5). And the most hyped Web product yet, Java, has been touted for its supposedly secure implementation. However, security looks set to be a big issue for a long time to come (see Section 4.6).

Advertising on the Web. A big difference between a company advertising its product on the Web and an individual publishing a home page, complete with pictures of the family cat, is that the company wants to see a return on its investment. It wants to know if its advertisements are having any real effect. The effect of traditional advertising (on television, in magazines, and other traditional media) is measured by sales and by surveys taken to gauge brand recognition. As noted in Section 6.10.6, these methods are not yet translatable to the Web since identifying repeat users is more problematic.

6.10.8 Subsidising Services

Creating, designing and maintaining a Web site takes time, and as the old adage says, time is money. Money is also required for the machines that run the Web servers, as well as for the costs of maintaining an Internet connection and for electricity consumption.

Many service-oriented sites (news summaries, search engines, non-profit organisations) have offset these costs by attracting sponsorship. In return for a "small" image touting a product, and a link to that producer's online shop, a site can subsidise its costs. The same principle applies to almost all of the traditional media, except for books.

The alternative, charging users for site services, has been extremely unpopular on an Internet where users traditionally had unrestricted access.

People remembering the "old days" of an advertising-free Internet have decried the invasion of crass commercialism. Others have accepted it as the only acceptable solution to the cost problem. Many new Web users, accustomed to advertisements everywhere else, probably don't even notice.

This creates another problem. Users may indeed be downloading the advertisements on a page, but are the advertisements really having any effect? We have so much practice at blocking them out in every other medium, that Web advertising may not be working! One site, the Netly News [URLo2], tried including parodies of advertisements on their pages – spoofs of other common advertisements. They eventually gave up this humorous effort when it became apparent that nobody had noticed – people glanced at the image, recognised it as an advertisement and ignored it.

6.11 Afterword

The World Wide Web is a marvellous, if chaotic, information system. However, its rapid growth is leading to some shortcomings and slowdowns. Even with fast HTTP connection, wading through mounds of irrelevant data leads to frustration. As the commercial sector gains an increasing proportion of both Web sites and Web traffic, we are seeing powerful backers controlling the direction of both standards and development. Nevertheless, as listed in Chapter 4, there are still many unresolved research issues which must be addressed if the Web is to continue to grow and be used for large secure projects.

7. Hyperwave – An Advanced Hypermedia Document Management System[1]

7.1 Introduction

7.1.1 The Concept

Hyperwave is a distributed hypermedia system developed at the Institute for Computer Science and Computer Supported New Media (IICM) at the Graz University of Technology in Graz, Austria. The principal architects are Prof. Hermann Maurer and Frank Kappe.

Hyperwave follows a more sophisticated concept than most available Web server systems. The project's aims are [Andrews et al., 1994a]:

- System access using hyperlinks, hierarchical browsing, and searching
- Reducing fragmentation of document collections over multiple systems and servers
- Support for multi-lingual documents
- User identification and access control
- Integration of existing Internet information systems
- Automatic enforcement of document consistency.

Hyperwave offers a self-contained working and navigation environment, and relies on the Internet as its base communication medium. A special machine sub-address (TCP port 418) has been reserved by the Internet community for communication to Hyperwave servers.

A full description of Hyperwave, including all technical details, can be found in [Maurer, 1996a].

7.1.2 History

Hyperwave's development started in 1989 under the name Hyper-G, about the same time as the development of the Web began.

Due to the parallel development, both "worlds" developed standards of their own for client/server communication, hypertext documents (HTF and HTML), and three-dimensional scenes (SDF and VRML). HTML and VRML were added to Hyperwave later, while the proposal for a new Web transport

---

[1] This chapter is written by Michael Klemme, HMU, University of Auckland.

protocol, HTTP-NG (see [URLd3] for a draft version) includes ideas used by Hyperwave since its inception.

The project has targeted the production of Web servers for large Web sites. This move is supported by the adoption of HTML as the markup language for hypertext documents and VRML for three-dimensional environments.

Due to a trademark conflict, Hyper-G was renamed Hyperwave in 1996. Its development as an Internet Web server system will be continued by a commercial company in Graz and the USA (see [URLm3] for further information).

7.2 The Hyperwave Server

Hyperwave was developed to store high-volume hypermedia resources, which can be spread over multiple servers. The long-term maintenance and development of databases becomes crucial when databases grow beyond a certain size. To expedite management, particularly of links, a more structured approach needs to be pursued right from the beginning.

The core of a Hyperwave server is formed by a set of object-oriented databases. It supports the customary database features such as the assigning of attributes to objects, indexing, and searching. The server also maintains a hierarchy of user and group entries. The following attributes can be assigned to a document:

- Read and write permissions for both groups and individuals
- Extra search keywords
- Titles in different languages
- Display properties
- Custom attributes
- Direct debit, from the user's account, of the cost of viewing a document
- Setting of a time period during which the document is visible to the public.

Since attributes are not stored within the objects (as in most Web servers), but in a separate database, they can be efficiently extracted and manipulated. In addition, objects can be locked to ensure they are not updated concurrently.

Each object is labelled with a globally unique object identifier that allows unambiguous referencing from every Hyperwave server. Since these identifiers will not be re-used when the document is replaced or deleted, remote Hyperwave objects can be cached without requiring a sophisticated cache update protocol.

Another feature of Hyperwave allows servers to be organised in *tribes* that share a common user hierarchy and keep the distributed data consistent within the group (e.g., within a corporate Intranet). The Hyperwave protocol is session oriented, i.e., it stores status information ("session information") about every user currently connected to the system.

7.2.1 Documents

A Hyperwave server can contain various types of documents. The most common types are:

- Text documents in HTML or HTF formats, or as unformatted text (HTF is the native Hyperwave document format)
- Still images in a variety of popular formats (JPEG, GIF, PNG, XPM, TIFF, etc.)
- Movies in MPEG format
- PostScript documents
- Three-dimensional scenes in VRML and SDF formats
- Programs, e.g., Java applets.

External documents stored on the Web, FTP, WAIS, and Gopher servers can be integrated as documents into the system. These documents are treated like native Hyperwave documents, but their content will be retrieved by the local Hyperwave server from the remote system.

It is possible to define links from and to all supported formats, including parts of documents. Thus, Hyperwave can claim to be a true hypermedia system.

Generic documents that are not known to Hyperwave and its client programs can be inserted into the server as well. However, an external viewer program is required to display them. Special pseudo-documents can be inserted for scripts that have to be executed on the server upon invocation by a client. Using this mechanism, content can be created on the fly and presented to the client. CGI scripts, as found on the Web, are supported in this category, as well as Hyperwave's HGI scripts that provide for the session-oriented gateway to external resources (such as access to SQL databases). Other databases can therefore be seamlessly integrated into the hypermedia system.

7.2.2 Collection Hierarchy

Hyperwave imposes a structure on the documents stored in the server. Every document is a member of one or more collections. These collections form a hierarchy (a directed acyclic graph) that is topped by the "Hyper Root", the collection of all servers worldwide. Figure 7.1 shows an excerpt of the collection hierarchy.

Hyper Root
    HyperMedia Unit Main Server, New Zealand
        Local Information
        The University of Auckland
            The University of Auckland
            NZ Educational Institutes on the Internet
            Library Services
            Common Work Space

            Contact Information
        Local Information
            Mail Archives
            Technical Documentation
    College of Engineering, California State University, Long Beach

Fig. 7.1. Hyperwave Collection Hierarchy (as Seen by the Harmony Client)

Clusters. A "cluster" is a special type of collection that allows tight integration of documents of different types and languages, such as storing different language versions of the same document. The client application requesting the cluster can select a version according to the preferences of the user. A client accessing a cluster might find an English and a German version of a document and decide to display the English version because English has a higher priority for this user. Documents of different types (e.g., a video and an explanatory text) that are stored in a cluster will be displayed in parallel by the client.

Distributed Storage. The collection hierarchy can be distributed over multiple servers worldwide, while documents and collections can be members of collections on different servers. The participating servers exchange information about shared objects and thus keep the system consistent[2].

The system can be used to coordinate and unify distributed projects and to provide a consistent entry point into a distributed information system. Unfortunately, it is not possible at the time of writing to directly modify documents on remote servers.

---

[2] For a detailed overview of internal communication within Hyperwave and the cost incurred in communication overheads, see [Kappe, 1995].

Searching the Collection Hierarchy. The collection hierarchy provides a search space for title, keyword, and full-text searches. Since all sub-collections of the selected collection will be searched, the search scope can be limited to the relevant parts of the database. If these collections are distributed over multiple servers, the servers will be queried in parallel and the result combined.

All text documents inserted into the server are added to a full-text index that allows fast access to the documents. External text extraction programs can be supplied to help the full-text server index the textual content of other documents. Extraction tools for PostScript and PDF documents will be available shortly.

Since Hyperwave is a multi-lingual database, searches can be restricted to certain languages. This applies to both the title and full-text search. Therefore, a separate full-text index is maintained for every language present in the system.

7.2.3 Document Sequences

As an example of the significant advantages of using collections, it is interesting to compare the process of maintaining sequential lists of URLs, first as it is done in most Web systems, and then in a Hyperwave system. For example, consider the steps that must be taken if a new document named Maurer has to be inserted into a list already containing Lanier and Nelson (see Figure 7.2). As shown, the document Maurer has to be inserted. Then

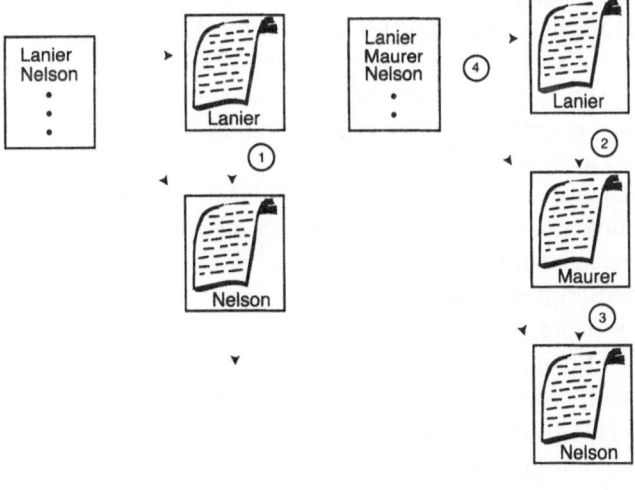

Fig. 7.2. Steps Involved in Adding to a Sequential Web List

the document representing the alphabetic list has to be updated to include Maurer; finally, the link labelled (1) between the Lanier and Nelson documents must be deleted, and the new links (2),(3), and (4) created. In sharp contrast, in a Hyperwave system sequences are maintained automatically. A *sequence* is a special type of collection that displays its content in a specified sort order. The references between consecutive members (labelled (2) and (3)) are generated dynamically when the documents are accessed. Therefore, only a single operation is needed, i.e., the document Maurer is simply inserted into an appropriate collection, and the system does the rest when the "sequence" attribute is set.

7.2.4 Links

Most Web servers store links between their documents as part of the document the link starts from. The link can therefore only be seen at its starting point – it is not bi-directional. This leads to the well known problem of dangling links: when a document is changed or deleted, the other documents pointing to it are not modified automatically (e.g., by de-activating, deleting, or redirecting the affected links) to reflect the change.

In contrast to other Web servers, Hyperwave stores links and documents in separate databases. Since links are bi-directional, changes in both source and destination documents of a link will automatically result in the modification of the link. If one of the documents is deleted, the link will be made invisible to the users.[3] It will be re-activated as soon as a document of the same type and title as the deleted document is inserted into the server. The same thing happens when the target of a newly created link is not yet available.

Hyperwave clients can extract all links to and from a document and display the document's "neighbourhood" as a local map. Figure 7.3 shows the local map for a node of the hypertext "415.708 Assignment One" as it is displayed by the Hyperwave client Harmony. As can be seen, these maps are useful for navigating through hypermedia systems and for designing and verifying the structure of these systems.

Since links are stored in a separate database, and thus are not embedded into the documents, they can be defined on all document types. So far, link types have been defined for text, images, video, three-dimensional scenes, and even PostScript documents. Links can point from and to parts of documents (e.g., a region of a page of a PostScript document) as well as to entire documents. Unfortunately, only native Hyperwave clients can visualise these links, since Web browsers only understand links to entire documents (except for standard HTML documents).

To create a link, the user needs to have write access to the document the link will start from, because adding a link changes the document. However, in contrast to other Web users, every registered Hyperwave user can create links

---

[3] In Hyperwave terminology the link is "open".

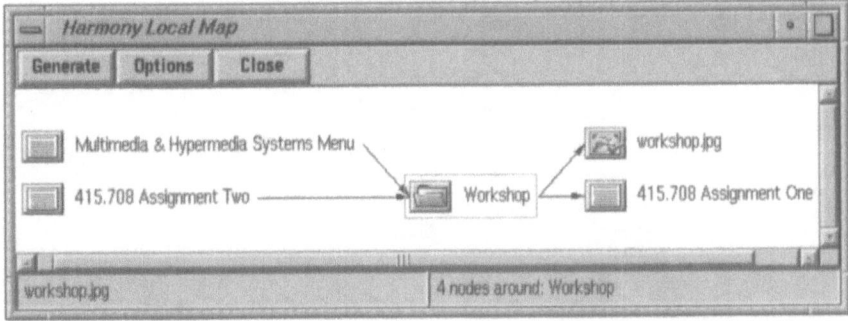

Fig. 7.3. Local Map for "415.708 Assignment One"

that point to parts of other people's documents.[4] The process of document
and link creation can be separated: documents can be created by the user's
favourite programs, and then afterwards inserted and interactively linked.

Link Types. Links in Hyperwave are typed – the type can be defined by
the creator of the link. The following link types are used by the system:

– *Referential links* connect documents and can be followed as normal hypertext links.
– *Inline links* point from a position in a text document to an image that is
  to be included at this position.
– *Annotational links* connect annotations to documents. Since links can be
  followed backwards, users can find all annotations connected to a certain
  document.
– *Texture links* add texture images to objects of VRML scenes.

Collection memberships are also internally represented as links.

7.2.5 User and Group Management

As mentioned above, Hyperwave features a built-in group and user hierarchy. Registered users, who identify themselves when contacting the server,
can view documents which have restricted read access, as well as modifying
documents they have write access to. Although other users can still connect
to the database as anonymous users, they will only see documents that have
no access restrictions specified, and they are not allowed to add or modify
documents.

User and group entries are objects within the database just like documents. Users can be members of one or more groups and each group can
have one or more parent groups. A group inherits all the rights of its parent

---

[4] This is a significant improvement on the system used in the Web, where creating
a link into another HTML document requires modification of the target document
to add a destination anchor.

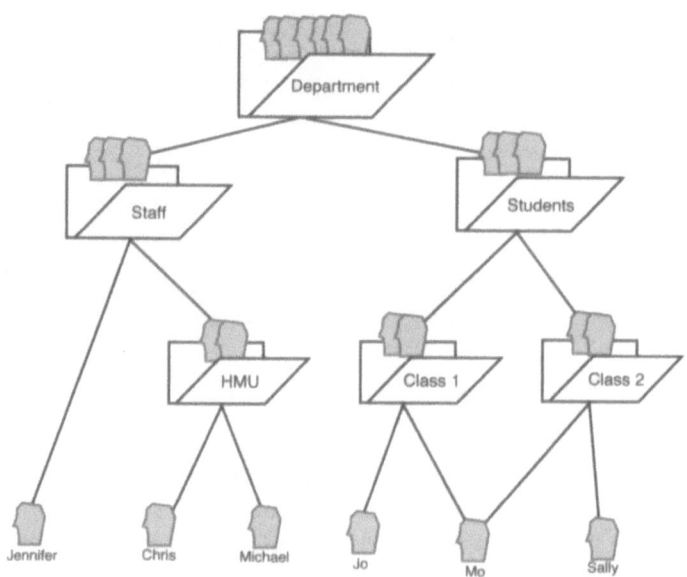

Fig. 7.4. Hyperwave's User and Group Hierarchy

groups. In the example shown in Figure 7.4, the user "Chris" can read all documents readable by the groups "Hypermedia", "Staff", and "Department".

Creating and updating user entries for many users is always a time consuming task. To minimise this problem, external identification servers can be used to identify users on the basis of information not stored in the Hyperwave database (e.g., UNIX passwords and group tables).

7.2.6 Copyright Enforcement

Hyperwave provides mechanisms to enforce copyright restriction and collection of royalties at the server level.

External providers of multimedia content will, in most cases, only allow a limited number of accesses at the same time to the material they provide (as is the case with conventional books and videos). These restrictions can be enforced by the Hyperwave server. In addition to the access rights on user and group basis as described in Section 7.2.5, every document can be a member of a license group that restricts simultaneous access to these documents to a defined number.

Hyperwave provides some basic functionality for collecting royalties from users. A price tag can be associated with each document. This tag can be different for different users and groups. Registered users each have their own account with (pre-paid) "points" they can spend on documents. Every time they access a document with a price tag, the appropriate number of points will be deducted from their account. In the event of insufficient funds, no document will be returned. Anonymous users do not have access to priced documents.

7.3 Hyperwave Clients and Their Functionality

To access the documents stored in a Hyperwave server, specially designed clients can be used, as well as gateways to programs that talk the Web HTTP and Gopher protocols.

The native Hyperwave clients will predominantly be used by information providers and server administrators, while the general public will be more likely to use the Web gateway through popular browsers such as Netscape Navigator. Native Hyperwave clients exist for the MS Windows and UNIX platforms.

7.3.1 Command Line Programs

Command line programs allow the automatic manipulation of vast quantities of documents. These programs exist for UNIX and Windows NT and allow searching, addition, modification, and deletion of documents. They are especially useful for the automatic creation and updating of documents.

7.3.2 Harmony

Harmony is the graphical client for Hyperwave that runs under UNIX and X Windows. It combines all the available functions under one unified interface.

The main window is the "session manager" (see Figure 7.5), which displays the collection hierarchy and the user's current position within that hierarchy. Every move the user makes within the database (link transfer, searches, etc.) is reflected in this display. Users will therefore always be able to get an impression of where they are in the database at any particular moment, so the "lost in hyperspace" phenomenon is less likely to occur. Furthermore, users can always explore the context in which a document is placed (provided the author created a meaningful collection hierarchy). Harmony marks all visited documents, providing users with the means to ensure that they have seen all the documents in which they are interested within that context.

Further navigation aids include a navigational log which helps in finding documents visited previously, and a search dialogue that allows users to specify search queries interactively. These are shown in Figure 7.6. Harmony's local map of a document has already been introduced in Figure 7.3.

Harmony also allows users to set up a priority list of preferred languages. Document titles are picked according to this order: if a cluster contains multiple documents of the same type (e.g., text) but different language attributes,

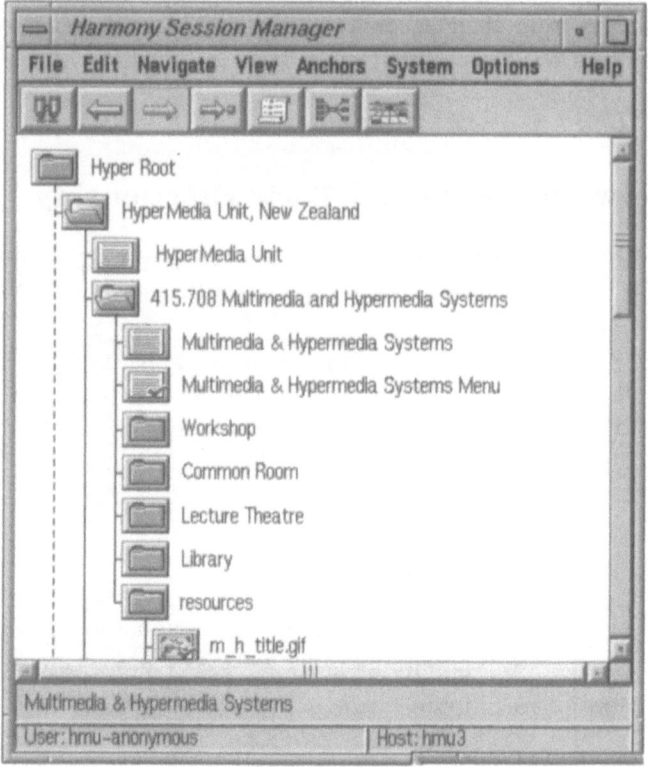

Fig. 7.5. Harmony Session Manager

the document with the most preferred language will be displayed. The first
selected language is used for the program's user interface.

Harmony contains separate document viewers for the different document
types.[5] Every viewer starts in a window of its own which contains all basic
navigation facilities as well as tools for interactively adding and removing
links. Figure 7.7 shows the Image Viewer when a link is being created from
this image to another document.

Documents can be edited interactively, during which they are locked
against other modifications and can be downloaded into the user's favourite
editor.

Links to and from HTML documents are preserved by inserting the links
into the text of the HTML document when exporting it and extracting them
when the changed version is inserted into the server.

Harmony also contains a viewer for three-dimensional VRML scenes (one
of the first of its kind), together with a three-dimensional collection overview

---

[5] See Section 7.2 for a list of types.

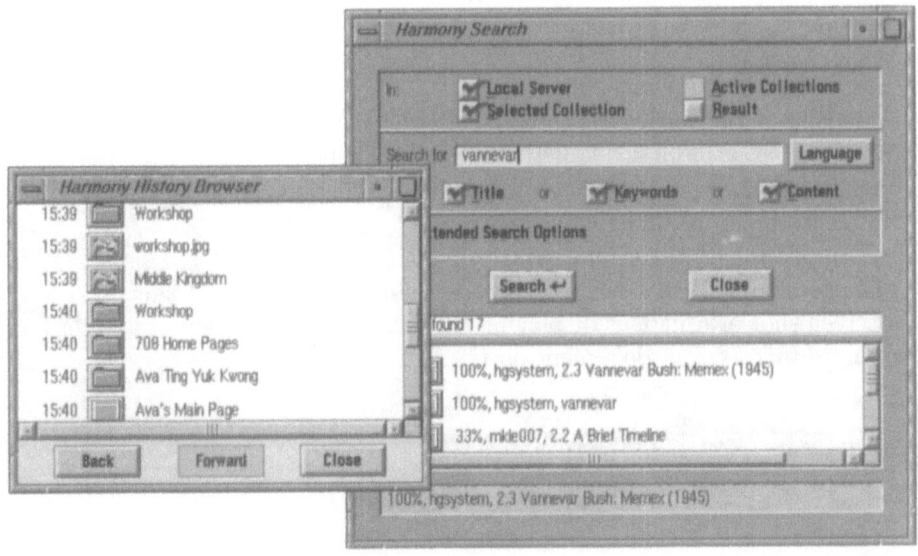

Fig. 7.6. Harmony's History and Search Mechanisms

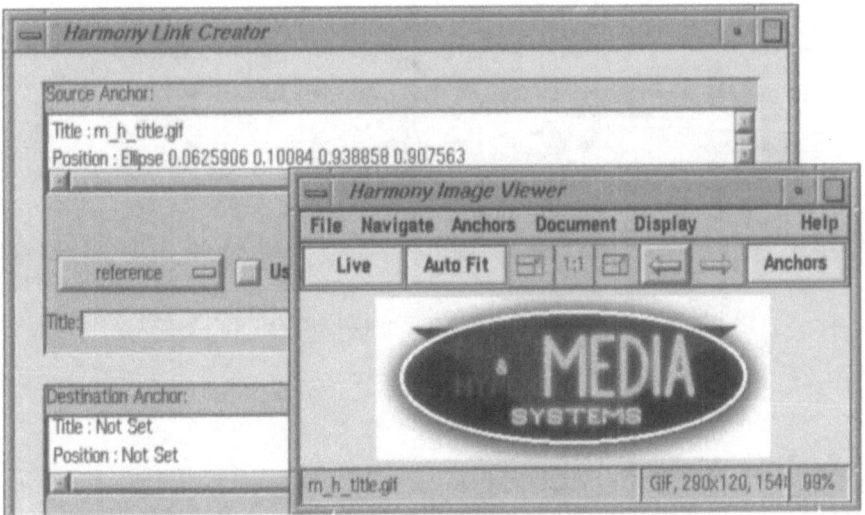

Fig. 7.7. Harmony's Image Viewer and Link Editor.

that allows users to "fly over" the collection hierarchy and replicates the functionality of the session manager.

7.3.3 Amadeus

Amadeus is the native Hyperwave client for Windows. It is available for Windows 95, Windows NT, and Windows 3.11. It has largely the same functionality as Harmony, although many of the functions are to be found under different names at different places.

Amadeus uses the same layout principles as Harmony, having one session manager and built-in viewers for different document formats. Figure 7.8 shows a screen shot of Amadeus displaying the collection hierarchy on the right and an introductory text document on the left.

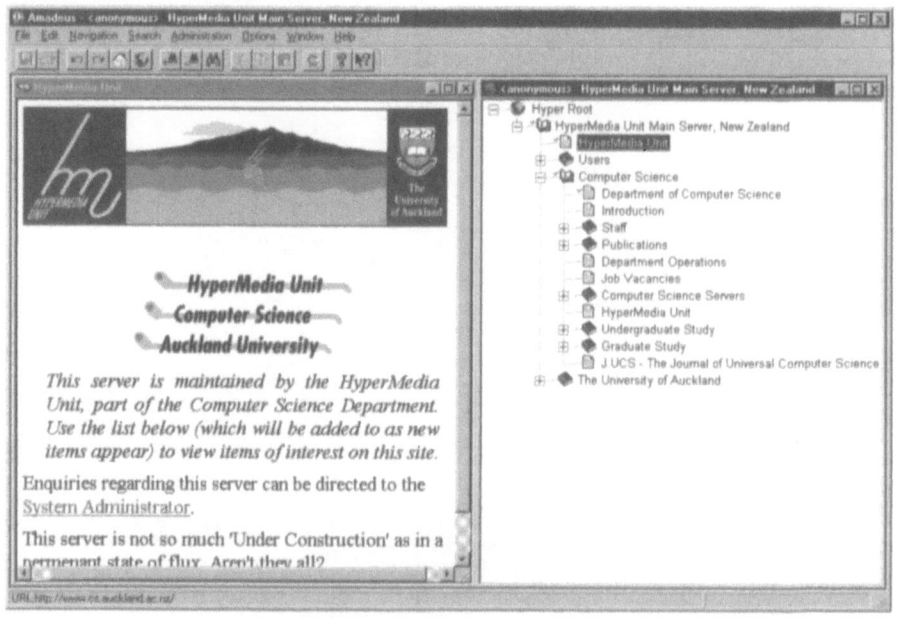

Fig. 7.8. Amadeus: Text Viewer and Collection Overview

7.3.4 WaveMaster

WaveMaster presents Hyperwave documents to Web clients. It is part of the Hyperwave server and acts as a "near standard" Web server. Figure 7.9 shows Netscape accessing the WaveMaster gateway. As can be seen, the head document of a collection is displayed at the top with the collection list underneath.

Fig. 7.9. WaveMaster

The WaveMaster interface can be accessed from all platforms providing a Web client and should thus be the main means of access for users who do not need to edit or add documents on a regular basis. Communication to and from WaveMaster can be encrypted using the *Secure Socket Layer* protocol (see Section 4.6.5).

In order to replicate a subset of the added functionality of Hyperwave some buttons and extra information are displayed with every document retrieved. These provide identification, search, language selection, server status, document attributes, and editing functions.

Documents are retrieved from Hyperwave's document server and delivered to the client. Text documents in Hyperwave's original HTF format are converted to HTML on the fly. For all documents that can be displayed by Web clients, a framework with the buttons described above and additional meta-information (e.g., document author and date, parent collections) is created on the fly and delivered via the gateway. This process can be customised to site-specific standards using Hyperwave's *PLACE* language, a set of template files that specify the layout and presentation of documents.

Hyperwave uses a connection-oriented protocol to maintain user identity and status information for the entire time a user is active. This is in contrast to the Web's connectionless protocol, where for every request we have a new connection. To overcome this restriction the WaveMaster asks the client on the first request to supply a certain information string (a "cookie") for all further requests.

By now, most of the functionality of the generic Hyperwave clients is present in the Web gateway. Documents and their attributes can be inserted, modified, and deleted. Existing documents can be annotated, copied, and moved. Documents can be directly uploaded to a Hyperwave server by using the "publish" function of Netscape Navigator Gold. Users of Microsoft Office programs can use Web Publishing Wizard to upload documents directly.

Other functions like user and group administration, and two- and three-dimensional visualisation of the document structures (e.g., collection overview and local maps) will be available soon. They will be based on a generic Java interface to the Hyperwave protocol and will allow replication of the functionality that is currently available only in Amadeus and Harmony.

7.4 Existing Applications

Several institutions have been using Hyperwave for quite a while now and some common fields of application have emerged. Some of these will be described in this section.

7.4.1 Electronic Publishing

Electronic publishing experiments are being pursued by many major publishers and organisations, including newspapers and scientific journals. The metaphors and interfaces used differ from experiment to experiment, but the researchers all agree on the following points:

- The new medium offers new presentation possibilities: The documents can contain the entire wealth of multimedia, where animations, simulations, and films can accompany traditional texts. Links to additional resources available over the Internet can be included.
- Articles can be kept up to date without requiring the publication of a new version or renaming further editions.
- Regular publications such as dictionaries can be updated continuously.

But there are still some unresolved problems. Electronic networks do not provide satisfactory mechanisms for the collection of royalties and enforcing copyrights. Publishers and libraries traditionally undertook the task of keeping publications available over a long period of time (centuries). The fifty years of computing so far have already left us with an overwhelming number of physical and logical data formats that cannot be deciphered any more. Furthermore, the role of publishers needs to be redefined from an information collector and re-distributor, to a mediator and evaluator of distributed resources.

The field of computer science, with its fast turnaround times and well equipped and educated readership, should be an ideal testing ground for new media. The Journal of Universal Computer Science (J.UCS) [Maurer and Schmaranz, 1994, URLz1] is a scientific journal that is only produced electronically, with Hyperwave being used as the base distribution system. Articles are submitted electronically, and, upon acceptance, both a hyperlinked HTML and PostScript version of the article will be uploaded to the server. An article will be included in the collection devoted to the actual issue as well as in a number of subject categories according to the ACM Computing Reviews classification of Computer Science subject areas. All collections allow keyword and full-text searches. At the end of each year a CD-ROM is produced containing all contributions for that year.

For reasons of scientific authenticity, articles in J.UCS are static, meaning they cannot be changed by the author after publication date. However, refereed annotations to existing articles are planned for the future [Maurer and Schmaranz, 1994].

7.4.2 Teaching and Learning Support Environments

Electronic teaching and learning environments can be realised using Hyperwave as a foundation. The working areas of the participants can be protected, if necessary, by the built-in user manager. A common collection hierarchy can contain documents of use to students and teachers and can be extended to a Virtual Learning Centre that can contain all the resources needed for the learning process. See Chapters 11 and 12 for more details.

Learning environment projects based on Hyperwave are underway at:

- Graz, Austria (see Section 12.8.1)
- Paderborn, Germany (see Section 12.8.2)
  [Brennecke and Keil-Slawik, 1995, Engbring et al., 1995]
- Auckland, New Zealand (see Section 12.8.3) [Klemme, 1996].

7.4.3 Digital Libraries

Increasing numbers of museums and libraries have added "electronic showcases" to their museums in order to offer their collections, or parts thereof, on the Internet. Since more and more information is available primarily in electronic form (e.g., Hypertext documents, technical manuals, theses), libraries are looking into presenting these directly though electronic interfaces. These electronic versions offer extensive search functions, they are dynamically extensible, and they may be annotated by users.

Issues arising from this include both how to ensure an institution's copyright on their work and how to charge for access. Copyright can be protected by the use of watermarking techniques, which add non-removable information about origin and ownership to a digital document [Anderson et al., 1996]. These can either be visible or invisible to the user of the system.

Image Libraries. Digital image libraries based on Hyperwave are currently being developed for The Museum of New Zealand and The National Library of New Zealand. Both institutions will present their libraries of photos, paintings, etc., on the Web. To ensure that their copyright and commercial interests are retained, only images with visible watermarks will be presented to the general public. High-quality unmarked versions will only be made available to customers who are willing to pay a fee.

General Electronic Libraries. Since electronic libraries are discussed much more fully in Chapter 9, we shall only mention one illustrative example here. The project LIBERATION (LIBraries: Electronic Remote Access To Information Over Networks) [URLn3] aims at adding a unified access mechanism for electronic resources to technical libraries and enabling publishing houses to operate successfully in the market of electronic publications. Resources include conference proceedings, electronic books, journals, courseware, manual pages and documentation, and bibliographies.

7.4.4 Corporate Document Repositories

Hyperwave is currently being used for corporate document repositories in corporate Intranets. Driving factors behind the acceptance of Hyperwave into the corporate environment include the ability to store vast quantities of documents, the structured search facility, and the user and group hierarchy. Companies known to use Hyperwave include Motorola, Boeing, and Daimler-Benz. The Hyperwave servers of the companies mentioned are company-internal and protected from the Internet by firewalls, so no more information is publicly available.

8. Hypermedia: Standards and Models

8.1 Introduction

Many of the important advances in hypermedia that we are discussing in this book are due to progress in data compression techniques (see Section 8.4) and in standardising network protocols (see Section 8.2.1).

In Section 8.4 of this chapter we outline two common image compression standards: JPEG and MPEG.

In Section 8.5 we describe several noteworthy hypermedia models that have become either de facto standards or standards approved by a standards body.

8.2 Networks, Access, and Services

To support multimedia applications, efficient and reliable transport networks are obviously of utmost importance – see [Koegel-Buford, 1994] for an introduction to Quality Of Service (QOS) for computer networks.

Wide area networks (WANs) such as the Internet are certainly of very limited use for applications such as video distribution, where slow transmission rates and narrow bandwidth negatively impact on the quality of both audio and video. Video-on-demand services, for example, are using very much more centralised approaches – such as Metropolitan Area Networks (MAN) [Sen, 1994].

A wide range of network access services are available. The following is a list given by Sen [Sen, 1994]:

- BSIDN or Broadband
  - Switch Multimegabit Data Service (SMDS): A connectionless cell-based (i.e., fixed-length packets) variable rate data service operating between 1.5 and 45 Mb/s (megabits per second).
  - Cell Relay Service (CRS): A connection-oriented cell-based data service operating from 45 to 150 Mb/s.
  - Continuous Bit Rate Service: A synchronous data service operating in the range 45–150 Mb/s (not standardised as yet).

- Private Line Access Service (T3): A synchronous data service at 45
  Mb/s.
- Wideband Services
  - Primary Rate ISDN: A channelised synchronous data service with 23
    times 64 Kb/s channels and one 16 Kb/s channel, for a total of 1.5
    Mb/s.
  - Frame Relay Service (FRS): A connection-oriented frame-based (i.e.,
    variable-length packets) data service operating at up to 1.5 Mb/s.
  - Private Line Access Service (T1): A synchronous data service at 1.5
    Mb/s.

8.2.1 Communications Circuits

Historically, hardwired communications circuits were leased from telephone
companies, where users paid for the connection whether they used it or not.
Nowadays, data packets travel between routing computers (nodes) along multiple paths (see Figure 8.1).

Communication circuits can be categorised as follows:

- Switched circuit. These can be compared with costed telephone networks.
- Packet switched. These are like personal courier services, where the user
  pays for each packet sent.
- Virtual circuits (X.25.OSI). These find the "best" way to send a complete
  ordered message to the destination.
- Datagrams (IP). These are analogous to ordinary postal mail.

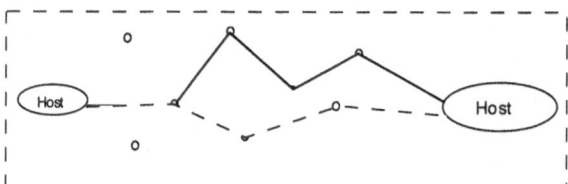

Fig. 8.1. Packet Switched Paths

8.2.2 IP (Internet Protocol)

IP is the low-level packet transmission layer. The path for the packets is
determined by the IP address, which is currently 32 bits long (but will soon
be 128 bits long). The path is determined by the current loading at each
node, where link loads and delays are read from routing tables.

However, if packets get corrupted or lost there is no error recovery mechanism built into the IP protocols – this is done by TCP (see next section).

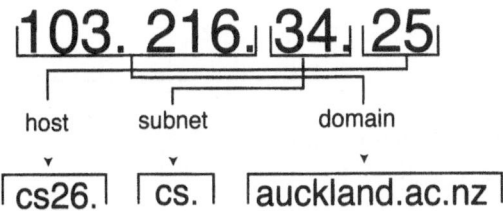

8.2.3 TCP Transmission

TCP (Transmission Control Protocol) provides reliable data flow on top of IP. This is achieved by the receiving machine requesting that corrupt or missing packets be retransmitted by the sender which then usually transmits all the following packets as well. As discussed in Section 3.2.2, each packet contains the final destination address. A node in the network either sends a packet to a directly connected host or to a "bigger" server (router). Messages may be broken into smaller segments each of which may travel along different paths. Hence they may be shuffled along the way and have to be reordered at the destination.

8.2.4 ATM (Asynchronous Transfer Mode)

ATM (Asynchronous Transfer Mode), also known as Cell Relay, is a modern development at the transmission level, which provides fast packet switching through the use of small fixed-size cells or packets. ATM currently works at speeds of 155 Mb/sec, and 622 Mb/sec should become standard in approximately 5 years.

8.3 Markup Languages

The HTML markup language was introduced in Section 6.4. In this section we look briefly at the SGML language, on which HTML is based.

8.3.1 Standard General Markup Language (SGML)

The Standard General Markup Language (SGML) is an ISO standard that grew out of the generic coding method GML (Goldfarb, Mosher and Lorie) that separates document format from its content. One of the stated aims of SGML is to "ensure that documents encoded according to its provisions should be transportable from one hardware and software environment to another without loss of information" [URLn1].

A good introduction to SGML can be found in the "TEI Guidelines for Electronic Text Encoding and Interchange" [URLn1]. The "TEI Guidelines" gives the following illustrative example, using a poem by Blake:

```
"<anthology>
   <poem><title>The SICK ROSE</title>
      <stanza>
                  <line>O Rose thou art sick.</line>
                  <line>The invisible worm,</line>
                  <line>That flies in the
                  night</line><line>in the howling
                  storm:</line>
      </stanza>
      <stanza>
                  <line>Has found out thy bed</line>
                  <line>Of crimson joy:</line><line>And
                  his dark secret love</line><line>Does
                  thy life destroy.</line>
      </stanza>
   </poem>

                  <!--more poems go here-->
</anthology>"
```

The significant advance that SGML made was the introduction of a Data Type Definition (DTD). A DTD is expressed as a set of declarative statements, each of which defines some aspect of the document. For example, the "TEI Guidelines" provides following example declarations:

```
<!ELEMENT anthology     - -  (poem+)>
<!ELEMENT poem          - -  (title?, stanza+)>
<!ELEMENT title         - O  (*PCDATA) >
<!ELEMENT stanza        - O  (line+)   >
<!ELEMENT line          O O  (*PCDATA) >
```

Note that as in HTML the element declarations are delimited by angle brackets. Each declaration consists of three parts: a name, two special characters governing the presence or absence of the start- and end-tags (O indicates optional), and a "content model" governing the form of the content. In the above example, an anthology consists of poems, which come down the tree to the type PCDATA.

8.3.2 HyperText Markup Language (HTML)

In the brief introduction to HTML that we gave in Section 6.4 we illustrated the following points:

- Each HTML tag appears within < and >
- Some tags include additional attributes (e.g., the IMG tag has SRC, HEIGHT, etc., attributes)
- Each tag is "closed" by a corresponding </tag> syntax.

Note that you cannot overlap tags eg. <HTML><BODY></HTML></BODY> is not allowed.

To illustrate HTML markup that includes a table, in addition to text and graphics, we have created a simple home page for an Online Music Store (see Figure 8.2).

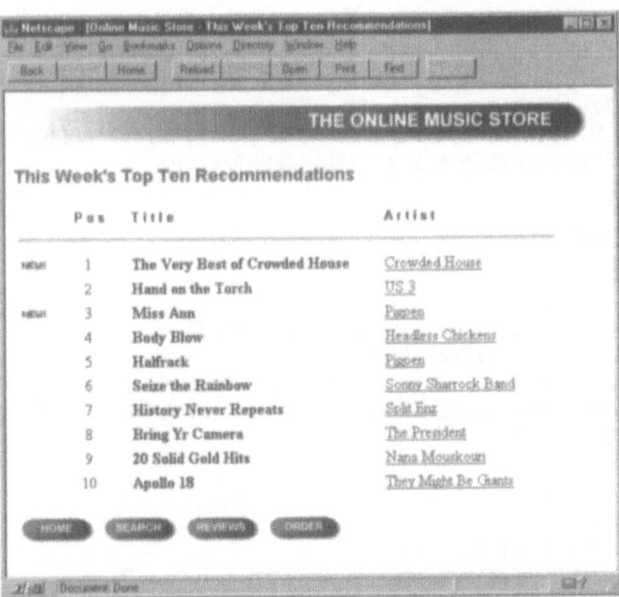

Fig. 8.2. Home Page For an Online Music Store

The HTML to produce the page shown in Figure 8.2 is as follows (a brief description of the tags used is given in Section 8.3.3):

```
<HTML>

<HEAD>
<TITLE>
 Online Music Store - This Week's Top Ten Recommendations
</TITLE>
</HEAD>

<BODY BGCOLOR="#FFFFFF">

<!-- First we display the main title graphic for the Online Music
     Store, as well as the title for this page -->

<IMG SRC="music_shop.jpg" WIDTH=590 HEIGHT=40 ALT="The Online Music
 Store">
<FONT FACE="Arial, Helvetica" COLOR="Green">
        <H3>This Week's Top Ten Recommendations</H3>
</FONT>

<!-- This table contains the information on the top ten recommended
     albums -->

<TABLE>
<TR>
        <TD></TD>
        <TD WIDTH=75 ALIGN="Middle"><FONT FACE="Arial, Helvetica"
          COLOR="#000088" SIZE=2><B>P o s</B></FONT></TD>
        <TD WIDTH=255><FONT FACE="Arial, Helvetica" COLOR="#000088"
          SIZE=2><B>T i t l e</B></FONT></TD>
        <TD WIDTH=175><FONT FACE="Arial, Helvetica" COLOR="#000088"
          SIZE=2><B>A r t i s t</B></FONT></TD>
</TR>
<TR>
        <TD COLSPAN=4><HR></TD>
</TR>
<TR>
        <TD><IMG SRC="new.gif" ALT="New"></TD>
        <TD ALIGN="Middle">1</TD>
        <TD><B>The Very Best of Crowded House</B></TD>
        <TD><A HREF="artists/crowded_house.html">Crowded House</A>
          </TD>
</TR>
<TR>
        <TD></TD>
        <TD ALIGN="Middle">2</TD>
        <TD><B>Hand on the Torch</B></TD>
        <TD><A HREF="artists/us3.html">US 3</A></TD>
</TR>
<TR>
        <TD><IMG SRC="new.gif" ALT="New"></TD>
        <TD ALIGN="Middle">3</TD>
        <TD><B>Miss Ann</B></TD>
        <TD><A HREF="artists/pigpen.html">Pigpen</A></TD>
```

```
</TR>
<TR>
        <TD></TD>
        <TD ALIGN="Middle">4</TD>
        <TD><B>Body Blow</B></TD>
        <TD><A HREF="artists/headless_chickens.html">Headless
        Chickens</A></TD>
</TR>
<TR>
        <TD></TD>
        <TD ALIGN="Middle">5</TD>
        <TD><B>Halfrack</B></TD>
        <TD><A HREF="artists/pigpen.html">Pigpen</A></TD>
</TR>
<TR>
        <TD></TD>
        <TD ALIGN="Middle">6</TD>
        <TD><B>Seize the Rainbow</B></TD>
        <TD><A HREF="artists/sonny_sharrock_band.html">Sonny Sharrock
        Band</A></TD>
</TR>
<TR>
        <TD></TD>
        <TD ALIGN="Middle">7</TD>
        <TD><B>History Never Repeats</B></TD>
        <TD><A HREF="artists/split_enz.html">Split Enz</A></TD>
</TR>
<TR>
        <TD></TD>
        <TD ALIGN="Middle">8</TD>
        <TD><B>Bring Yr Camera</B></TD>
        <TD><A HREF="artists/the_president.html">The President</A>
        </TD>
</TR>
<TR>
        <TD></TD>
        <TD ALIGN="Middle">9</TD>
        <TD><B>20 Solid Gold Hits</B></TD>
        <TD><A HREF="artists/nana_mouskouri.html">Nana Mouskouri</A>
        </TD>
</TR>
<TR>
        <TD></TD>
        <TD ALIGN="Middle">10</TD>
        <TD><B>Apollo 18</B></TD>
        <TD><A HREF="artists/they_might_be_giants.html">They Might Be
        Giants</A></TD>
</TR>
</TABLE>

<P>
```

```
<!-- The following displays the buttons at the bottom of the page -->

<A HREF="index.html"><IMG SRC="home.jpg"
WIDTH=81  HEIGHT=30 BORDER=0 ALT="Home"></A>
<A HREF="buttons/search.html"><IMG SRC="search.jpg"
WIDTH=81 HEIGHT=30 BORDER=0 ALT="Search"></A>
<A HREF="buttons/reviews.html"><IMG SRC="reviews.jpg"
WIDTH=81 HEIGHT=30 BORDER=0 ALT="Reviews"></A>
<A HREF="buttons/order.html"><IMG SRC="order.jpg"
WIDTH=81 HEIGHT=30 BORDER=0 ALT="Order"></A>

</BODY>

</HTML>
```

8.3.3 Description of HTML Tags used in Online Music Store Example

As noted in Section 6.4, many good HTML tutorials can be found on the Web [URLh2, URLi2, URLj2], and here we just include descriptions for the illustrative few that we have used in our music store example:

HTML	This tag tells the browser that the document contains HTML-coded information.
HEAD	Indicates the beginning of the HTML header.
TITLE	This tag, which appears in the document header, gives the HTML document a title. This appears in the title bar of the browser window only.
BODY	Indicates the beginning of the main body of the HTML document.
BGCOLOR	This BODY attribute specifies the background colour for the document. In this case, #FFFFFF (which describes the RGB colour values in hexadecimal) means white.
IMG	Insert an inline image.
SRC	The location of the source image (either on the local system, or stored remotely and accessed via a URL).
WIDTH	The width of the image in pixels.
HEIGHT	The height of the image in pixels.
ALT	The alternative text which is displayed instead of the image when the user turns off the browser's ability to automatically display images.

FONT	Changes the current font attributes.
FACE	Specifies which font to use, such as Arial or Helvetica.
COLOR	The colour to use for this font.
SIZE	The size of the font.
H3	A heading of level three. Headings range from level one through six, with one being the largest and six being the smallest.
TABLE	Starts a table of data contained in row/column format. A table is split into rows, and each row can contain a number of cells.
TR	Starts a new row in the current table.
TD	Inserts a new cell into the current row.
WIDTH	Specifies the width of the cell.
ALIGN	Specifies how the text will be aligned within the current cell.
B	Change the text style to bold.
COLSPAN	Indicates how many columns this cell will occupy in the current row.
HR	Displays a horizontal ruled line.
A	Turns the following text or image into an anchor, i.e., an end of a link.
HREF	Gives the filename or URL for the other end of the link.
P	Inserts a paragraph break.
<!-- -->	Everything enclosed within these two tags is a comment and is ignored by the browser.
BORDER	Determines whether or not a border will be displayed around the image.

8.4 Digital Compression

Compression techniques fall into two categories:

1. *Lossy*: Lossy compression is usually used where a reasonable approximation of the original is satisfactory, i.e., for the human user. Lossy compression intelligently removes some of the original data, often without any discernible loss of quality. Examples of lossy compression include JPEG (see Section 8.4.1), MPEG (see Section 8.4.2), and Wavelet [URL12] compression.
2. *Lossless*: Lossless compression is needed for computer data compression where data must be recovered "bit for bit". It exploits similarities (regularities, redundancies) of data in a localised area. LZ-77 [Ziv and Lempel, 1977] is an example of lossless compression.

8.4.1 The JPEG Still Picture Compression Standard

The fact that many modern hypermedia systems are able to cope with huge quantities of data is in large part due to recent developments in data compression – both for digitised still pictures and, more particularly, for digitised video (see Section 7.5.2). Since even one still picture, on a 640×480, 24-bit colour screen (NTSC standard), can eat up over 7 Mb (7,372,800 bits), a movie playing at 30 frames a second can gobble over 210 Mb/s. A European (PAL) video sequence requires similarly large quantities of data. A 768×576, 24-bit video stream running at 25 frames a second requires 253 Mb/s. Thus, in order for digital movies to be practical in either large-scale systems or desktop machines, highly efficient methods of compression have to be utilised.

The stated aim for the Joint Photographic Experts Group (JPEG) – whose name their compression method bears – is the development of a standard for continuous-tone image compression that meets certain requirements [Wallace, 1991]. These requirements may be summarised as follows:

1. To obtain "state of the art" compression rates (circa 1991).
2. To be applicable to "practically any kind of continuous-tone digital source image".
3. "To make feasible software implementations with viable performance on a range of CPUs, as well as hardware implementations with viable cost for applications requiring high performance".
4. To have the following four modes of operation:
   – Sequential encoding (e.g., DCT-based coding).
   – Progressive encoding.
   – Lossless encoding where the decompressed output is identical to the input of the compression process.
   – Hierarchical encoding where the image is encoded at multiple resolutions.

Lossless Encoding. The lossless coding scheme of the JPEG standard is rarely used in practice. It makes use of a simple predictive and difference encoding method, which can give 2:1 compression on moderately complex scenes. The lossless compression scheme can compress source images which have between 2 and 16 bits per pixel of colour or grayscale information.

If the image is of a multi-component type (e.g., RGB), the compression sequence is applied to each plane separately. Images are scanned sequentially, left to right, top to bottom, with the value of each pixel being predicted from pixels in the previous column and/or row. Eight prediction schemes are available to the encoder, as shown in Figure 8.3. The difference between the actual value of a pixel and its predicted value is calculated and entropy encoded using Huffman or arithmetic methods.

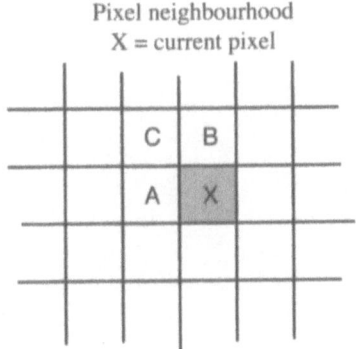

Pixel neighbourhood
X = current pixel

Encoder type	Prediction method
0	no prediction
1	A
2	B
3	C
4	A + B - C
5	A + ((B - C) / 2)
6	B + ((A - C) / 2)
7	(A + B) / 2

Fig. 8.3. JPEG Lossless Mode Predictor Types

DCT-Based Coding. The Discrete Cosine Transform (DCT) lossy encoding method of the JPEG standard uses a completely different encoding method to the lossless mode. It allows a variable amount of compression to be applied to each image, making it suitable for many applications.

The image is first transformed into a suitable colour space (see Figure 8.4). If the image is a simple grayscale picture, no conversion is necessary. Colour (RGB) images are transformed into a Luminance/Chrominance (YUV) space. The luminance component (Y) is the grayscale and the other two are the colour components (U and V). The reason for this transformation is that there is little visible loss in quality if information is lost from the chrominance components (note the lower contrast of the UV images in Figure 8.4). The UV components are then optionally compressed by merging adjacent pixels horizontally and vertically ("downsampled" by a factor of 2). The size of the image is halved in both dimensions. The YUV image is now 75% of the size of the original RGB image. Colour images thus compress more than their grayscale counterparts. Each component is then encoded separately, but all use the method below.

Pixels are grouped into 8 × 8 blocks for the DCT transformation. Real numbers $F(u,v)$ are obtained by the following formula, where $f(x,y)$ is the intensity value of the pixel at (x,y).

$$F(u,v) = \frac{1}{4}C(u)C(v)\left[\sum_{x=0}^{7}\sum_{y=0}^{7}f(x,y)\quad\cos\frac{(2x+1)u\pi}{16}\quad\cos\frac{(2y+1)v\pi}{16}\right]$$

$$\text{where}\quad u,v = 0\ldots 7 \text{ and } C(u),C(v) = \begin{cases} \frac{1}{\sqrt{2}} & \text{for } u,v = 0 \\ 1 & \text{otherwise.} \end{cases}$$

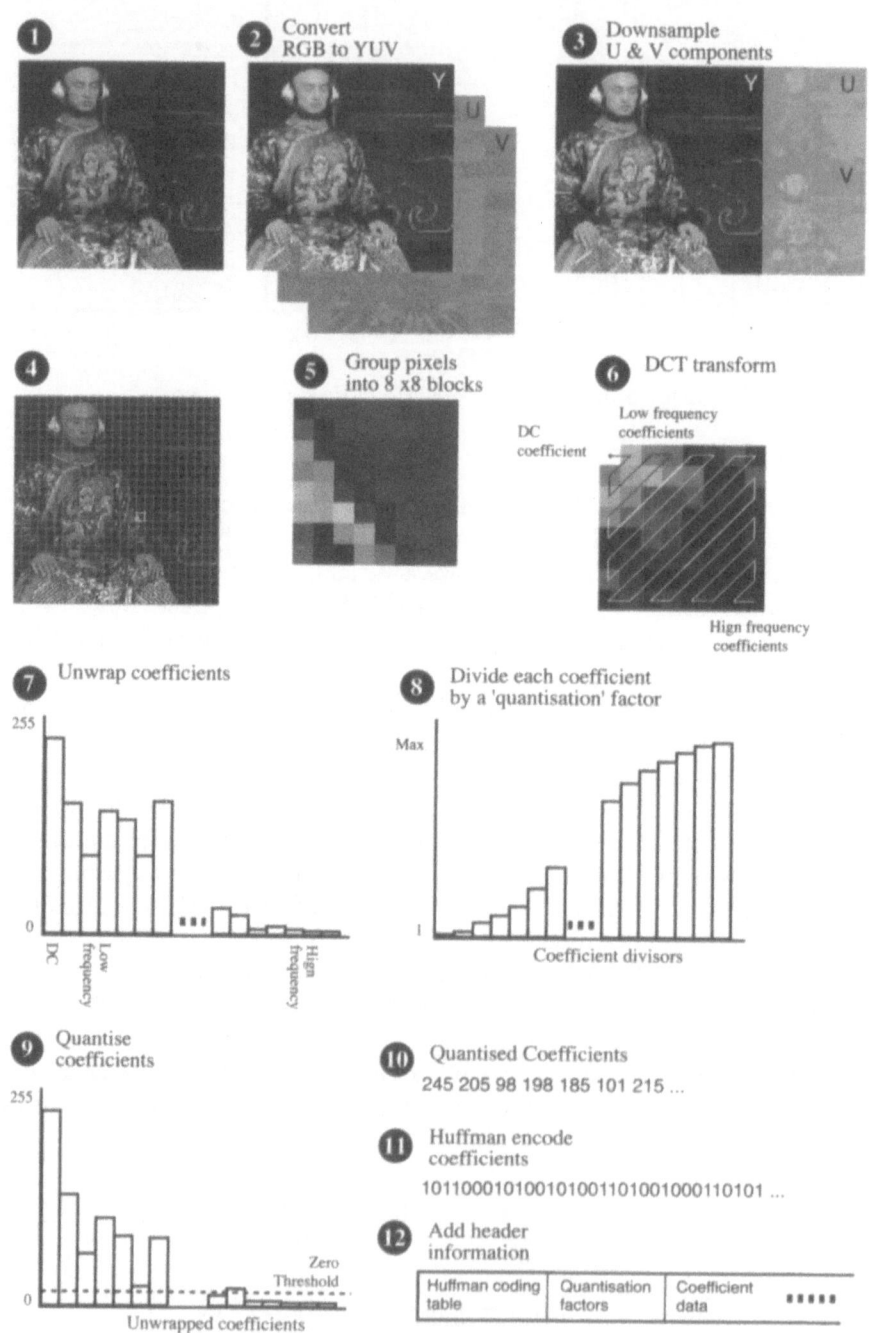

Fig. 8.4. JPEG Compression Steps

By Fourier Transform theory, $F(0,0)$, the DC component, is eight times the average value of intensity over the block and the other 63 coefficients give the frequency components of the variation in intensity. If the source image does not contain many high contrast areas, the values of $F(u,v)$, for the larger values of u and v, will be near zero. The coefficients $F(u,v)$ are always sorted into order of increasing $u + v$, in a zig-zag pattern as shown in Figure 8.4(6), so the (normally) near-zero coefficients come last.

Each real coefficient $F(u,v)$ is then divided by a quantisation factor taken from a 64-element quantisation table and rounded to an integer. It is this step where most compression takes place and many low-value, high-frequency coefficients will be rounded to zero. The values in the quantisation table can be linearly adjusted to give variable compression, although the actual tables used are not part of the JPEG specification (example tables are given, however). The larger the values in this table, the more compression takes place.

The resulting reduced and quantised coefficients are then entropy encoded, using Huffman or arithmetic encoding. This step is actually lossless and efficiently compresses the coefficient data. In the final step, the Huffman encoding table and quantisation factor table used in compression are placed as headers to the coefficient data.

Decoding a JPEG image is essentially a matter of performing the compression steps in reverse. The Huffman encoded coefficient data is decoded and scaled up using the quantisation factors, the DCT coefficients are used to reconstitute and 8×8 pixel block (using the Inverse Discrete Cosine Transformation given below), and the colour planes are converted back into an RGB format (if required).

$$f(x,y) = \frac{1}{4} \left[\sum_{x=0}^{7} \sum_{y=0}^{7} C(u)C(v)F(u,v) \quad \cos \frac{(2x+1)u\pi}{16} \quad \cos \frac{(2y+1)v\pi}{16} \right]$$

$$\text{where} \quad C(u), C(v) = \left\{ \begin{array}{ll} \frac{1}{\sqrt{2}} & \text{for } u, v = 0 \\ 1 & \text{otherwise.} \end{array} \right.$$

Progressive Encoding. Several different methods for producing series of partial images are supported by JPEG (see Figure 8.5). These methods are of particular interest in limited bandwidth situations where a quick, but low-detail, view of the image is needed. Blocks of data may be processed (and transmitted) in "slices" whose order is determined by either the coefficients (called spectral selection – where only a subset of the DCT components are encoded for each scan) or corresponding bits (successive approximation, which encodes only certain bits of each DCT coefficient). A further advantage of progressive encoding is that a custom Huffman table can be used for each scan, resulting in slightly smaller files.

For example, if only the $F(0,0)$ coefficient for each 8×8 block is transmitted, then the original image may be reconstituted using pixels 8 times larger horizontally and vertically than the original. As successive $F(u, v)$ coefficients are transmitted for all blocks in the image, more frequency components may be added to the image and a better approximation to the original obtained. Most images become readily recognisable after just a few coefficients have been transmitted. The final few coefficients affect only the most high-frequency areas of the image.

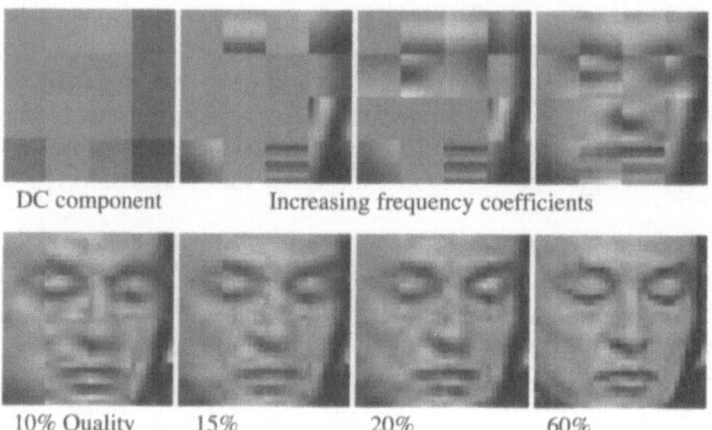

Fig. 8.5. Progressive JPEG with Increasing Frequency Coefficients

8.4.2 MPEG (Moving Picture Experts Group)

The Moving Picture Experts Group have expanded on the work done by JPEG to give even greater compression ratios for moving pictures [Le Gall, 1991] and to incorporate audio streams. Like JPEG, they have tried to create an open standard that can be used with a wide range of storage devices. Their original premise was "that a video signal and its associated audio can be compressed to a bit rate of about 1.5 Mb/s with an acceptable quality" [Le Gall, 1991], which would allow streaming video off a CD-ROM.

MPEG activities are divided into the following three categories:

– MPEG-Video
– MPEG-Audio
– MPEG-System (considers issues such as the synchronisation of video and audio)

The compression of audio and video each have their own particular problems to overcome. For example, consider the problem of video throughput. As mentioned previously, video at 25 frames/s requires over 253 Mb/s on a

PAL system (or 210 Mb/s for a 30 frames/s NTSC system). It is fortunate that, since there are often areas of continuous colour or pattern and limited areas of motion in any video, much of the information is either spatially or temporally redundant.

While the audio component of an MPEG data stream is one-dimensional and of a much lower bandwidth than video, it is no easier to compress. This is due partially to the faster response rate of the human ear, compared to the visual system. The human eye could be described as a low-speed parallel input device, with 25 "samples" per second delivering apparently smooth motion. Similarly, the human ear can be thought of as a high-speed serial input device, requiring at least 44 thousand "samples" per second for high fidelity sound.

In addition to good compression, the following encoding features were identified as being important for any audio/video encoder [Le Gall, 1991]:

- Random access
- Fast forward/reverse searches
- Reverse playback
- Audio-visual synchronisation
- Robust handling of errors
- Coding/decoding delay
- Editability
- Format Flexibility
- Cost tradeoffs.

There are currently three different versions of MPEG video compression in use or under development. MPEG-1 was the original format specification, designed to operate at 1.15 Mb/s and run off a CD-ROM. This is by far the most commonly used of the MPEG compression schemes. MPEG-2 was an extension of MPEG-1, and is aimed at high resolution video at much higher data rates. It also addresses the problems of video interlacing. MPEG-4 is optimised for very low bandwidth video streams, of the sort used in video conferencing.

There are also three different MPEG audio compression methods, called layers. MPEG audio Layer-1 is the original compression method for use with MPEG-1 and operates at around 256 Kb/s. Audio Layer-2 is an improvement on Layer-1, allowing similar quality to Layer-1 at slightly lower bit rates. Audio Layer-3 is optimised for low bandwidth applications running at 64 Kb/s or lower.

8.4.3 MPEG-1 Video Compression

The MPEG-1 format, in one form or another, is currently the most commonly used type of MPEG compression and is actually very flexible in terms of the video resolution and bit rates at which it can operate. It is theoretically possible to compress images up to 4095 × 4095 in resolution, with bit rates up to 100 Mb/s.

The standard video image size used by MPEG-1 is based on the CCIR-601 digital video standard. This is an image 720 × 288 by 50 fields (with two fields making up one frame) for PAL television, and 720 × 243 by 60 fields per second for NTSC. The images are downsampled 2:1 horizontally to 360 pixels for both standards.

The common source input for MPEG-1, called SIF, is based on a CCIR-601 standard image, downsampled 2:1 in time (25 instead of 50 fields per second), and another 2:1 horizontally and vertically in the chrominance components. Thus, a source PAL image has 360 × 288 at 25 fields/s, with a chrominance resolution of 180 × 144 and NTSC has 360 × 240 at 30 fps, with chrominance 180 × 120. Note that these figures give an identical source data rate for both formats, since (360 × 288 + 180 × 144 × 2) × 25 = (360 × 240 + 180 × 120 × 2) × 30.

MPEG video compression makes use of three methods of encoding information, one purely spatial, and two a mix of spatial and temporal. All methods work on blocks of pixels, called macroblocks, which are 16 × 16 in size.

1. I frames (Intrapicture), not dependent on other frames.
2. P frames (Predicted), dependent on previous frames (I or P).
3. B frames (Bidirectional predicted), dependent on previous and/or future frames.

Intrapicture frames essentially encode the source image in the JPEG format (with some differences). Blocks of pixels of size 8 × 8 (4 per macroblock) are run through a Discrete Cosine Transform and can be quantised on a per-macroblock basis. This macroblock grouped quantisation greatly increases the control over the final size of the compressed image, which is important to maintain fairly constant data rates.

Intrapicture frames are not dependent on any other frames and are used as "jump-in" points for random access.

Predicted frames make use of the previous I or P frame to predict the contents of the current frame and then compress the difference between the prediction and the actual frame contents. The prediction is made by attempting to find an area close to the current macroblock's position in the previous frame which contains pixels similar to those found in the current macroblock. The resulting motion vector essentially describes the movement of the macroblock and may legitimately be a null vector if there is no motion.

The difference between the predicted pixels and their actual values is calculated, DCT-encoded and the coefficients quantised (more coarsely than I frame DCT coefficients). If a sufficiently similar group of pixels cannot be found in the previous frame, a P frame can simply spatially encode the macroblock as though it were an I frame (see Figure 8.6).

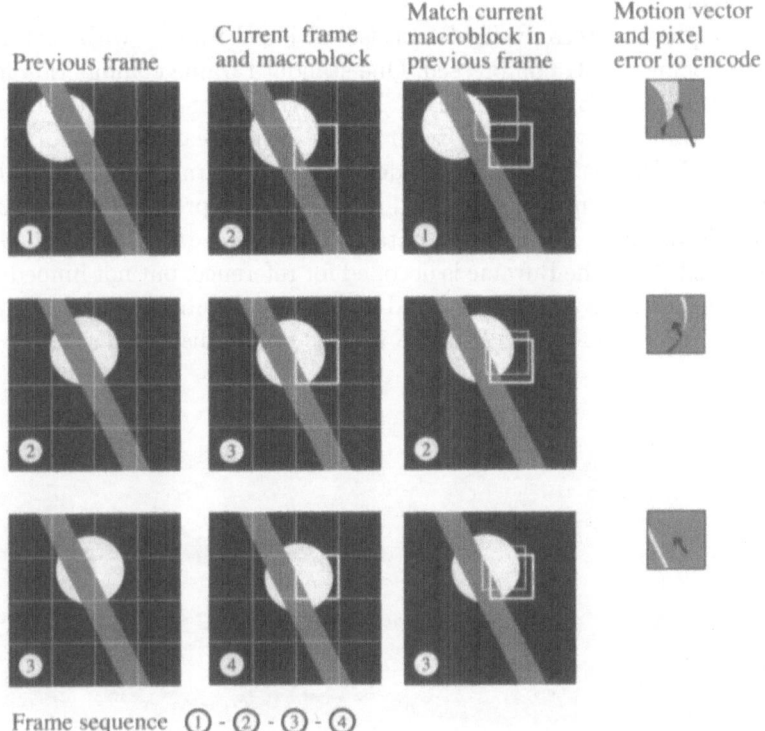

Previous frame | Current frame and macroblock | Match current macroblock in previous frame | Motion vector and pixel error to encode

Frame sequence ① - ② - ③ - ④

Fig. 8.6. Motion Vector and Difference Encoding

Bidirectional frames can use a number of different methods of encoding. Each macroblock may be encoded as though it were an I frame or a P frame. Furthermore, it can predict the contents of the current macroblock from the closest *following* I or P frame. This works in the same way as a P frame except that it attempts to find a motion vector to a similar set of pixels in the following frame, rather than the previous.

The final method available to B frames for pixel prediction uses both the previous and following frames. The best matching pixel groups in the previous and following frames are found and averaged. The difference between these averaged values and the actual pixel values is calculated, DCT-encoded and quantised (see Figure 8.7).

I, P, and B frames may be mixed in virtually any sequence – with some semantic and practical restrictions. If the video stream is to have adequate random access, then I frames must be periodically inserted into the frame pattern. While P frames add detail to previous I or P frames, the information described by a B frames does not persist beyond the lifespan of the B frame itself. In this sense, B frames merely increase the apparent frame rate of a video stream.

The simplest pattern available consists of just I frames, with each frame essentially being JPEG compressed. One standard frame combination for an MPEG stream is IBBPBBPBBPBB. This is the order in which the frames are displayed, not in which they occur in the data stream (see Figure 8.8).

Because B frames may be dependent on I or P frames occurring later, these I and P frames must be decoded first. Thus the previous frame pattern IBBP would occur as IPBB in the data stream. The I frame is decoded first and displayed. Next the P frame is decoded for reference, but not immediately shown. The B frames are decoded and displayed, possibly using information from the P frame, before the P frame itself is finally displayed.

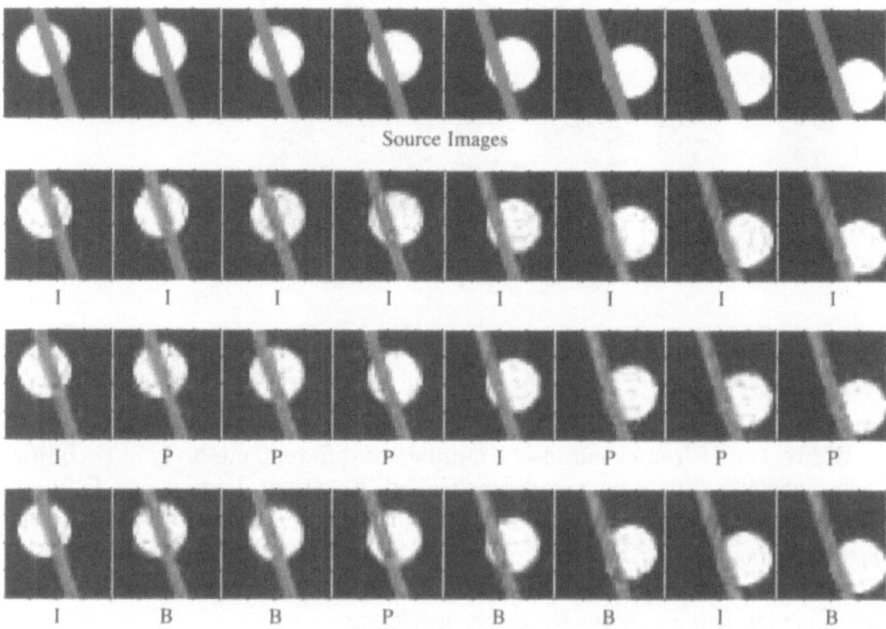

Fig. 8.7. MPEG Frame Combinations (with emphasised errors)

8.4.4 MPEG Audio Compression

Like JPEG and MPEG video compression, MPEG audio compression is lossy. It uses psychoacoustics principles to discard masked sound and assign higher fidelity where it is required the most. This means that MPEG audio compression doesn't concern itself with traditional audio sound parameters like

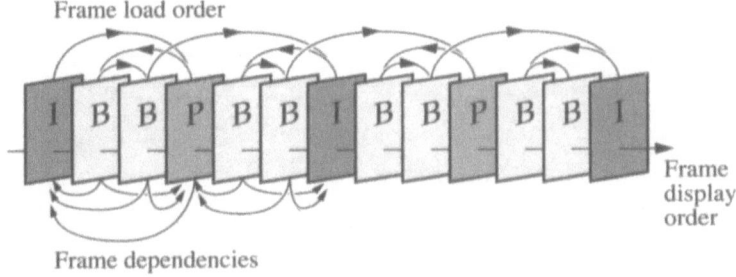

Frame load order

Frame display order

Frame dependencies

Fig. 8.8. Display and Load Order of MPEG Frames

signal-to-noise (s/n) ratios, total harmonic distortion or bandwidth. Essentially, if it sounds 'good enough' to a variety of listeners, then it is good enough.

MPEG audio can use a number of different source sample rates: 32, 44.1 (CD quality), and 48 kHz (DAT quality). Nyquist's theorem states that the highest reproducible frequency is equal to half the sampling frequency (hence the 20–22 kHz frequency range on CD). Each sample has 16-bit precision, which gives a good s/n ratio of 96 decibels (dB). Note that each extra bit of precision added to a sample increases the s/n ration by around 6 dB (see Chapter 4 in [Koegel-Buford, 1994]).

The reason why 16-bit (or greater) samples are used in most high fidelity digital sound systems is to achieve the maximum s/n ratio possible. An 8-bit sample results in noticeable *quantisation* noise, and background noise in quiet passages. This noise is less noticeable and often impossible to hear in louder passages. The loud sounds *mask* out the quieter noise. This psychoacoustics principle of masking is what MPEG audio uses to discard inaudible sounds.

The human ear is most sensitive to frequencies in the 2–4 kHz range, which is the same region that the human voice occupies. There are regions in which quiet sounds will not be apparent to the human ear at all (see Figure 8.9). If there is a strong tone with a frequency of 1000 Hz and a second tone at 1100 Hz, quieter by 18 dB, the second tone will be completely masked by the louder and cannot be heard. A third tone introduced at 2000 Hz and 18 dB quieter than the first will be heard, as it is a sufficient distance away from the louder (see Figure 8.9).

There are two ways to mask a tone: place a louder tone close to it, or place a tone of the same power but increased frequency band near it (see Figure 8.10). Masking can also occur before and after a strong sound (pre and post-masking, respectively). Pre-masking require a great difference in sound level (around 30–40 dB). The pre-masking window is only 2–5 ms, whereas post-masking can occur up to 100 ms after the initial sound (see Figure 8.10).

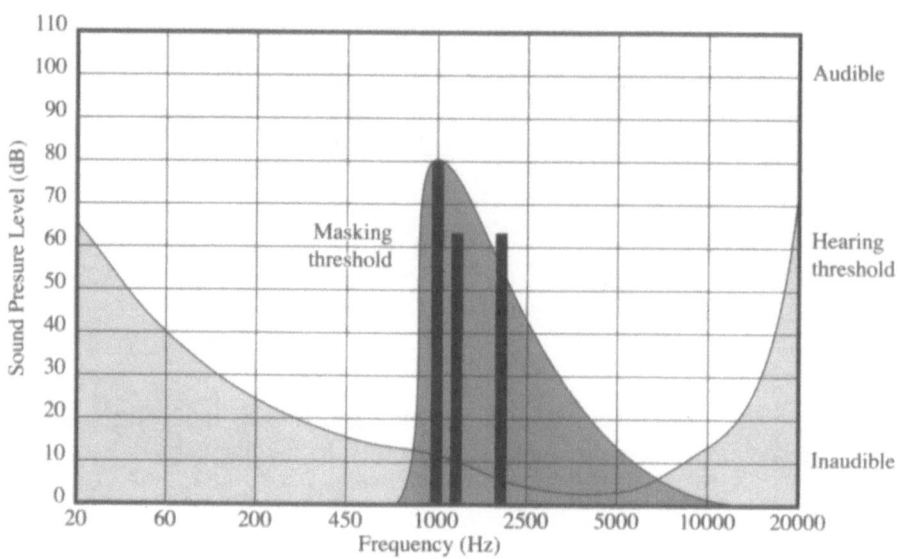

Fig. 8.9. Loud Tone Masking a Quiet Tone

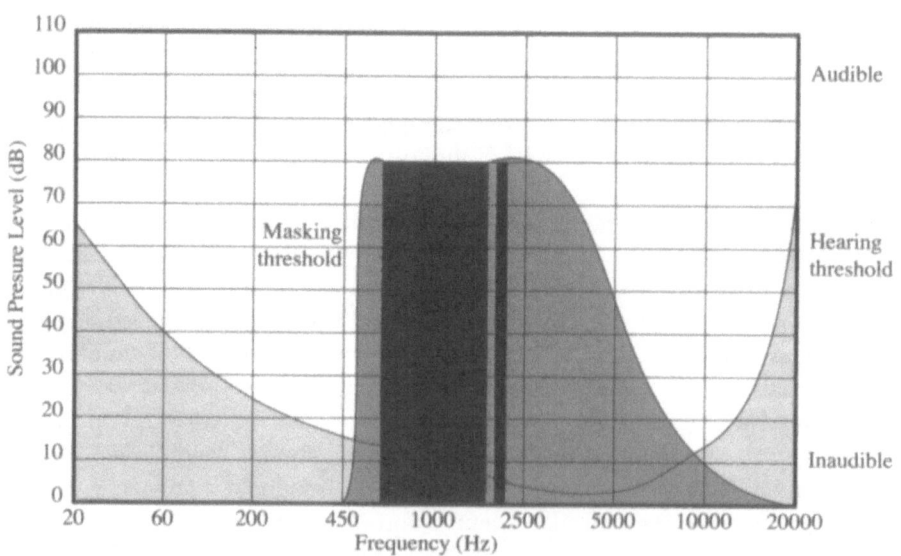

Fig. 8.10. Increased Energy and Increased Frequency Band Masking

MPEG Layer-2 compression performs a masking calculation about every 23 ms (for 44.1 kHz sample rate), on a group of 1024 samples. In each sample group, the intensities of the frequency components are calculated by a Fourier Transform and split into 32 sub-bands, with more sub-bands at lower frequencies than higher ones. Masking within a sub-band is then calculated, with precedence being given to the loudest sound. Masking effects across adjacent bands, and pre- and post-masking effects, are also taken into account (see Figure 8.11).

For each sub-band a standardised set of intensities is used to select a maximum intensity factor which is close to the frequency component of greatest intensity in the sub-band. The intensities of non-masked frequency components are expressed as a fraction of this maximum intensity factor. The number of bits used for the accuracy of this fraction varies for the sub-bands; the fewer bits used, the more quantisation noise will be introduced. The allocation of the number of bits of accuracy to use for each band is done so that more bits are used in regions of the spectrum where the ear is more likely to notice any changes, but the total number of bits, for all the sub-bands, is kept roughly constant.

All MPEG layers can encode mono and stereo audio channels in a number of ways, some of which make use of the commonality in stereo left and right channels. These can be either single (mono), dual (two mono channels), stereo or joint-stereo (intensity or "m/s" stereo for Layer-3 only). The dual-channel method stores the left signal in one channel and the right in another. The m/s method has one channel containing the sum signal $(L + R)$ and the other the difference signal $(L - R)$. Intensity stereo combines the high frequency part of the signal (above 2 kHz).

MPEG style audio compression is also used in other commercial audio systems. The first large scale commercial implementation of these compression methods was used by Philips in their Digital Compact Cassette system. Their PASC (Precision 360/ Adaptive Sub-band Coding) system was essentially an MPEG Layer-1 audio compression and playback system. Sony's more recent offering for MiniDisc uses a more advanced method of compression, called ATRAC (Adaptive TRansform Acoustic Coding). The ATRAC system has much in common with the MPEG Layer-2 and 3 coding scheme.

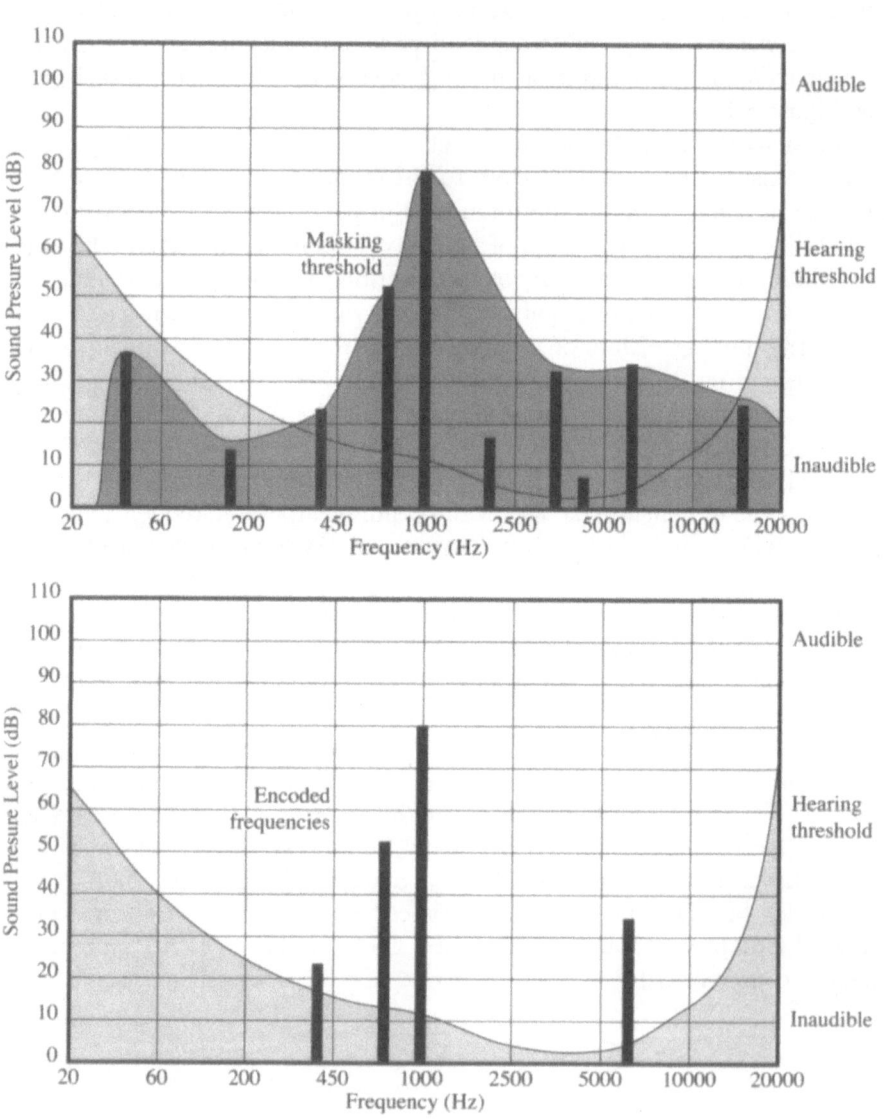

Fig. 8.11. Before and After Sub-band Masking

8.5 Hypermedia Models

The successes and shortcomings of hypermedia systems have been discussed both by Halasz in his "Seven Issues" paper [Halasz, 1988] and in Chapter 4 of this book. This section will focus on several hypermedia models that have been developed to address some of the issues. We begin with the Dexter Model since it is of historical importance.

8.5.1 The Dexter Hypertext Reference Model

In 1988 a group of hypermedia experts in hypermedia system design met at the Dexter Inn in Sunapee, New Hampshire, with the goal "to hold discussions that might lead to consensus on the terminology and semantics of basic hypermedia concepts" [Grønbæk and Trigg, 1994]. What evolved was a "reference standard against which new hypertext systems could be compared" [Grønbæk and Trigg, 1994]. The formulated goal for the model "is to provide a principled basis for comparing systems as well as for developing interchange and interoperability standards" [Halasz and Schwartz, 1994]. The special issue of the Communications of the ACM on Hypermedia [Communications, 1994a] describes the original model and several extensions such as AHM (Amsterdam Hypermedia Model, see Section 8.5.2) and a "cooperative hypermedia system."

The authors have taken pains to avoid ambiguity. For example, they use the term *component* instead of *node*, *card*, or *frame*. Components, besides including text, graphics, sound, video, etc., also include links (of arbitrary arity with attributes such as keywords or link types associated) and hierarchies (directed acyclic graphs). A globally unique identifier (UID) is assigned to each component, but indirect addressing is also supported.

The model is careful to distinguish between run-time, storage, and *within-component* aspects of any hypermedia system. It distinguishes between what "is handled by the system and what is the province of external applications" [Halasz and Schwartz, 1994]. Although it is the storage layer that receives the most consideration, the interfaces between the layers are also focussed on. For example, as shown in Figure 8.12 [Halasz and Schwartz, 1994], anchoring is considered to be outside the storage layer which contains the nodes and links.

The model also defines a set of database management functions such as "CreateComponent, DeleteComponent, LinksTo....".

8.5.2 AHM: The Amsterdam Hypermedia Model

The Amsterdam Hypermedia Model adds time and context attributes to the Dexter model [Hardman et al., 1993, Hardman et al., 1994]. In particular, AHM considers multiple streams of multimedia data, i.e., movie, sound,

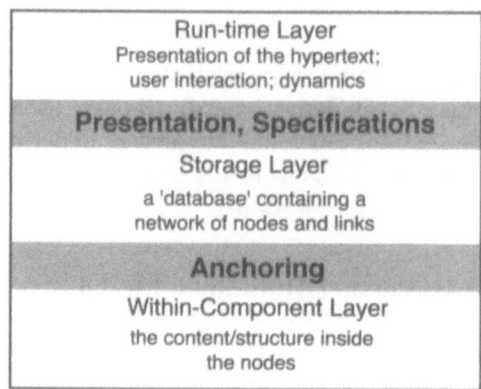

Fig. 8.12. Layers of the Dexter Model [Halasz and Schwartz, 1994]

graphics and/or text, being played along a time-line. Although temporal aspects are commonly assigned to the within-component layer, the authors maintain that this practice falls short for large and complex systems.

The major differences between the Amsterdam Hypermedia Model and the Dexter model are highlighted in Figure 8.13, adapted from [Hardman et al., 1994].

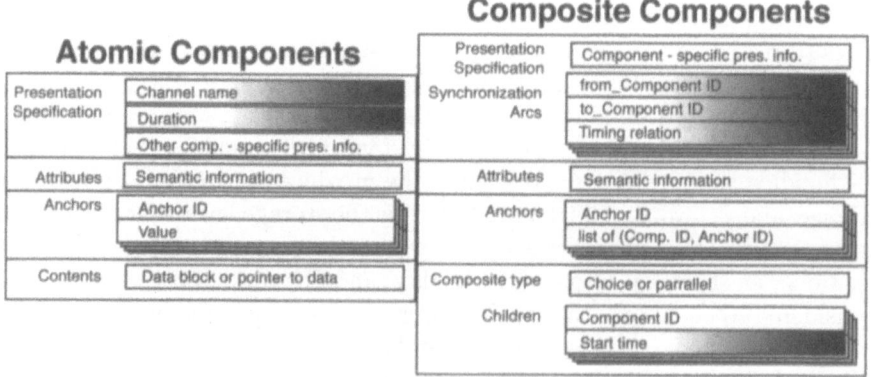

Fig. 8.13. The Amsterdam Hypermedia Model (AHM) [Hardman et al., 1994]

Abstract channels are proposed in AHM [Hardman et al., 1993]. Since on/off attributes are associated with each channel, users can specify, at run time, their preferred viewing options.

In addition, AHM components can have start-time offsets (see Figure 8.14), duration attributes, and synchronisation arcs (see Figure 8.14), as well as the usual links and anchors.

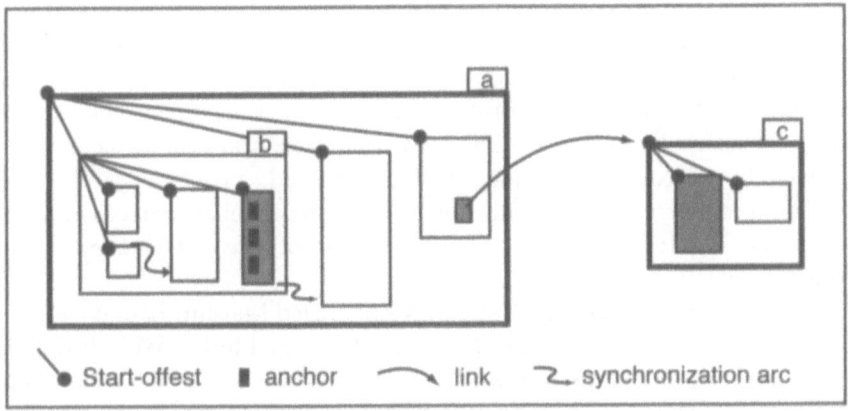

Fig. 8.14. AHM Components and Timing Relations [Hardman et al., 1994]

8.5.3 HDM: Hypertext Data Model

In the paper "HDM – A Model-Based Approach to Hypertext Application Design", the authors suggest that representations such as the Dexter model "should be regarded as more 'system' oriented" whereas the HDM aims at "modelling applications rather than systems", particularly "large and complex applications" [Garzotto et al., 1993]. They define classes of *entities* that consist of hierarchies of *components*, where the components are abstractions for sets of data units.

Of particular importance is the notion of *perspectives*. Any entity may have multiple perspectives associated with it. For example, a collection may have Italian/English perspectives or Textual/Graphical perspectives.

The model allows three categories of links:

- Application links to connect different entities, e.g., between "Orfeo ed Euridice" and a biographical work on Gluck.
- Structural links to connect components, e.g., between acts.
- Perspective links to connect units, e.g., between Italian and French versions.

The authors state "One of the central advantages of HDM... is that defining a significant number of links can be left implicit – being induced from structural properties of the model – or can be defined intentionally and algorithmically derived" [Garzotto et al., 1993].

8.5.4 HyTime

HyTime is a "Hypermedia/Time-based Document Structuring Language for representing hypermedia, including time and space based documents" [Newcomb et al., 1991]. It has been developed at an abstract level but in such a way that it is hoped it will encourage application developers to produce hypermedia applications that can communicate across both software and hardware boundaries. It is hoped that such an architecture will "be used as a means of integrating the information management of a diverse enterprise, so that, for example, innovative ideas, their sources, and the obstacles those ideas have to overcome can be identified and tracked.... HyTime can be used to facilitate concurrent engineering and other forms of collaborative research" [Newcomb et al., 1991]. Much emphasis is placed on the interchange of time dependent data.

HyTime, based on SGML (Standard Generalized Markup Language), has many features of markup languages such as those used in the Web. It defines *architectural forms*, instances of which can be used to create Document Type Definitions (DTDs). HyTime extends SGML to include "real" hypermedia, i.e., it supports the placement and interrelation of objects within coordinate spaces that can represent space, time, or space and time.

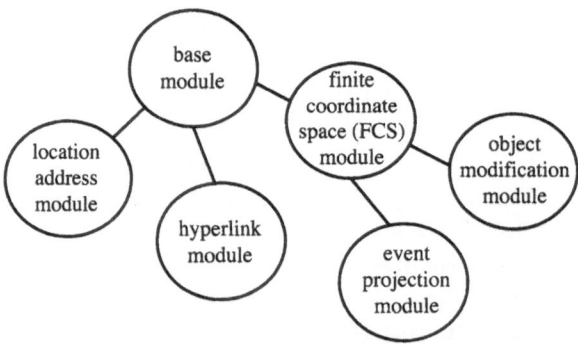

Fig. 8.15. Hytime Module Interdependencies [Newcomb et al., 1991]

The model includes at least six modules. These modules and their dependencies are shown in Figure 8.15.

1. The Base Module. The Base Module includes general management, coordinate addressing, and activity tracking facilities.
2. The Location Address Module. Unique identifiers are defined within documents and documents inhabit *name spaces*. However, HyTime "allow[s] literally anything to become an end of a hyperlink" [Newcomb et al., 1991].

3. The Hyperlink Module. Five types of links are supported: independent, property, contextual, aggregate, and spanlink.
4. The Finite Coordinate Spaces module defines Finite Coordinate Spaces (FCS) "by combining any measurable domains on any number of axes (e.g., seconds, meters, moles, lumens, grams, dollars) [Newcomb et al., 1991]. Objects are scheduled in the Finite Coordinate Spaces and are bounded by *events*.
5. The Event Projection Module. This maps events from one FCS to another according to the units in the corresponding FCS.
6. The Object Modification Module. This provides for the modification of scheduled objects according to user-defined rules.

8.5.5 MHEG: Multimedia and Hypermedia Information Encoding Expert Group

The MHEG group began as an ad-hoc group in 1989 to "address the coded representation of final form multimedia and hypermedia objects that will be interchanged across services and applications, by any means, e.g., storage media, LAN, wide area telecommunication or broadcast networks" [Price, 1993].

In contrast to HyTime, the sets of objects are intended for "final form presentations". MHEG is particularly aimed at "large scale telematic applications: training and education, simulation and games, sales and advertising, ... [and] medical applications" [Price, 1993].

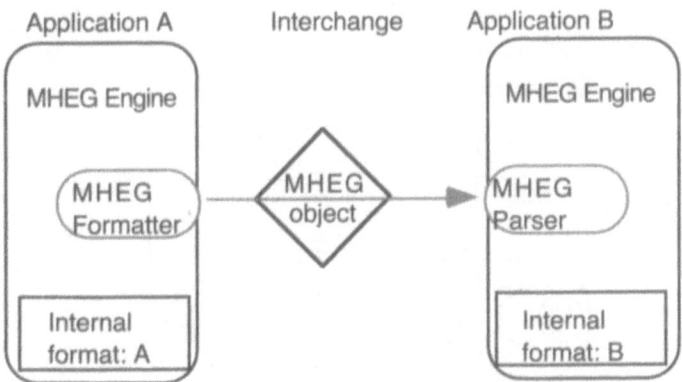

Fig. 8.16. MHEG Engine (redrawn from [Price, 1993])

MHEG Interchange Format. The MHEG interchange format allows for applications with different internal formats to exchange objects. This, of course, requires that each application can convert between its native internal format and a standard MHEG format. An example of this is shown in Figure 8.16, where the MHEG formatter in Application A's engine converts from A's internal format to the MHEG standard format. Application B's Parser then converts the MHEG object to B's internal format.

MHEG Support for Interactivity. MHEG supports interactivity by defining application-independent interaction objects such as "buttons, text entry, and scrolling areas." [Koegel-Buford, 1994].

MHEG support for Synchronisation. MHEG "identifies four levels of synchronisation":

– Scripting
– Conditional: e.g., "when the audio has finished, ask the question"
– Spatio-temporal: e.g., "show the product name 2 cm above the image"
– System: e.g., lip synchronisation for movies [Price, 1993]

8.5.6 The HM Data Model

The HM-Data model supports the structured browsing of hypermedia databases [Maurer et al., 1993a].

The databases consist of a set of structured collections called S_Collections (or just collections for short) [Maurer et al., 1995]. An S_Collection encapsulates both a chunk of multimedia data (content), and a particular internal structure.

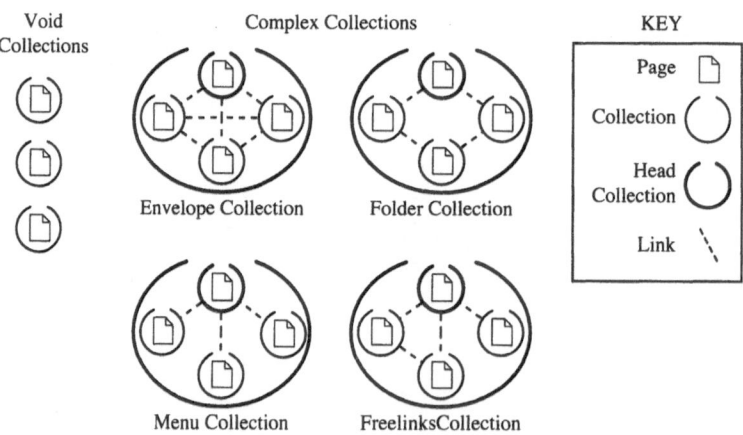

Fig. 8.17. HM Data Model Collections

The internal structure consists of a *pseudo-hierarchical* group of other collections. We use the term "pseudo-hierarchical" because in fact the structure is a directed acyclic graph of parent and children nodes, where a child may belong to more than one parent. This means that any document can belong to multiple collections – without duplication of content.

The HM Data Model provides a number of predefined subclasses of S_Collection (see Figure 8.17) as follows:

1. An Envelope where all members are inter-linked
2. A Folder which is essentially an ordered list
3. A Menu which is a simple hierarchical structure
4. Freelinks where members may be arbitrarily connected

An imposed condition in the HM-Data Model is that all links must be encapsulated within S_Collections. Browsing is achieved via three operations ACCESS, ZOOM-IN, and ZOOM-OUT. When any S_Collection is ACCESSed, its content are displayed. ZOOM-IN opens a collection to display the underlying content. ZOOM-OUT takes the user back to the collection that was accessed just prior to the most recent ZOOM-IN.

The ZOOM-UP function is extension of the ZOOM-OUT operation. In this case, the user can switch up to any S_Collection of which the current S_Collection is a member (see Figure 8.18).

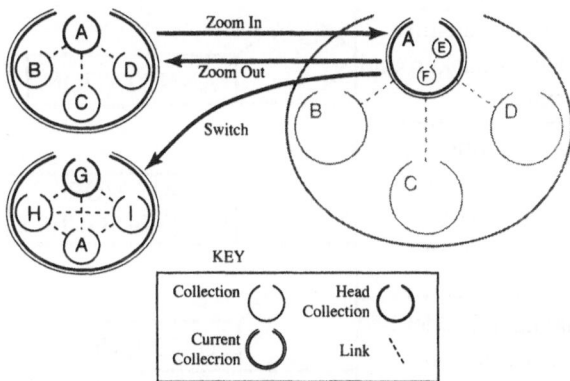

Fig. 8.18. Switching Up to Another Collection

We thus have a structure, which does not have to rely on explicit links, where users can browse up and down the hierarchies while keeping a "well defined sense of the current location" [Maurer et al., 1993a]. Also, since at any moment of time a stack of open S_Collections may exist, it is easy to generate a meaningful graphical trace.

It is important to note that although any collection can be a member of other collections, this does not mean that the data has to be duplicated:

pointers may be used instead. Also, recursive membership is both possible and meaningful.

Besides supporting multi-metaphor browsing [Maurer et al., 1993a] the HM-Data model incorporates a powerful query mechanism in the navigational paradigm [Maurer et al., 1993b], thus providing users with an integrated environment.

The HM data model [Maurer et al., 1993a, Maurer et al., 1994c] is designed as a model for very large hypermedia systems that may contain mega-quantities of documents. In systems such as this the problems associated with links, from both the user's and the author's perspectives, magnify almost exponentially – "getting lost in hyperspace" and dangling links are serious problems. The HM data model emphasises alternative approaches as shown in Figure 8.19.

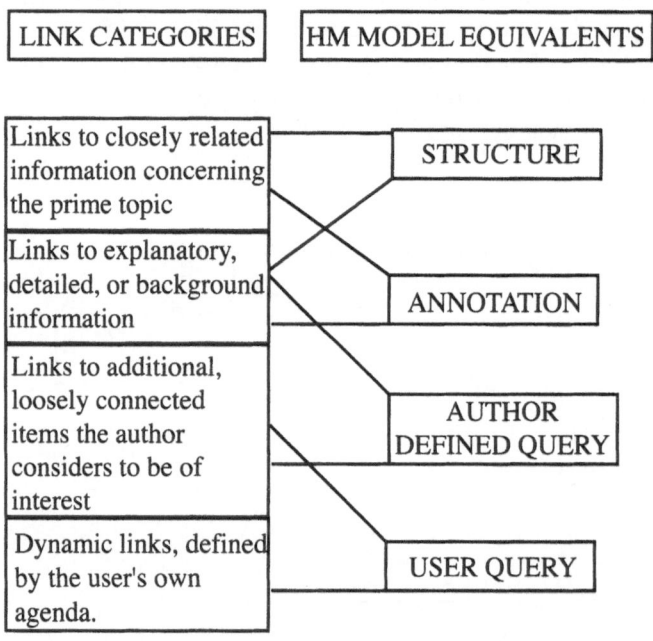

Fig. 8.19. HM Model Equivalents [Maurer et al., 1994c]

Thus in a HM model database links are "encapsulated within a particular S-Collection", as shown in Figure 8.17. In practical terms the advantages of providing structures such as these far outweigh any disadvantages associated with the absence of global links. Because links are not embedded it is easier to provide maps and tours to aid user navigation.

Part III

Advanced Applications and Developments

9. Electronic Presentation, Publishing, and Digital Libraries

9.1 Introduction

Any complexity to be understood, let alone conveyed, must be structured. It may be that the human brain needs it actually modelled as a structure, visual or conceptual. Moreover, anything new, particularly anything abstract, can be most comfortably met by meeting it in terms of something familiar. Computing, accepting all this, has had fun with metaphors. The concept of "navigating" is itself a metaphor. For multimedia presentations "travel" is only one of several available metaphors discussed in Section 9.2.

As discussed previously, multimedia and Internet technologies are converging. However, since in practice the Web still does not provide the quality of service needed to generate and present sophisticated multimedia presentations, most people are still reliant on stand-alone resources and processes. Accordingly we shall discuss stand-alone presentation and publishing before considering general electronic publishing.

Finally, having the world's reference resources at one's instant call in digital libraries has become a possibility – and a near-necessity for researchers, authors, presenters, and students. Digital libraries are being developed with all haste by the powerful projects discussed in Section 9.8.

9.2 Multimedia Presentations

Several different presentation metaphors have been implemented:

- Stacks of cards, as popularised by Hypercard [Hypercard, 1989].
- Hierarchical folders as used, for example, in Hyperwave (see Chapter 7).
- The book metaphor, as in Dynabook (see Section 2.9).
- The library metaphor, as used in the PC-Bibliothek application (see Section 9.3).
- Travel through 2D or 3D landscapes (see Section 7.3.2).

Any good authoring package should give authors the chance to choose the paradigm most appropriate to the needs of their targeted audiences. The authoring package will also need to provide the following navigational aids needed in any multimedia implementation:

- An index into the pages.
- A bookmarking system.
- The facility to iconise any particular page needing to be referred to more than once.
- Helpful features like a graphical icon indicating the total number of pages and the number already viewed.

The system should also support sophisticated viewing opportunities such as:

- Annotation. It is important that the presenter be able to annotate the material as freely as in any traditional environment. The annotation system should provide suitable drawing support in perhaps a variety of forms.
- The facility to zoom into parts of diagrams, maps, and pictures.
- Multiple windows.

The software used to produce the presentation should be on line so that real-time additions or deletions can be made. There should be an option to determine which changes are to be permanent and which are just temporary.

The usefulness of all this to researchers is worth illustration: imagine the geologist or oceanographer presenting dozens of maps, wishing to show some rapidly, hold several in view, and relate data in them – probably data needing magnification of parts. Then imagine side by side on the screen a section of topographical map and an infra-red photograph of the same small area. It is features such as these that are needed.

At any stage the presenter should be able to capture any page or pages of information and have the option of either distributing them electronically to the audience (or to any other interested group, e.g., the disabled who weren't able to attend) or having the pages printed out as hard copy for people to take away. This helps to minimise mindless note-taking.

Presenters should be able to access electronic encyclopedias to enhance the lecture as well as answer questions. Art teachers have a particular problem in that they currently rely heavily on slide carousels for illustrating their talks. It is difficult to move backwards and forwards through the slides to find a particular one they need to refer to, and they cannot display slides from previous lectures in response to students' questions. Furthermore, they often need to show two slides at the same time to compare and contrast them.

Information in the sciences can often be most clearly shown by displaying uncluttered diagrams, where additional details are not shown until required. Lectures in medicine can benefit by incorporating photographic quality images and by studying the body not only in various ways (e.g., by looking at bone structure or blood or lymph systems) but by viewing each system under increasing (and decreasing) degrees of magnification. Students of engineering and architecture receive extensive training in the use of computer-aided design (CAD) tools. CAD is not only being used in the initial design phases of projects but, coupled with good HM systems, it is being incorporated into training sessions for new staff, retraining for current staff, building and maintenance specifications, and high-tech troubleshooting.

Electronic libraries of pictures such as IconBazaar on the Web [URLi3], and CDs such as Microsoft's "Art Gallery", provide an Aladdin's trove for authors.

9.2.1 Presentation Packages

Packages are available which make it possible to step from preparing transparencies by computer to actually using a computer for presentations. Reasonably sophisticated presentations are possible, although no currently marketed presentation package is ideal. One widely used presentation package, for both the PC and Macintosh, is PowerPoint [PowerPoint, 1992], which allows direct access to the Access database and spreadsheet package. Authorware Professional [Authorware, 1991] and MacroMind Director [MacroMind, 1991] are available for Macintosh and PC. HM-Card [Maurer et al., 1995] (see Section 2.18) is a well-designed package now available for the PC.

A good presentation package should facilitate preparation of presentations using a combination of media, including animation, and the presenter should have convenient tools to show the material, including special pointing devices such as an airmouse.

9.3 Electronic Publishing

Certainly a considerable amount of electronic material is currently being distributed using CD-ROM technology. Electronic books distributed on CD-ROM include such titles as *The Oxford Textbook of Medicine on CD-ROM*, *Sinkha* (a 3D novel), *The Complete Works of Shakespeare*, and several encyclopedias [Barker et al., 1993] as well as a wide variety of games such as Gadget, Loon, Star Trek, Journeyman Project, Myst, The 7th Guest, Space Quest V, and Secrets of the Luxor.

CD-ROM World ("The World's First and Oldest CD ROM Store") has a full catalogue, search, and ordering facilities [URLp1]. *Digital Planet* is a commercial site dealing with "multimedia and edutainment" products [URLq1]. It advertises a "full slate of original CD-ROM products".

PC-Bibliothek [Maurer et al., 1994b] is a commercial product that comes on floppy disks or CDs with an extended manual. The material of the *PC-Bibliothek* is also being integrated into Hyperwave [Kappe et al., 1993]. It is currently available for PCs running Windows, and Unix and Macintosh versions are under development. It offers a powerful generic user interface for electronic multimedia reference works. At any time, the user can choose a set of reference books from the system's virtual bookshelf in order to look up information using keyword and full text search. Features available for searching include logical operations for query definition, spelling error tolerance in queries, and creation of a personal alphabetical keyword list. The system allows personal annotations to be made. Access from other Windows applications is available, together with data export and import routines. It certainly gives us a tantalising taste of things to come once complete reference systems are integrated into our commonly used applications.

9.4 Electronic Publishing on the Web

The early Web concentrated – as it had to – on content and structure, ignoring aesthetics. Now Web pages are passing rapidly into the early stages of aesthetic exploration that echo the history of book production, both the hand-written and the printed. We see pages crafted with heavy decoration, diversified typefaces, and illustration.

The first HTML standard, version 1.0, concerned itself with the logical structure of a written document – paragraphs, headings, titles, and links. At that stage the Web was mostly used by academics, for distributing papers and working collaboratively. The focus on logical document structure allowed for a variety of presentation styles – for example, one user might wish Level One headings to be 36 point bold, another might wish links to be coloured bright green. It also allowed for variety in the capabilities of browsers – one could use a text-only terminal and still retain all the meaning written into the document. The concept of a document's independence from its representation on a screen was important.

As the Web moved from its position as a kind of electronic journal to a plaything for any computer-literate user, more demands were placed upon HTML. Users wanted (and got) the ability to include embedded graphics into their documents, the ability to write programs that produced Web pages (thus, CGI was born), and other features. HTML 2.0 provided users with more control over the layout of their documents on the viewers' screens. The emerging CGI (Common Gateway Interface) standard allowed users to link the Web to databases and provide search facilities, dynamically create pages according to users' preferences, and get feedback from users via forms specified in HTML.

However, with the extension of the Web into the areas of advertising, sales, formal publishing, and entertainment, this was not enough. In early 1996, according to generally held belief, around 80% of Web users were browsing with Netscape, a browser provided (free of charge) by the company of the same name. Netscape Communications Corporation had devised new HTML tags, designed to extend the flexibility of the web to things like background and link colours, background images, simple animations, and automatic page reloading. Since part of the HTML standard dictated that an unrecognised tag should be ignored, thus allowing an HTML 2.0 document to be viewed by an HTML 1.0 browser, Netscape's extensions were extremely popular, not least because they provided still more control over screen layout.

HTML 3.0, incorporating many of Netscape's extensions as well as other innovations, was released in early 1996. A cynical commentator at the time noted that 3.0's designers had, one drunken night, planned to include tags named (PEEK) and (POKE) to finally appease the layout control freaks. (It is not suggested, here or in the original comment, that this is true). HTML has come far from its beginnings as a structural specification, and is now a sophisticated user-interface design tool.

9.5 Electronic Publishing Houses

Although so much information is being "published" daily on the Web the fact remains that much, if not most, of the information is simply trivia – certainly not properly edited, let alone refereed! Just as publishing houses evolved for distributing paper books we hope that prestigious electronic publishing houses will arise. Unfortunately, as Maurer and Schmaranz [Maurer and Schmaranz, 1994] state, "Authors, readers and publishing companies have to deal with some major disadvantages:

- Special file formats are used for hypertext. Thus authors are forced to give up their favourite wordprocessing software.
- Data has to be transmitted over very long distances: during rush hours the transmission rates are unacceptably low.
- Electronic journals today are too similar to their paper-based counterparts. They could also contain non-printable information such as animation and sound as an explanatory add-on to the text.
- All large Hypermedia systems such as WWW are missing billing mechanisms making it unattractive for publishing companies to distribute electronic journals."

Nonetheless, most publishing houses see some form of electronic publishing as inevitable, and compelling arguments can certainly be advanced in support of information systems that:

- Support fast text searches (see Section 4.4.1)
- Support versioning
- Support annotations
- Have special dictionaries and encyclopedias implemented
- Save time, money, and library space
- Save tons and tons of woodpulp.

Where server and network costs and/or licence agreements are involved, it is frequently necessary to pass charges down to the users. Several mechanisms have been suggested, among them the following [Maurer, 1994b]:

1. Subscriptions, based on passwords of single users, with mechanisms to prevent passwords being circulated.

2. Permitting to copying by organisations, and charging on the basis of maximum number of simultaneous users.
3. Charging each user for each page displayed.

Option 1 is unacceptable for the occasional reader. Option 2 is the most desirable for the publisher but not for the user unless the system is easy to use. Option 3 is also doubtful since users will probably look at it as similar to renting a car with a charge to be paid per kilometre driven: most people prefer "unlimited" mileage [Maurer, 1994b].

9.5.1 New Forms of Sponsoring

The charging problem may be partially solved by new forms of sponsoring which are emerging. For example, corporate sponsors back Web search engine providers in return for flashing "one liner" advertisements. Sponsors can also provide publishing organisations with their licence fees in return for special advertising privileges. For example, electronic publishers may distribute lists of titles to potential sponsors who will select titles, paying a certain amount for each. They will then have their advertisement placed in the titles of their choice where the amount of "air" time may be proportional to the amount paid. It may be that overt advertising may well be prohibited from certain publications, but discreet and well targeted advertisements, such as an icon or a small amount of text, perhaps with links to the full advertisement, may be tolerated.

9.6 Repercussions in the World of Advertising

Can we really hope for the disappearance of unsolicited, one-size-fits-all advertisements? If the current growth of trading on the Web is anything to go by, the answer may possibly be "Yes." As consumers, we can search for what we want when we want it – although, as suggested above, we usually find advertisements embedded in it.

Users may have much more intelligent access to publicity material. We see interests ranging from sports fitness centres to adult education courses being targeted to reach specific audiences. Printed advertisements may become as obsolete as town criers. See Section 5.5.5 for other aspects of this question.

As described in Section 9.10.1, access to electronic magazines and journals may have to be controlled by license agreements based on usage. Popular journals may require more than one license just as traditional libraries buy more than one copy of books in demand. As described above, these licenses may be provided by sponsors in return for some form of carefully targeted advertisement such as a small but clickable icon on the cover of the book.

9.7 Electronic Newspapers

News can be really news on the Internet – flashed around the globe before it appears on conventional news channels. Electronic newspapers range from one line "fliers" to full brightly coloured hypertext papers such as the Electronic Telegraph. The Telegraph comes complete with pictorial front-page headers, plus the hypertext sections: Home News, World News, City News, Sport, Features, email to the editor, and Weather – complete with colour maps. It does, however, require user registration.

9.8 Digital Libraries on the World Wide Web

In an excellent talk at the Webnet'96 Conference, Ian Witten [Witten, 1996] began by asking the question "What is a digital library?". Should the whole World Wide Web be considered a digital library? Or large American National Information Infrastructure (NII) initiatives [URLh3]? Or anyone's home page?

Witten concluded that there was no real answer, but for discussion purposes digital libraries can be considered to be:

– A collection (chosen and focused),
– of information sources (including, for example, virtual museums),
– stored in some logical space.

When the sources are physically dispersed, there must be a uniform interface that allows the information to be located and accessed.

Witten categorised Web-based libraries as follows:

1. Libraries where librarians have selected and organised the electronic books, e.g., the Bartleby library (see Section 9.8.1).
2. Libraries that authors contribute to, e.g., Hypatia (see Section 9.8.2).
3. Libraries that search engines generate (see Section 9.8.5).
4. Other libraries that display characteristics that are a combination of the above categories, e.g., NZDL (see Section 9.8.3) and J.UCS (the Journal of Universal Computer Science, see Section 9.10.1).

Examples of libraries in each of these categories are given below.

9.8.1 The Bartleby Library

In contrast to so much on the Web, the Columbia University Bartleby Library has a surprisingly erudite feel to it [URLe3]. Although it is a small site (approximately forty books) the items are carefully selected, accurate, and faithful editions, e.g., William Wordsworth's complete poetical works.

The rare book and manuscript library, certainly warranting the subtitle of "Treasures", includes, for example, scans of the original manuscripts of Galileo's drawing of a compass, and a picture of a late seventeenth century Japanese papier-mache celestial globe, 10 inches in diameter.

Fig. 9.1. The Bartleby Library [URLe3]

9.8.2 The Hypatia Electronic Library

The Hypatia Electronic Library contains both a directory of researchers in computer science and mathematics, and a library of their papers [URLf3]. Both categories are searchable using a Web form.

Researchers register (by form) and provide a list of their research interests and the URLs of papers they have published.

Fig. 9.2. The Hypatia Library [URLf3]

9.8.3 The New Zealand Digital Library (NZDL)

The New Zealand Digital Library (NZDL) is a research project led by Ian Witten at the University of Waikato, New Zealand [URLg3]. It maintains its own full text indexes. To date, the library consists of over 27,000 documents from 300 sites worldwide. Files are stored in PostScript (the conversion is done in Calgary because of a small pipe to New Zealand).

The library includes Computer Science technical reports, German technical reports, The Computists' Communique, the Oxford Text Archive, the Project Gutenberg Collection, a FAQ archive, and the HCI Bibliography.

Fig. 9.3. The New Zealand Digital Library [URLg3]

9.8.4 LIBERATION

The LIBERATION (LIBraries: Electronic Remote Access To Information Over Networks) project is a joint venture among several European universities, libraries, and publishers [URLm2]. The members of the LIBERATION consortium are:

Universities:

– IICM (Institut für Informationsverarbeitung und Comptergestützte neue Medien), Graz University of Technology (Director of the LIBERATION Consortium)
– IfI (Institut für Informatik), University of Freiburg

Libraries:

– Hallward Library, University of Nottingham
– Universitätsbibliothek, University of Freiburg

Publishers:

– Addison-Wesley, Bonn
– Bibliographisches Institut & F.A. Brockhaus AG, Mannheim
– Springer-Verlag, Berlin, Heidelberg, New York (Sponsoring Partner)

The project is investigating several important issues such as:

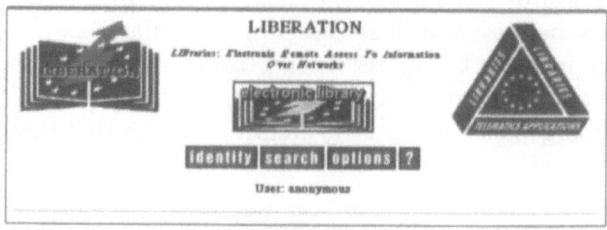

Fig. 9.4. The LIBERATION Project [URLm2]

- How library material should be distributed: over the Web, on local servers, or on CD-ROMs?
- What the best paradigm is for charging, so that well-refereed material can be published in a cost-effective way.

9.8.5 Web Crawlers

Web Crawlers, e.g., those employed by search engines such as Infoseek, are discussed in Section 6.9. Here we must underline the fact that these programs gather indiscriminately – as the various companies vie with each other to have the "Web's largest" collections.

Some digital libraries, like WAIS (see Section 3.5.3) and NZDL (see Section 9.8.3), have always maintained full text indexes, i.e., the index is formed from the entire body of the text as well as the headings. Others, such as Infoseek [URLx2], use engines like the Harvest Broker [Bowman et al., 1994] to create indexes. Still other indexes are, unfortunately, well kept commercial secrets.

Fig. 9.5. Infoseek [URLx2]

9.8.6 Searching Digital Libraries

As discussed in Section 6.8, advances in scripting for the Web have made it easier to search large databases such as libraries, display the results rapidly, and also tailor returned documents to fit the users' requirements. This last point, the ability to customise search results to reflect users' preferences, is most important. In the original Web paper, [Berners-Lee et al., 1992], Tim Berners-Lee et al. foreshadow this effect with the statement, "The documents in the Web do not have to exist as files; they can be 'virtual' documents generated by a server in response to a query or document name. They can therefore represent views of databases." This is particularly necessary in library settings where users range from young school children, through the general public, to erudite scientific researchers.

9.9 Electronic Support for Paper-Based Libraries

In the foreseeable future it will become standard practice, on cataloguing a new book or journal, to fax (i.e., scan) the table of contents into a hypermedia system so that borrowers can rapidly access the new information. This much at least can be done without infringing copyright laws (see Section 9.11). Some Web servers such as Hyperwave [Kappe et al., 1993], support library systems, integrating services, and fast efficient searches of titles, tables of contents, etc. Users can also define the scope of their searches by defining "active collections" within the information database [Kappe and Maurer, 1994].

When the new book or journal has been electronically catalogued, information in email form can be sent to all members of a library according to their personal "information profile". Such an action can be almost entirely automated using suitable systems.

Once people have found a paper relevant to their work (e.g., by using the electronic table of contents) they will no longer have to go to the library to read or copy the papers. Rather, just by clicking at the paper selected in the electronic table of contents, the enquirer can send a message directly to the library. Library staff now copy the paper and send it to the person concerned; the copy may even be sent in electronic form, again using a scanner exactly like a photocopying machine.

Although this approach does place an additional burden on library staff, looking at it from a global point of view it is much more efficient than all the present legwork put in by physical users, and time spent searching for journals that would be found by library staff much more quickly. Other aspects of the library may be automated by:

– Subscribing to electronic publications rather than paper publications
– Introducing automatic recall where the user, wanting to use a book and finding it is out on loan, can by a single click initiate an email message
– Keeping more information in electronic form.

All of this will free library staff from other work so that the proposed much more efficient library might not need a substantial increase in staffing.

9.10 Electronic Journals

One of the most comprehensive reports to date is published under the title "Tragic Loss or Good Riddance? The Impending Demise of Traditional Scholarly Journals" [Odlyzko, 1994, Odlyzko, 1995].

In spite of the many advantages of electronic publishing, electronic journals have, until recently, been rather slow to take off – even though there have been many attempts. Here we mention just a few:

- EJournal by the University of Albany. Information may be obtained by mailing EJOURNAL@ALBANY.bitnet.
- Digest of Physics News Items from the American Institute of Physics. This is posted in the Internet newsgroup scol.research, and back issues can be downloaded by FTP from NIC.HEP.NET.
- MSRI [URLa1]. This is comparatively well established, and supports the following four mathematics journals:
  - Electronic Journal of Combinatorics
  - Electronic Journal of Differential Equations
  - Electronic Transactions on Numerical Analysis
  - Ulam Quarterly
- MUSE [URLd1], a Johns Hopkins University joint venture with the Milton S. Eisenhower Library and Homewood Academic Computing. It will allow networked electronic access to their electronic journals. The project was begun in 1993, and in February 1994, three JHU Press journals were made available on the network as a project prototype.

Maurer and Schmaranz [Maurer and Schmaranz, 1994] list the following factors for the slow acceptance of electronic publishing:

- Poor quality, with little or no inclusion of hypermedia
- Lack of refereeing, leading to lack of prestige
- Lack of support for navigation – surely the essence of hypermedia
- Lack of page numbering, so that quotation and citation is difficult
- Poor distribution methods: journals use a wide variety of formats (LateX, PostScript, ASCII, etc.) and articles are frequently obtained using FTP. They are then no better than their paper counterparts since no cross-linking is supported.

9.10.1 Journal of Universal Computer Science (J.UCS)

There is no doubt that any journal that addresses these problems will have many significant advantages over traditional journals. The Journal of Universal Computer Science (J.UCS) [Calude et al., 1994, Maurer and Schmaranz, 1994, URLz1] is one such journal. And since it is based on Hyperwave [Kappe et al., 1993], powerful search facilities are available (see Section 4.4.1). J.UCS also has the following advantages:

- An editorial board consisting of over one hundred computer scientists will ensure that the acceptance of a paper in this journal will carry the same prestige as acceptance in any other reputable journal [URLz1].
- Accepted papers are kept in stable form, i.e., changes to published papers are not allowed.
- Refereed annotations are allowed. Thus errors can be corrected and notes made about further research.
- Both multimedia and PostScript versions of papers are supported.
- Graphics, hyperlinks, and annotations are all incorporated.
- Powerful full-text searching is possible.
- And most significantly, since it is fully supported by Springer-Verlag, printed versions of the journal will be available, as well as CD versions, at the end of each year.

Electronic Billing for J.UCS. Electronic billing is provided as an integral part of Hyperwave, in a sophisticated form that even registers simultaneous readings of any particular issues of J.UCS. "Thus organisations can manage the access to J.UCS issues just as is the case in libraries. The organisation can pay fees for a specified number of J.UCS versions – and access to one issue of J.UCS is then limited to this specified number of simultaneous readers. J.UCS, although not intended to be a free publication, will certainly be less expensive than comparable printed journals. As a result of the electronic nature of J.UCS all costs of printing and mailing will disappear".

9.10.2 Back issues of Journals From Swets and Zeitlinger

Swets are international library suppliers and information providers [URLn2]. On their home page they also mention that they are "involved in library automation, scholarly publishing, psychological and educational tests, optical disk and microfilm production as well as a comprehensive backsets and reprints business." Their volume of back issues of journals is certainly large – "1500 scholarly journals". The home page also provides alphabetical lists of links to other publishers' home pages. For example, under "A" you can find publishers ranging from the ACM to the Auckland University Law Review.

9.11 Copyright and Intellectual Property Issues

The issues involved in copyright and intellectual property are undoubtedly far from clear. Many issues pertaining to electronic copying have still not been defined, laws can vary from country to country, and important decisions are still tied up in law courts. The protection needed by multimedia developers is discussed in [Fernandez, 1994].

Tables of contents of magazines, journals, etc., can be stored and publishers can make arrangements for certain selected pages to be copied, or notably, abstracts or the first few pages of a novel.

In schools and universities there are additional problems because it is difficult to predict how far a document will actually be distributed – to a single user (or dustbin) or campus-wide.

It is a very sad fact that in many countries there has been extensive electronic sellout of national treasures due to insufficient governmental legislation [Maurer et al., 1994d]. Because many art museums were unaware of the ramifications, they have sold the exclusive rights to the digital copies of great art works (or practically given them away) to the first applicant.

The protection of intellectual property can be regarded as part of the general security issue (see Section 4.6). The issues are still being formulated and it will be interesting to see what solutions are implemented.

9.12 Version Control

Much research remains to be done on systems that support version control. It is necessary to keep track of versions for both backup and archival purposes (future historians will have a difficult time tracing document life cycles if valuable annotations are lost) [Halasz, 1988, Neuwirth et al., 1992]. Of course, when two or more people work on the same document, at the same time, it is essential that all users are notified of the status of other users' changes, and for the system to provide appropriate lockout.

A sophisticated versioning system is currently under development at Graz University of Technology as part of their Hyperwave development [Gaisbauer et al., 1995]. The various versions of a document are grouped together in a cluster [Kappe et al., 1993]. The user will determine what is a new version. The system can automatically port source anchors from the older version. For a successful port the new anchor has to be at "nearly the same position" in the document as in the old version. The system also updates a special type of link called the "version link". Version links are used to correlate corresponding sections in old and new versions. This means that when users browse versions they can have corresponding sections automatically displayed side by side for comparison purposes.

9.13 Afterword

Just as Web pages have evolved from simple text, to gimmicky flashing pages, to professionally crafted and styled pages, we hope to see Web sites continue their development from disordered collections of miscellaneous information, to fullscale publishing platforms where authors can be proud to have their work published.

Most of all, we watch with interest the evolution of scholarly libraries that promise to provide high quality Web pages, including properly refereed electronic books and journals.

10. Integrated Learning Environments

10.1 Introduction

Integrated learning environments, based on Web-based digital libraries, will allow remote access to resources from home, work, and learning centres, thus breaking down physical barriers [Marchionini and Maurer, 1995b].

Marchionini and Maurer [Marchionini and Maurer, 1995a] categorise learning under three headings: Formal, Informal, and Professional – not that these are intended to compartmentalise reality. The authors describe how information technology in general, and digital libraries in particular, can underpin all styles, fields, and environments of learning [Marchionini and Maurer, 1995b, Communications, 1995]. In this chapter we discuss aspects of formal and professional learning from this point of view.

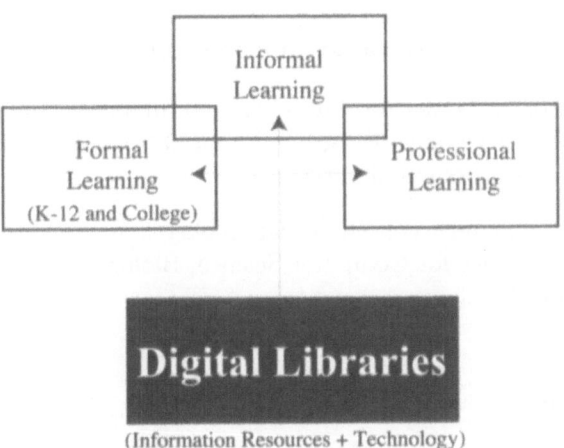

Fig. 10.1. Support for Integrated Learning Environment [Marchionini and Maurer, 1995b]

10.1.1 The Shift From "Teacher Centred" to "Student Centred" Education

It has been argued that, for a successful future, education must shift from being teacher centred to being student centred [Petruk, 1992]. To survive in the information age, students will need to be proficient in navigating various information pathways, and they must be provided with the necessary skills. Once they have these skills they will be able to take control of their learning to a much greater degree than ever before. For example, in the area of medical research, new knowledge about treatments is becoming available at such a rate that no general practitioner has a hope of keeping up to date. Nowadays members of the public are able to query the Web's medical databases and bring the most up-to-date information (or misinformation!) to their own doctor's attention, so that the best treatments available may be chosen.

In the paper "Multimedia: We Have the Technology but do we have a Methodology?" [Alty, 1993] the author describes a study indicating that peripheral or parallel streams of information containing redundant information can be of importance in helping students understand complex ideas. He also argues that the users of multimedia systems should be given flexibility to determine which particular medium suits their purpose best, and concludes that a great deal more work needs to be done in this area. However, a note of caution is needed here. Experience has shown that students need encouragement and even gentle discipline to form the new study habits required for mastering the new learning environment.

10.1.2 Access to Background Information

A by-product of the "quiet revolution" in desktop publishing is the increasing amount of easily accessible background information. Well designed graphical interfaces can let users readily access:

– All types of manual – computer, car, cookery....
– Scientific glossaries for Computer Science, Biology, Engineering
– Detailed specifications
– Price lists
– Dictionaries
– Encyclopedias

10.2 Professional Learning

Professional learning comes under a wide variety of headings, including:

– On-the-Job Training (see Section 10.2.1)
– Just-in-Time Learning (see Section 10.2.1)

- Computer Based Training (CBT) (see Section 10.2.2)
- Computer Aided Instruction (CAI) (see Section 10.2.2)
- Computer Managed Instruction (CMI)
- Computer Supported Collaborative Work (CSCW) (see Section 10.2.4)

10.2.1 Just-in-Time Learning

Many large firms such as Boeing and AT&T have "need to know" training programs already in place. Where projects are as large as these, no trouble-shooter can expect to know everything. "Just in time learning" has taken on new dimensions with the introduction of multimedia programs to help technicians diagnose faults literally on the fly!

10.2.2 Computer Courseware (CBT and CAI)

It is not our contention that the human teacher will ever be completely re-placed by Computer Based Training (CBT) or its academic counterpart Computer Aided Instruction (CAI); but computers can complement a teacher's activities and they have many unique parts to play in education.

A large number of applications have been written. Early on, Apple Macintosh encouraged its educational users to produce lessons written in Hypercard by giving the application away free. Much good software has been produced, often in the long hours of busy teachers' nights. This is certainly an area which needs more coordinating and cataloguing so that excellent work doesn't get lost in proverbial "bottom drawers". A good example of using computing in higher education is the Athena project at the Massachusetts Institute of Technology [Balkovich et al., 1985], [Murray and Malone, 1992].

We believe that specialists involved in the preparation of courseware material should get recognition for their work on a par with time expended on writing books. It should be possible to publish courseware packages just as books are published. However it is an unfortunate fact that a great deal of misplaced enthusiasm and effort has been put into producing courseware. To create high quality courseware an author needs to combine the skills of educator, graphical designer and computer specialist [Augenstein et al., 1993]. Unfortunately many courseware packages break even the most fundamental rules of good design:

- Too much text cluttering the windows (at worst, page after page copied straight from books!)
- Cluttered diagrams
- Flagrant abuse of colour combinations
- Too little or too much flexibility in navigation paths through the material
- Inappropriate or patronising computer generated responses.

A seemingly unavoidable risk is that the material produced may become out of date quickly – particularly in the notoriously changing arena of information technology. For example, graphics that were of acceptable quality just a few years ago may no longer be so.

Courseware programs that make good use of multimedia can certainly provide captivating and effective learning experiences. In the article "Why Hypermedia Systems Are Important" [Maurer, 1992b] the author states:

"It is to be understood that the visual component of a computer supported multimedia system is not limited to ordinary digitised photos and movies: such photos and movies of real-life situations are valuable in some cases but lack the necessary level of abstraction in others. At least as important are other techniques for visualisation, among them:

1. diagrams, maps, and abstract pictures;
2. process visualisation tools;
3. data visualisation tools;
4. 3D modelling, animation, and abstract movies."

These techniques, discussed further in Sections 5.3.2 and 5.3.3, enable specialists to create exciting and effective learning environments. It is unfortunate that, even coupled with modern authorware packages, most lessons incorporating multimedia still need an immense investment of time to produce.

10.2.3 Groupware

Groupware appears to be the best term to cover the wide range of electronic collaborative communication tools that include:

– Email (see Section 3.4.1)
– Computer Supported Collaborative Work (CSCW) (see Section 10.2.4)
– Computer Conferencing (see Section 10.2.5)
– Group Decision Support Systems (see Section 10.2.6)

Whether the electronic communication is formally supervised by a complete computer conferencing system (see Section 10.2.5), or is just an informal exchange of ideas between two colleagues, the impact of computers on collaboration is already being felt across the world.

10.2.4 Computer Supported Collaborative Work (CSCW)

Computer Supported Collaborative Work (CSCW) ranges from simple email communication to the joint preparation of hypermedia documents [Dewan, 1993, Derycke et al., 1993, Ellis et al., 1991].

Within a CSCW system computer screens can provide a shared workspace (textual and graphical) so that all participants can literally work on the same document at the same time and all simultaneously see the result [Elrod et al., 1992]. Obviously when two or more users simultaneously work on the same document there has to be a carefully constructed means of ensuring that the document always reflects a valid state. Successful work is already in place ensuring proper lockout.

Traditionally, collaborative work has been divided into two separate categories:

1. Asynchronous: An asynchronous CSCW system has the advantage of enabling users to collaborate when they are separated not only by distance, but also by time constraints. This is obviously an advantage when workers are in countries separated by a twelve-hour time difference.
2. Synchronous: In a synchronous system the participants are logged on to the computer system at the same time even though they are not necessarily all in the same room together, as in Teleconferencing. There will normally be either an audio or video link between participants.

However the boundaries between these two categories are blurring as new systems allow users to take part simultaneously in both types of collaborative work.

Although computer supported collaborative work is a rapidly expanding discipline, it is still a particularly difficult research area because the human interactions are so complex. Many untested and ad hoc systems have been implemented (we can't even say designed) by computer programmers with little knowledge of real-world workplace conditions. One problem is the fact that a solution that works in one situation, with one group of users, may not work in other cases. For example, two experienced programmers may be able to work collaboratively on the same document, at the same time, without even an audio link between them. Or a group of students may work on a project efficiently with only an audio link between them (although they may miss the feeling of presence that face-to-face communication provides). However, there are often more critical requirements in industry, or in life support situations such as fire or accident emergency services. In these cases decisions can depend on body language such as a shrug or eye movement. For example, there are times when workers may well have to pass on judgements, particularly about colleagues, that they are not prepared to verbalise, let alone set in text. In these cases a video link may be essential.

Finally, since few workers these days work in a vacuum, and many work in multiple groups, a CSCW system should be designed to support personal work spaces alongside a variety of group work spaces [Fitzpatrick et al., 1996].

10.2.5 Computer Conferencing

Technology that supports conferencing can range from the simplest (often just email) to full video conferencing, circumstances determining what technology is appropriate. Recently there have been significant improvements in the quality of large-scale projected images [Berends, 1993]. However when bandwidth is a limitation, experience has shown that a small video clip of a speaker's face can provide at least an illusion of "presence". In fact, work done at Dartmouth College suggests that small sequences of video may be repeatedly reused without users detecting the lack of synchronisation between video and voice [Cheyney et al., 1994]!

A computer conference can provide a highly structured discussion [Conklin and Begeman, 1988]. When a topic or proposal is presented, the system can force contributions of the required type: extended topic or generalisation, supporting argument, supporting example, counter argument, counter example,.... Varying levels of anonymity can be supported, from complete anonymity to every contribution being identified by the sender's real name. Often pen-names are used.

There are also times when documents require such a high level of security that all communication is not only anonymous but encrypted (see Section 4.6).

An important variable is the real or delayed time aspect. As in CSCW, conferencing systems can be classified into synchronous and asynchronous systems:

Synchronous Conferencing. Modern synchronous conferencing systems can provide a highly stimulating environment for both brainstorming and collaborative work, particularly in the final stages of completing a project. Many systems provide good graphical interfaces and support both text and graphical shared workspaces. They also give several levels of participation control:

- "Free-for-all" participation – with appropriate lockout
- Cyclic participation around the participants
- Moderator controlled participation

However synchronous systems have the obvious disadvantage of requiring participants to be online at the same time – often requiring difficult timetabling logistics.

Asynchronous Conferencing. As pointed out by Harasim [Harasim, 1990] and Hiltz and Turoff [Hiltz and Turoff, 1994], asynchronous systems solve some of the real-time problems. However, they can cause delays in turn-around time for project completion.

Several interesting combinations of the above technology are evolving – such as using asynchronous communication at the beginning of a project and then switching to synchronous collaboration for the final stages.

10.2.6 Supporting Decision Making

A special case of synchronous conferencing is seen in electronic decision support centres [Nunamaker et al., 1991, Sheffield, 1993]. All participants are physically in one room, usually with a facilitator, and may communicate normally at any particular time. However, everyone is also linked to a computer system, and discussion usually takes place anonymously with immediate feedback. Unstructured Bulletin Board discussions have worked, where there are only a few participants, but they quickly get out of control with more than a few. In a *Card Passing* system messages are passed to members chosen at random and each successively adds to the "card" until either the facilitator or a member calls a halt at a point where a vote on the issue might be taken.

In the paper "The Impact of Electronic Meeting Systems on New Zealand Organisations" [Sheffield, 1993] the author states: "Participants using simultaneous computer input may work throughout the meeting without being 'blocked' by other participants. Because there is no competition for air-time, task focus is increased. Persuasion and advocacy are less necessary in achieving consensus. The combination of high task focus, high participation and expert facilitation appears to produce a more informed consensus." The ability of participants to access and organise information is enhanced and surveys show that participants claim a time saving of sixty or more percent – a factor of great importance to administrators. Although the electronic meeting rooms do not themselves generate decisions (these may need human interactions including eye contact), the decisions reached are proving very workable and highly satisfying, as shown by detailed follow-up surveys [Sheffield and Gallupe, 1993].

10.2.7 Contract Preparation

In the above discussion we have assumed that the various collaborators have had the same basic aims. But there is one application of CSCW in which the participants may have quite different objectives: contract preparation. The different parties to the document are both – or all – working on it. But in this case each has to obtain a version that is best for their own interests, and there can be a tendency for each to slip in changes it is hoped the other party will overlook. In this case the computer system's supervisory role is to ensure fairness.

10.2.8 Meeting Support

When calendar functions are integrated with email systems, meetings can be electronically timetabled. Although we feel that some scheduling systems intrude too much on users' privacy, other systems, not exposing personal calendars, can be just as effective. One user will suggest a time for a meeting, and the system, after browsing at appropriate calendars, can report back the number of clashes if any. Since the attendance of certain members may be critical, a weighting may have to be placed on certain entries. To help communication further and to engender a feeling of camaraderie (to help offset feelings of computer-generated alienation) the screen may also show video images of the participants.

10.2.9 Electronic Support for Conference Administration

As described in the article "Conferencing – Do It the Hypermedia Way!" [Maurer and Schneider, 1994], conferences of all types can be supported in many ways: issuing invitations, distributing preliminary programs, submitting contributions, handling registrations and administrative details, etc.

Conference organisers can also provide registered delegates with electronic versions of the Proceedings before the conference starts. To avoid misuse, delegates will probably need to be restricted in the number of times they can download material. Having the proceedings available early like this enables participants to make intelligent decisions about which one of the parallel sessions they want to attend. They can also engage in discussions with authors before the conference starts – possibly giving valuable feedback, from which authors may want to adapt their presentations.

Many publishing houses are already accepting manuscripts in electronic form for in-house editing, or for inserting directly into edited volumes such as conference proceedings.

10.3 Formal Learning

In Chapter 11, ideas are discussed that will take future lecturing techniques far beyond the use of computers for simply giving presentations. There have been many highly innovative ideas on how to use computer-based teaching theatres [Norman, 1993, Shneiderman, 1993b, Gilbert, 1993, Fisher, 1993]. As personal computers become smaller, cheaper, and consequently more widely used, increasing numbers of students are bringing their own laptops to class and connecting to the teacher's computer via a network. This opens many interesting possibilities, just a few of which we list here:

- Students and teachers can interact electronically – from wherever they are located.
- Students can electronically download the teacher's notes and then individually annotate them from the teacher's explanations.
- Electronic question and answer sessions allow lecture forums in which the teacher simply acts as facilitator.
- Instead of bringing just a tape recorder into lectures, students have the choice of voice recorders, electronic cameras and even video recorders, and they can store the data directly into their own computers for perusal at their leisure.
- Computer supported collaborative work is provided for.
- Computer conferencing is supported.

– Lectures may develop into anonymous group discussions similar to those which take place in decision rooms.

Since many people experience a significant mental barrier to asking questions in large class situations where they feel self-conscious, it may be desirable to provide each student with some sort of electronic signalling device [Maly et al., 1994]. This could enable students to anonymously indicate to the teacher that they did not understand a point or that the pace was too fast or too slow. In large classes this may mean that the teachers would need some computer support to analyse the incoming data without impinging too much on their concentration.

10.3.1 Distributed Learning Environments

In Chapter 11 we describe how, almost as a corollary of the electronic lecture room, we have a system that supports distance teaching [Hewitt, 1993, Rajasingham, 1988]. In difficult economic climates more students have to be handled with smaller financial resources, and distance teaching may be a viable solution. The system we suggest achieves the following objectives:

– Generating high quality computer-aided instruction material in the form of hypermedia lectures that are coupled with question and answer material electronically captured from students' interactions with teacher or tutor. This material may be multi-authored.
– Enabling students to plug their own personal computers into a LAN to play and replay lectures at their own convenience.

It is an important truth that only through education does a country make any real progress. An estimated 80% of US college students now have access to networks. For everyone from kindergarten children through to university administrators the new worldwide network links provide educational possibilities undreamt of.

10.3.2 Intelligent Tutoring Systems (ITS)

Currently much research is being directed into the development of general tutoring systems involving artificial intelligence. Systems, coupled with discourse languages, have been developed to interactively set up knowledge bases (lessons, examples, tests, etc.) in many fields. The Exploring System Earth Consortium is a group of universities and industries in the United States currently developing intelligent science tutors. The group is addressing the problems associated with choosing appropriate teaching strategies based on students' backgrounds and tutorial experiences [Woolf, 1992].

Because a significant investment of time is still needed to create an ITS or to tailor any general program to a specific domain, a system is urgently required that will enable staff to find out readily what existing work has already been done in any area of interest.

10.3.3 Exploratory Learning

There is still an immense amount of work to be done to determine just how students learn best when confronted with a large information system. There may be as many different answers as there are students. However there has been some good work done in providing students with tours and maps [Davies et al., 1991].

Programs enabling students to experiment by directly manipulating graphical objects can provide fascinating learning experiences. In his paper "Direct manipulation: a step beyond programming languages" [Shneiderman, 1993a] the author asks, "Why not teach students about polynomial equations by letting them bend the curves and watch how the coefficients change, where the x-axis intersects, and how the derivative equation reacts?"

Many virtual instrument systems exist to support the real-time plotting of data in forms that can be manipulated on the computer as required. In medical applications, for example, they can generate plots reflecting conduction in nerves or forces in muscles.

10.3.4 Student Study Aid Programs

It is a universal problem that the very students who would benefit most from assistance programs are the least likely to volunteer for them – or even to hear of them. An attractive, non-threatening, multimedia environment is likely to have such wide appeal that significantly more students will learn how to obtain help before it is too late.

10.3.5 Resource Centres

Well designed hypermedia systems can guide users to the various campus facilities to find out what is available. It is a fact that most students today have no idea of the many resources available to them: audio and video tapes held in other departments, computing services, teaching resources, sports equipment, and of course hypermedia programs of many kinds.

10.3.6 Tutorials

Fully networked tutorial laboratories provide a wide range of learning environments:

- Teacher-directed learning. Students new to the computerised environment can be guided step by step until they are proficient.
- Teacher-guided learning. Students can be given increasing control over what and how they learn. They can be encouraged to explore at their own pace with the teacher acting as guide.

- Student-directed learning. Mature students can benefit from being given control over their environment. The teacher's role will be that of a mentor or supervisor.
- Working in groups. Many students prefer to do computer work in groups rather than alone. This preference is seen in many minority groups and particularly amongst women.

It can also be argued that all students benefit by a certain amount of group activity since there is so much team work in the workplace. Work can be divided up among the group members, results compared and combined, and the final version prepared in professional form.

Wide-area networks can provide an immeasurable resource base for tutorial work. Many groups will benefit from having brainstorming sessions with various degrees of anonymity.

10.3.7 Self-Testing

Computer Based Training (CBT) modules can provide unique ways for students to assess themselves in a relaxed and non-threatening environment:

- Incoming students can determine whether they are well enough prepared to embark on their selected courses of study.
- Students who attain a required standard by sitting self-administered preparatory tests are able to sit formal examinations with considerably less stress.
- Advanced students can use tests to determine what background reading they must do before embarking on their projects.

More advanced modules can help students assess their level of understanding on key topics and direct them to appropriate material.

It may not be necessary to build electronic marking of the students' answers into the courseware packages. In fact it may be best for the answers to be written or drawn on paper. Since the self-assessment results do not influence the students' final results, it is in the students' own interests to get as accurate an assessment as possible. Thus the tests can provide model answers and let the students determine the correctness of their responses. Alternatively, two students may work on a quiz together and mark each other's work using the computer's answers as a guide.

Several types of self-test exist. Perhaps most easily adapted from standard tests are multi-choice tests. More interesting are tests asking the user to draw their answers or indicate them on diagrams. Tests involving interactive animation can frequently test students' understanding of processes more reliably than standard testing methods. For example, in the assembling of complex pieces of apparatus the various parts can be dragged across the computer screen to test correct assembly order.

In an interactive medical simulation, complete with awe-inspiring hospital sound effects, medical students are tested on their knowledge of operating room procedures using computer-controlled time constraints and lifelike animations.

Attempts have been made to design systems in which the questions themselves are computer generated. However the results to date have not been encouraging. In the paper "Question/answer specification in CAL tutorials (automatic problem generation does not work)" [Maurer et al., 1991] the authors describe two programs: one to generate functions to give students practice in differentiation, and the other to provide sets of linear equations for solution practice. The authors found that it was difficult to control the generation of undesirable functions and sets of equations, and they conclude that "with present methods, the use of such procedures is neither cost-effective nor desirable. Better results, with less effort, seem to come from random selection of 'fixed' problems from a (possibly large) database of such problems."

Since it is often desirable to let a student re-sit a test, groups of questions need to be defined so that the program can randomly select from each group during any particular run.

10.3.8 Examinations

We believe that traditional examinations must gradually be replaced by much more effective "on-the-job" programs, where students continue studying, with either a teacher or CBT, until they are able to show by practical demonstration that they have mastered new sections of a subject. After all, we cannot afford to rely on 60% good doctors or 90% good aviation technicians!

As in the case of self-administered examinations there are several different types of testing programs available:

- Multi-choice examinations that can accept answers in words, numbers, or diagrams.
- Simple graphic examinations where, for example, the students can graph points or indicate the correct answer on a graph.
- Examinations designed so that the student indicates the required answer by circling a region.

There is a problem with administering computerised examinations to large classes: where there are not enough computers for each student to use one simultaneously, multiple tests have to be devised and this too is time-consuming. The sharing of work among colleagues from different campuses can alleviate the problem a little, but alternative methods of marking may have to be used. For example, if questions are answered on well designed paper forms they can be scanned and marked electronically.

10.4 Research

Computer networks link my office to the office next door, to facilities across the campus, to databases in other universities, to the American Library of Congress catalogue,.... Most academics see computers as a way to improve teaching, research, management, and general university life. Scientists are developing visualisation tools that provide effective student training without expensive laboratory equipment and chemicals. Biological scientists, who are now very aware of the environmental impact that their students make on nature, are experimenting with computer simulations in "dry laboratories".

Heavy use is being made of the Web in many disciplines: chemists (particularly cell biologists who cannot work without up-to-date information on the thousands of new compounds), the medical profession (keeping up to date with the daily emergence of new, lifesaving drugs) and lawyers (with endless cases to look up for precedents). In addition to all this, today's networks contain databases of patent registers as well as collections of abstracts and much more.

There is no question that having material available in electronic form may be as important as having it available in print – or more important. The statement "more important" may be justified since the perusal of electronic information, at least for "entry point" research, is much more efficient than the use of printed volumes (and much of the material available on CD-ROM is of the "entrypoint" type: collections of reviews, abstracts of papers, dictionaries, etc.). A wealth of bibliographic data and several complete encyclopedias of information now exist in electronic form and are available on the Web.

10.4.1 Comparing Documents

Research, by its very nature, frequently involves comparative work. In English Literature, for example, it can be highly desirable to have two documents on the screen at the same time: if one document is a validated Chaucer text then the other can be compared to determine whether it was likely also to have been written by Chaucer – and whether it was written by Chaucer some ten years later. In Law, many cases have to be carefully compared to see whether an existing case is a precedent. Tools should do some of the comparing.

10.4.2 Cross-referencing and Checking

This is an area where a supervisory program, like the Personal Assistant (PA) discussed in Chapter 14, will have a big impact. A PA program will provide intelligent cross-links enabling better use to be made of today's huge databases. Not only will the PA make continuous searches for cross references on what we are reading but it will also make cross checks on what we are writing. One such system, Ways 2, produced by the Swiss researcher Keller, has been marketed in Germany with considerable success. Having such checking done automatically, in whole or in part, is the only way to ensure that the increasing amount of stored work taken to be authoritative is at least relatively free of errors.

10.5 Afterword

Once students have access to an integrated learning environment they can access information as and when they need it. We expect students to be better motivated not only to make intelligent use of basic information but to probe more deeply into areas they find particularly interesting.

Recently, interactive hypermedia programs have made accessing information from CD, or from databases via the Web, very much easier. CSCW research is developing into more of a science than an art. We trust that these factors will foster integrated learning environments that are truly student centred [Petruk, 1992].

11. From Traditional Lectures to CAI[1]

11.1 Introduction

In this chapter lecturing technologies past and present are considered and then several conjectures are made about future developments based on recent advances in hypermedia systems. The advantages and disadvantages of present day techniques are discussed, so that the ideas developed are soundly based on past experience. A single system is posited integrating technologies as diverse as multimedia presentations, computer-assisted learning, computer conferencing, distance teaching, and decision rooms.

11.1.1 The Traditional Approach

Reading at the podium or using blackboard and chalk: these basic lecturing techniques have been used for hundreds of years. But lecturing styles have changed in the last ten years as overhead projectors have pushed blackboards into the background. Now computer-based presentations are in the process of replacing overhead transparency presentations. And this is a mere beginning; we believe that lecturing techniques are going to change much more radically and much further in the next ten years or so.

However, until now many computer-based training schemes have not been the successes their authors hoped they would be. We believe that this is frequently due to:

- Lack of time, money, and resources
- The poor quality of many "quick and dirty" implementations
- Rapidly changing technology causing material to look out of date even before it has been completed
- Lack of professional input.

11.1.2 A New Approach to Electronic Learning Environments

In Chapter 10 we introduced the idea of an integrated learning environment as it is formulated by Marchionini and Maurer [Marchionini and Maurer, 1995b].

---

[1] A previous version of this chapter was published in Educational Technology ([Lennon and Maurer, 1994b], ©(1994) by Educational Technology Publications, Inc.).

In this chapter we describe a lecturing scenario that can form part of such an environment and describe how we can produce high-quality computer-based training material almost "on the fly".

11.2 Lecturing Facilities Past to Present

For generations blackboard and chalk set the style of lecture presentation. The past ten or twenty years have seen considerable changes in style with the addition of whiteboards, flip charts and overhead transparencies.

11.2.1 A Comparison Between the Manual Technologies

Blackboards, whiteboards, flip charts, and overhead transparencies: each of these four technologies has some advantages and some disadvantages, and the blackboard should not be underestimated. For certain purposes it is actually best. This is worth noting because it is easy to assume that whiteboards, flip charts and transparencies are better than chalk and blackboard in all respects. Yet, as we shall point out in following sections, each technique has its disadvantages.

If you want to computerise lecturing technology then surely you want to develop a system that incorporates all the advantages while avoiding the disadvantages of each. So we think it is important to analyse carefully, at least once, what are the advantages and the disadvantages of the various techniques.

Work Space. Blackboards have one great advantage: there is ample room to write. A typical big lecture theatre is well equipped with blackboards – several blackboards, immediately available and ready to use. This means that everything important that you write or draw during one hour of lecturing can be kept displayed and accessible throughout the hour.

In comparison with this, overhead transparencies are a nightmare. One sees people using strange crutches such as two parallel projectors, or desperately searching through the pile of transparencies to pull out one they have used before. Difficulties like this show clearly the limitations of transparencies.

Working space is not such a limiting factor when using flip charts because after all you can take the pages you have just written and hang them up somewhere else. On the other hand we have been amused to see whole rooms become draped with flip charts – which all crashed when someone opened a window.

Whiteboards, as far as space is concerned, are somewhere between blackboards and overhead transparencies. Of course, there is no particular reason why there should not be lecture rooms with whiteboards as large and plentiful as blackboards, but we have never seen any.

Editing and Erasing. One aspect of blackboard work which will have to be incorporated in a computerised version is that blackboards allow intensive editing. For example, it is very easy to show on a blackboard a process involving slow multiplication: you just erase a number and replace it by another number.

Whiteboards can be used in a similar fashion but there is limited space and erasing is much more difficult. These are serious limitations for a lecturer to work with, especially if the teaching involves repeated re-writing on one spot – for example, in explaining the working of the arithmetic register in computer subjects. After a few erasures the writing becomes illegible, unless a major clean-up operation is carried out.

Overhead transparencies, of course, are still worse for such tasks. There are erasable pens, but they are not very satisfactory. Some pens can be erased by using another pen with an alcohol tip, but they only work with very moderate use, for the alcohol tip retains the colour.

As far as flip charts are concerned, changes are not normally attempted. Have you ever seen white-out for flip charts?

Sometimes people say that writing on a blackboard with chalk produces too much dust, which gets everywhere. Whiteboards and transparencies do not have a clear advantage: it is very annoying to have the pens dry out or stain one's hands or clothes. Chalk may well be preferable, after all.

Overlaying Material. Overlaying of material is one of two facilities that transparencies have and blackboards do not. Overlaying allows dynamic processing which is quite different from the kinetic process on a blackboard. Showing superimposed images is an inherent property of transparencies. We have never seen flip charts with transparent layers between pages but it is conceivable.

The Use of Markers. We have seen some memorable talks using markers, or coins, which are put on transparencies and moved around. We have occasionally seen markers on magnetic bases for blackboards and whiteboards but not very often because the markers tend to get lost. Coins you may have in your pocket. A flip chart can be marked with pins, but since they must all be removed to turn over a page, they are unsatisfactory. All these things are very trivial, but the point we are trying to make is that certain things can be done with this and certain things can be done with that, but with a computer they can all be done.

Copying and Archiving. One big drawback of blackboards is the fact that the end product cannot be archived in any reasonable fashion except by using a clumsy technique like taking photos. The lecture material cannot be taken home by the student except by copying down notes. With whiteboards the situation is a little better. There are some whiteboards available which allow a printout – but they are fairly expensive. Flip charts can be archived but not copied. Transparencies, of course, are easily archived and copied. It is really strange that blackboards and overhead transparencies behave so differently in this respect!

Preparation of Material. The most important difference between blackboards and whiteboards on the one hand and flip charts and overhead transparencies on the other hand is the fact that transparencies and flip charts can be prepared ahead of time. (It is only in special cases that a blackboard or whiteboard may be prepared in advance.)

Between flip charts and transparencies the big difference is that transparencies are much easier to prepare: copying machines, including colour copiers, can be used to incorporate extant text, diagrams, and even photos; and computer programs with ever better presentation software allow the preparation of high quality transparencies. Prime examples of such software are CorelDraw [CorelDraw, 1992], PowerPoint [PowerPoint, 1992], Hypercard [Hypercard, 1989], and More [Symantec, 1990].

Thus, although transparencies have many positive points, their use is not without drawbacks, as is well known.

Further Drawbacks of Transparencies

- As we all know, there are limits to the number of transparencies it is practical to try to use in one lecture.
- There can be a clash between the uses of transparencies during and after the presentation. Since straight reading from transparencies is poor teaching technique, transparencies rarely contain whole sentences, just key words. Yet, this creates a problem if copies of the transparencies do not contain enough material to learn from afterwards. This means that if something is to be distributed it should not be a straight copy of the transparency – a point often overlooked.
- Talks using transparencies alone tend to be rather passive experiences unless they involve the audience in writing or some other activity. Many people need physical involvement for focus. This is missing in the typical transparency talk. The ideal talk with transparencies probably contains some keywords and important material but leaves enough room between points for the students to expand them. This provides the haptic component. However, there is another problem which is usually overlooked: different learning styles prevent any single solution from suiting everybody. At this point we must be content to use a lecturing style suitable for the majority of our audience. A deeper individualisation is probably only possible with small groups or maybe if computers are used.

Summary of the Advantages of Transparency Talks

- Transparencies are reproducible and copies can be handed out to students.
- Preparation is easy using a computer.
- Pictures and diagrams are easily included.

Summary of the Four Basic Technologies. An analysis of the four technologies (blackboard, whiteboard, flip charts and overhead transparencies) shows that a simple ranking is impossible. Certain things can be done better with one technique, and certain things can be done better with another technique.

	Black board	White board	Flip charts	Overhead transparencies
1. Work space	🙂	😐	🙂	🙁
2. Editing and erasing	🙂	🙁	🙁	🙁
3. Overlaying material	🙁	🙁	😐	🙂
4. Use of markers	🙁	🙁	🙁	🙂
5. Copying and archiving	🙁	🙁	🙁	🙂
6. Preparation of material	🙁	🙁	🙂	🙂
7. Color	🙁	🙂	🙂	🙂
8. Inclusion of pictures	🙁	🙁	😐	🙂
9. Structure visiblity	🙂	🙂	🙁	🙁

Fig. 11.1. Summary

11.2.2 Increasing the Use of Computers

Computers are already being used to generate excellent material for presentations. Using computers to generate pictures for transparencies is the first step in the right direction. The next step, already in limited use, is to run computer applications directly in the lecture room for teaching purposes. A further step is to include animations to a much greater extent than is currently done.

Projection Equipment. There are at present two technologies for projection of computer presentations, both clumsy. One is the RGB projector which is heavy and hard to adjust and needs dim light. The other is the transparent

LCD screen on an overhead projector. The newest versions of colour LCDs provide an image which is almost good enough; however, the resolution the LCD projectors can handle is still somewhat limited. Modern LCDs also have the possibility of video input, so that they can be used to project clips of movies. However, set-up procedures are still unsophisticated: the user is frequently faced with a conglomeration of heavy expensive hardware connected by a spaghetti of hanging wires.

Additional Requirements. Firstly, most presentation packages at the moment show the same thing to the lecturer and the student. Sometimes this is not desirable – sometimes the lecturer wants additional notes which the student should not see.

Secondly, there is not enough interaction possible for the presentation. When material is displayed on the screen, it should be possible to move things around during the explanation, highlighting and pointing to items. The activation or use of other programs is still usually fairly clumsy.

All the positive features of our existing facilities, and more, should be supported in future lecturing techniques. In addition to using such lecturing techniques, an altogether different approach can also be used: the decision-room style. Future technologies will have to pull together all the advantages we have discussed above, plus all the advantages computers and networks provide, plus all the advantages of a decision-room setting. As we shall demonstrate, this kind of integration results in very powerful teaching and learning environments.

Basic Specifications For Future Systems. Our experience suggests that any computerised system must support:

1. A good working window which gives the lecturer a feeling of control over the complete presentation. The lecturer must be able to refer effortlessly to any part of the lecture using a system of footprints, trails, etc.
2. A good projection system able to project wall-sized pictures or a suitable alternative.
3. Annotation, editing, scribbling, and erasing.
4. Overlaying material (tiling and/or cascading windows).
5. The placing and moving of graphic markers and icons.
6. Efficient search and data retrieval algorithms.
7. Easy access to reference material (dictionaries, encyclopedias, reference books, journals, video clips, etc.) for both preparing presentations and for real-time backup and support material.
8. Reasonably high resolution colour and professionally designed templates.
9. Acceptable response times for the loading of digitised video, animations, pictures, etc.
10. Easy access to other programs.
11. Methods for displaying the structure of the presentation.

11.3 Lecturing Technologies of Tomorrow

In this section we are going to broaden the current definition of an electronic classroom. There have been many highly innovative ideas on how to use computer based teaching theatres [Fisher, 1993, Gilbert, 1993]. None of the ideas go as far as we suggest, not even those in the excellent paper by K. L. Norman [Norman, 1993] in the volume "Sparks of innovation in human-computer interaction" edited by Ben Shneiderman [Shneiderman, 1993d]. We base our projections on the success of work such as those.

Let us make a jump into the future and describe a typical scenario. We are not claiming that this is what future lecturing will actually look like, but the essential ideas will be the ones we describe.

11.3.1 Physical Layouts

In the future lecture room the lecturer will have a computer the screen of which is visible only to the lecturer. This computer also controls the projection computer which projects its images onto a large screen in a room that is bright enough to allow reasonable working. The screen of the projection computer is visible in one of the windows of lecturer's computer. This means that lecturers do not have to crane their necks all the time to see what is projected but see on their screen what the students see projected. The lecturer's screen has a number of windows, so the lecturer can concentrate on that screen and still have some attention free for the students!

All students have their own portable PCs, and at the beginning of the lecture they plug them into the network sockets.

The lecturer can also control all these student computers to a certain degree, as follows:

The lecturer computer delivers what we shall call basic screens. Thus, some basic information comes from the lecturer, but the student machines may also contain information or do things hidden from the lecturer. This basic screen is visible on the lecturer's screen in a window. So the lecturer sees what is projected, and the lecturer sees what the students have as basic screens. The students can add things to the basic screens, and the lecturer can look at each of these changed basic screens. This means that the lecturer can say, "I want to look at screen number 5". However, the students can also put on their screens other notes which are invisible to the lecturer and they can also carry out other actions. For example they can look up a term they do not understand, to research in an encyclopedia or database, go back in the sequence of basic screens, perform calculations, send comments (see below), and do much more.

It is apparent that there must be a fairly powerful system in the background which is at the disposal of the student and the lecturer. A structured hypermedia system such as Hyperwave [Kappe et al., 1993] might be suitable.

The computers which we have discussed, the lecturer's computer, the projection computer, and the students' computers, are not only networked with each other but are also networked beyond the lecture room with the hypermedia system, in which there is general and specific information, such as collections of examples and solutions, collections of pictures, video and audio clips, and simulation programs. Both lecturer and student can access some of this information, perhaps with varying degrees of authorisation. As a typical case, example problems could be accessible to both, but the solutions accessible only to the lecturer.

11.3.2 The Lecture Scenario

The actual lecturing now works as follows. The lecturer activates, one after another, the sequence of basic screens. These screens are multimedia screens. That is, they consist of text, graphics, and pictures; and, of course, these pictures can change dynamically, and can be video clips or computer simulations and the like. The change can be governed by the choice of certain parameters or by other activities of the lecturer. For example, the lecturer can show something slower or faster or can repeat certain actions or can adjust parameters. The screen contents can also contain audio clips, and these audio clips can be heard by the students exactly as if the lecturer were talking. Everything that has been selected by the lecturer for the students and modified by the lecturer reaches them in the form of basic screens as mentioned.

During all this the lecturer talks and comments about what is happening. The lecturer's speech, digitised, is transmitted to the student computers. The student computers store all basic frames and all the comments and other information as we shall describe in detail.

This means that the student, when leaving the lecture room, has all the material available for repeating the lecture. A video picture of the lecturer as he/she is talking, can be digitised and shown in a window of the student screen. If the lecturer is filmed working at a whiteboard a full length picture may be appropriate. As mentioned in Section 10.2.5, a small picture of the lecturer's face in one corner of the screen may suffice to give an impression of the lecturer's mannerisms. Obviously methods such as these help reduce overload on the archive database. Observe that in this way the students get high-quality dynamically changing screens of all kinds of information including video and audio clips, at the same time hear the lecturer, and have all this stored on their PC for later learning.

Of course it makes little difference whether the student sits in the same lecture room or is geographically in another place as long as the student is connected on a network.

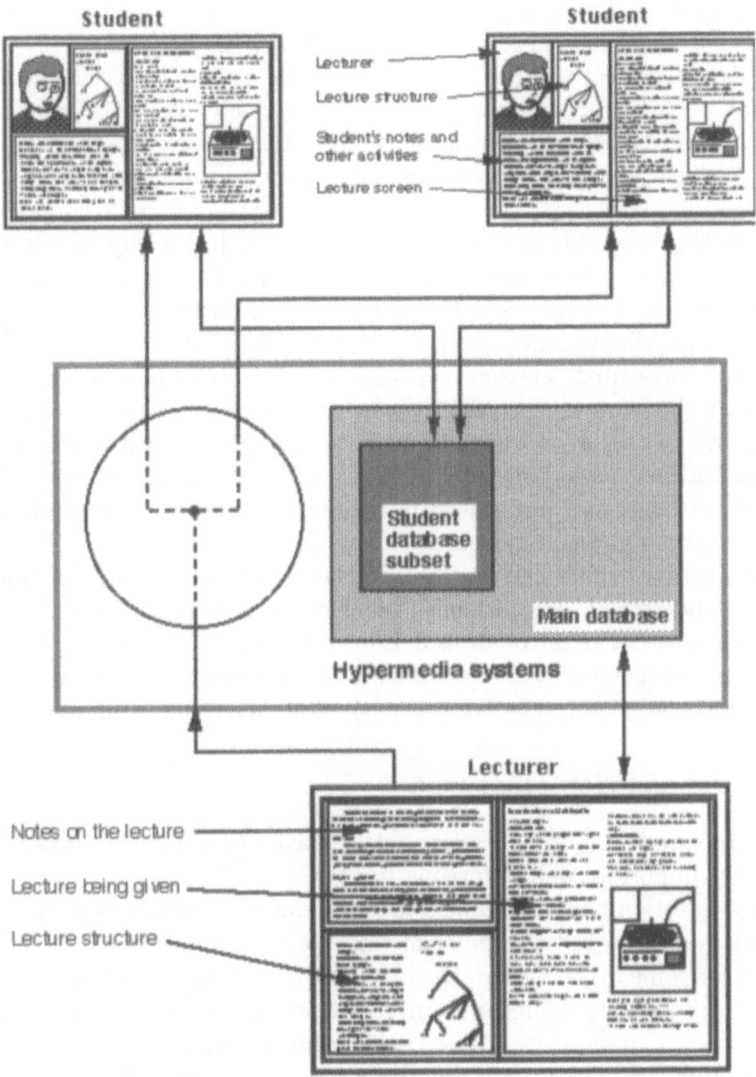

Fig. 11.2. A Network of Lecturer and Student Screens

11.3.3 Additional Possibilities

The description so far still hides many other possibilities of the system. We continue with a number of other consequences.

Lecturers not only have the option of sending basic screens to students: they can modify these basic screens by putting notes on the screens or highlighting things and zooming in to certain parts. They can also tie in material from sources such as encyclopedias or a library of video clips, on the fly, as they go. The lecturer has all kinds of tools available to help in finding material, such as indexes, searching algorithms, etc. What is important is that whatever the lecturer does, all modifications, even clips inserted from encyclopedias, are stored locally in the student's computer, ready to take home.

Up to here it sounds as if this new technology is just a very nice assuaging kind of lecturing, which does not really help students to work actively or to interact with the lecturer. But this is far from the truth.

First of all, the students can make arbitrary notes, they can look at details in pictures presented, or they can consult other information sources. For example, if there is a word on the screen that they do not understand they just click it, and this action starts an immediate lookup in appropriate supporting information databases. This will be of immense value to students with English as a second language, and indeed to everyone in this world of proliferating technical jargon and acronyms.

The reactive facility can be taken further: students can put questions like "I don't understand this formula" or "I don't understand that diagram". They can also either select from a FAQ (Frequently Asked Questions) list or send a text message. For the students this represents a fundamental shift from traditional lecture-theatre passivity to an active listening role.

11.3.4 Old and New Questions

Having the students pose questions, as we have just explained, makes something very important and surprising happen.

If the question happens to be a foreseen question, that is a question that has already been asked a number of times or has been taken care of by the lecturer for some other reason, then this question is answered by the system without the lecturer doing anything. Picture the students simply pointing to a formula and pressing a question option to indicate that they do not understand it. If it is a standard question, then the system can reply and the student may not even know if it is the system or the lecturer who replies.

However, if the question is a "new" question, then it is relayed to the lecturer; or, even more important, it is actually relayed not to the lecturer but to another person, typically a tutor.

Once it is answered, each new question has become an "old" question, and so next time the answer will be given by the system.

It is important to note that it is human intelligence, not AI, that compares new questions with old questions and judges answers.

The potential use of further persons, of tutors, has two very important consequences. First of all, a single lecturer can work with arbitrarily many students if the lecturer is supported by a number of tutors. All questions asked by the students can be answered individually. Better still, if tutors are used then students who have questions as they repeat the material can ask these questions as long as they are attached to the network, independent of when the lecture was delivered. This means that the time limitation to work through the material while the lecturer is present also disappears – if students work through it at midnight, provided they are attached to the network and there is a good tutoring system set up, they will still get individual answers. What is more, this works even if the student working through the material is seeing it for the first time.

Tutors can assist in editing the questions and answers, omitting one-off questions, and using fuzzy search techniques to filter out duplicates [Ukkonen, 1985, Wu and Manber, 1992]. They will then add to the database all genuinely new questions, together with their answers.

In other words the recording of the lecture in the way we have just described is nothing but the preparation of excellent computer assisted instruction (CAI) material.

11.3.5 Generating CAI Material

The procedure that we have described will indeed produce excellent CAI material. Pages of good material have been prepared, shown to students, and annotated. Furthermore some students have asked questions and the answers to these questions have automatically become available through the help system. This means that the student takes home a very good CAI package. And such packages are available even if the students have never attended the lecture but have obtained them by mail. Looking at the material may be the next best thing to sitting in the lecture room because you see the lecturer, you hear the lecturer, you see the transparency, you see the modification of the transparency. If you don't understand this diagram then the answer comes up immediately. And if it is not a standard answer and you are hooked onto the network, and if it is a course for many students, then there will be an online tutor, even at 4 o'clock in the morning, who can give an individual answer. So without much effort we are actually producing very high-quality CAI material. Lecturing and preparing high-quality CAI material are merging; teaching and teleteaching become one!

11.3.6 The Integration of Three Different Forms of Teaching

The technology that we have described actually provides lectures, long distance teaching [Stewart et al., 1988] and CAI. Things which are considered different disciplines today merge into one. And we are going to merge still more things, as will be seen shortly.

The fact that well-prepared teaching material presented in an appealing way with a commentary in acoustic form will actually give excellent CAI material can also be looked at from a different point of view. Because of this, CAI may finally have the success it has not had on a large scale in the past.

11.3.7 The Production and Use of Commercial Teaching Modules

When lecturers are trying to create CAI material, it will be much easier for them to include existing and commercially available teaching modules. Imagine that you are going to teach a course on Data Structures. The only thing you do initially is to prepare some professional-quality transparencies with your computer. You then use them in your class, commenting on them acoustically. By the questions asked, you learn what the students do not understand, and additional information is entered. After giving the course a couple of times you sell the product as an electronic book. Other lecturers who have to teach Data Structures will teach their own course but they will be able to take certain parts of yours as they stand and just tie them into theirs.

Whether the CAI material is distributed on CD or via a hypermedia database there will be important decisions to be made concerning billing. For example, what role will editors play? Certainly, as the Dartmouth group found [Cheyney et al., 1994], removal of noise and "umm's" and "ahh's" can be essential – and the edited talks can be only "half as long as the originals, and much more listenable." Then again, what will the role of publishers be? All the range of options for electronic publishing that were discussed in Section 9.4 must be considered – from the publishing free of charge (for just the honour and glory) to user-pays royalty schemes, as suggested by Ted Nelson in his Xanadu project [Nelson, 1987].

11.3.8 Further Extensions of the Lecture Scenario

Now let us go back to how the lecturing actually works. As we have explained, the students can ask questions, and these questions will be answered either by the system or by a person. In this, as in a number of other situations, students can either remain completely anonymous, or be identified by one or more pen-names, or be completely identified. Usually the choice is left to the student except in certain examination situations.

Levels of Anonymity. There are more than three levels of anonymity [Maurer and Flinn, 1994], but we restrict ourselves to the three most common.

- Complete anonymity:
Complete anonymity ensures that the students do not hesitate to ask "stupid questions" and the lecturer thus will get many more questions. The quality of the material produced will benefit by this, for every question that has been asked once is answered and is therefore available automatically on the system. In addition it allows the lecturer to carry out quick-fire tests and see from the students' responses whether it is necessary to explain a little more. And the lecturer can use it to control lecturing speed without stress. It also creates decision room conditions for stimulating uninhibited discussion. Again the dialogue is recorded for take-home purposes.
- Partial anonymity:
Using pseudonyms is much better than complete anonymity in certain situations as it allows dialogue between people without giving away their identity. Participants in dialogues must have names and addresses for each other.
- Complete identification:
Complete identification is sometimes preferred by students because they want to shine, and of course it is sometimes necessary for exams.

But for the real learning process anonymity is usually the best technique.

Formulating Questions. So that the system can react to certain standard questions it is reasonable to assume that these questions are formulated in written form, with a simple syntax, or generated via a menu.

The student defines the area of interest by clicking or dragging on the screen and then makes the appropriate choice from the menu. Questions which cannot be handled automatically by the system will be sent to the tutor, who can either respond directly to the student or pass the interesting and important questions on to the lecturer.

Questions may be formulated acoustically and can be archived acoustically; the sound of the voice can be changed to preserve anonymity. Unfortunately, the system cannot answer an acoustic question automatically at the present state of the art.

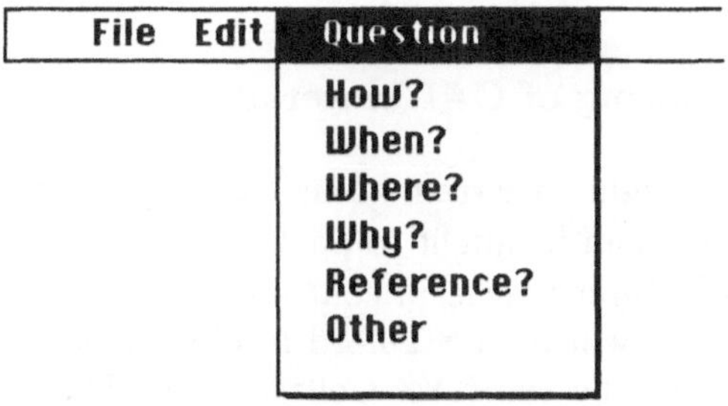

Fig. 11.3. Generating Questions by Menu

Automatic Response Metering. The interaction of students with the lecturer is not restricted to asking questions: much simpler interactions are possible and may be even more important. For example, students can anonymously signal "Please slow down," "Please give an example," "I don't understand the explanation," "I'm of a different opinion," etc. The lecturer sees on the Lecturer computer how many students, or what percentage of them, are making such remarks and can act accordingly. A display at the bottom of the Lecturer computer can also show warning icons at levels determined by the lecturer. Students can indicate when they need an adjustment to be made to the theatre lighting, the projector focus, or the volume of the sound system. At the pre-determined level of demand the particular icon "lights up" – perhaps red for too high or fast, blue for too low or slow.

Light   Sound   Focus   Pace   Questions

Fig. 11.4. Interaction Indicators

Decision Room Style Discussions. Further examples and additional explanations can be given, or a discussion can be instigated. And here is the point at which such a system incorporates all the experiences of groupware, computer conferencing systems, computer supported cooperative work (CSCW) and decision rooms [Dewan, 1993, Ellis et al., 1991, Elrod et al., 1992]. All the kinds of discussion that are possible in a decision room, including straw voting, are now possible in the lecture situation.

Thus, an ordinary lecture suddenly turns into an anonymous electronic discussion in which perhaps the lecturer plays the part of a moderator or possibly not even that role any more. On the other hand, by using quiz questions or little tests (and again because of the anonymity this does not increase the stress for the students) the lecturer can test which things have been understood and for which further explanation is necessary.

11.3.9 Multi-authoring of CAI Material

The same material taught to certain groups of people may look considerably different a year later than if taught to another group. This is very valuable. It means that if a lecturer teaches a course on 3rd level Data Structures at Stanford University it will be a Stanford level CAI package. If it is taught at XYZ College it will be the XYZ College level. The original material is the same but because of the various questions that the students ask and the fact that in some cases the lecturer is forced to repeat and insert things the

CAI material suddenly becomes available on various levels, and this quite effortlessly.

Just imagine what this may mean! It will be something like multi-authoring of CAI material. A real expert in data structures writes "A First Course in Data Structures". This is used by a number of universities. It may be that a number of professors sign an agreement with the original author that if they use it for three years then the resulting course is distributed jointly under the names of the original author and the additional professor(s), and it gets a certain qualified title such as "Data Structures for College Level" or "Data Structures for Advanced Graduate Students". So the original course nucleus will have been transformed by the interactions into different fully developed courses designed for specific levels of learners, whether needing more examples and repetitions or looking for further information from other sources.

Once again, unfortunately, the most difficult phase of development may well be sorting out the nightmare concerning copyright (see Section 9.11).

11.4 Lecturing "On the Fly"

It is really not surprising that lecturers absorbed in their own subjects cannot keep up with developments in communication technology. The system we have proposed in this chapter lets lecturers develop, refine and define their own material much more readily than ever before – almost "on the fly". There have been several initiatives to implement these ideas – see Sections 12.8.1, 12.8.2, and 12.8.3.

11.4.1 Incorporating Lecture Material on the Fly

A wide variety of lecture material is now available in electronic databases (pre-prepared slides, animations, dictionaries, encyclopedias, and journals, as well as new style "interactive and annotated" movies [Jayasinha et al., 1995]). Lectures from previous years, complete with video clips of the lecturer, and, most important, questions and answers (see Section 11.3.4) are also stored in the database.

Much useful material containing pictures and diagrams is available on the Web [URLi3], and on CD-ROM, e.g., CorelDraw [CorelDraw, 1992]. In addition scanners, whether large fixed models or lighter hand-held ones, can capture pictures to a remarkably high degree of accuracy.

However, lecturers should also have easy options for determining how the data objects (video, sound, graphics, etc.) are to be labelled – textually or graphically. They may decide, for example, to have a key scene from the video iconised.

Since sound can make or break any presentation, the option of having it ultimately under the user's, rather than the author's, control is extremely important. Lecturers will decide what icons they want to open depending on circumstances, skimming over some to find more appropriate ones.

What we also need is an environment that helps us select the best of a range of pictures efficiently, and links them into our documents. Research concerning graphical queries on pictorial data is still in its infancy [Bordogna et al., 1989] but miniaturised versions of pictures can be displayed in groups of up to one hundred on the screen to aid selection. Double-clicking will enlarge them for closer inspection. Ideally, at this stage, the user should be able to have full editing facilities such as those provided by applications like Adobe Photoshop for cutting, scaling, touching up, and adding graphics. Once the selected photo has been edited, the user will be given the choice of how to integrate it into the document. The photo can appear either in its actual size or as an iconised representation. Clicking on the photo icon will, of course, open it to the full picture. The icon may either be labelled with text or, if it is clear enough, be a miniaturised version of the picture.

11.4.2 Capturing Video and Sound on the Fly

To capture lectures on the fly the lecturer, concentrating on the material being presented, needs a highly efficient data capturing system – ideally with professional audio-visual staff assistance. However, to avoid extensive editing, the lecturer should be given a certain amount of control over the capture. A small menu of buttons at the bottom of the browser page could provide controls for capturing the video, sound, and lecture material. Fortunately, the new "add-on" cameras that look like little more than a small standard lamp are easily adjustable – and are no more threatening!

11.5 Afterword

In Section 11.3 we introduced a projection computer. At this point it should be clear that it will become redundant: it will not be necessary once improvements in resolution allow small screens to replace the projection screen. The original idea of the projection screen was to show the structure of the presented material. While the lecturer goes through the individual parts, on the projection screen the student can see the whole structure of the lesson displayed – and the lecturer can refer to it saying, "I am now at point 5.2" Once this can be shown clearly on the student's screen, either visible or available in a window (see Figure 11.2), physical attendance at a lecture may be unnecessary – perhaps the only advantage of going in person will be for personal contact with other students and with the lecturer.

The kind of technology described integrates various strands of developments which are already visible today but are still separate: computer presentation software, media corners, CAI, distance teaching, computer conferencing systems, and decision rooms. Tying all of these together may result in the most powerful tool for teaching mankind has ever known. It may well have ramifications far beyond the confines of teaching. We believe that these powerful tools could provide the facilitation vital for handling the tremendous problems facing mankind and our planet.

12. Hypermedia and Distributed Learning Environments

12.1 Introduction

The statement "Millions of students take courses electronically" [Rossman, 1992] is no exaggeration. Even back in 1990, the National Technical University (NTU) in the US, for example, had more than 1,100 graduate students in their electronic learning programme, and most of those who completed the Masters programme said that they would not have been able to do so in any other way [Rossman, 1992].

The items of software and hardware available to support distributed learning environments are already "legion" [Wells, 1993]. Even the terminology has proliferated: Computer Mediated Communication (CMC), Online Education, Computer Supported Collaborative Work (CSCW), Groupware, etc. Wells goes on to state, "However, what is striking is how much of it is designed for generic communications purposes rather than for specific user groups like distance students and instructors." There is certainly no one-size-fits-all answer, and care must be taken in choosing the right combination of technology to support specific learning requirements.

In the first third of this chapter we give a general overview of current trends in distance education. The middle section of the chapter is an illustrative survey of existing distributed learning environments. The last third of the chapter concentrates on several high tech projects for hypermedia learning environment using broadband networks.

12.1.1 Tailoring Facilities to Needs

Online courses are certainly not an easy way out for the staff! Systems have to be carefully researched, while organisation and planning time almost inevitably increases as well [Rumble, 1992]. All the various options, advantages, and disadvantages of electronic publishing systems that we mentioned in Section 9.4 have to be considered. There is no "right" answer. However, for the students the advantages of the modern systems can be significant, provided we pay particular attention to details that will optimise success – such as guarding against the feeling of alienation that frequently occurs in traditional distance learning situations.

People are asking whether the Internet is to "become a planetary nervous system or an electronic tower of Babel?" [Rossman, 1992]. We believe a form of global "university" is emerging, and that with appropriate hypermedia support including the formation of specialist *hubs* [Rossman, 1992], it will be one of the most exciting developments of our century.

Good design for learning networks is obviously imperative. The paper "Learning network design: a methodology for the construction of co-operative distance learning environments" discusses one method of attack [Davies, 1994].

There is little doubt that much time and money has been sunk into amateurish computer-aided instruction programs. The system we described in Chapter 11 will tend to give control back to the professionals: good lecturers will create high quality lectures, top class tutors will provide first-rate tutoring services, and video producers will produce high-quality video.

12.2 From Teacher Centred to Student Centred Learning

Many well established distance learning centres, such as the Open University, UK [Daniel, 1994], are now heavily involved with electronic teaching. As with traditional school learning, online teaching was initially a one-to-many activity – active on the teacher's part, but unfortunately all too passive on the student's part. Recent advances in technology have expedited a change from one-to-many teaching to many-to-many [Harasim, 1990]. Bates [Bates, 1993] states, "Teachers then will increasingly be advisers, and managers and facilitators of learning, rather than providers of information."

12.2.1 From Passive to Active Learning Environments

It is clear that, ideally, a distributed learning environment is not a passive environment where students simply sit in front of a screen receiving broadcast information – multimedia or otherwise. Interactivity can be of paramount importance. Certainly the amount of interaction will vary, depending on factors such as economics, distance, group size, learner maturity, and so on, although it is usually possible to add at least some degree of interactivity using audio or email connections.

The importance of peer tutoring has been well documented [Harasim, 1990, Johnson and Johnson, 1975]. Remote learners, in particular, can benefit greatly from computer-mediated collaboration that helps offset feelings of alienation.

12.3 Why So Much "Distance Education" in Urban Areas?

Traditionally, distance education has been the poor sister – the only option for rural children. Now we are seeing an ever increasing number of city-based people of all ages choosing it as their preferred option. Many reasons are given for the setting up of online courses, just a few of which are listed here:

- Facilitating market-driven retraining programs for business professionals [Rossman, 1992]
- Retraining teachers [Lupton and Rushby, 1994]
- Providing access to specialist centres [Rossman, 1992]
- Providing equal opportunities – economic, age, gender, race [Hiltz and Turoff, 1994]
- Bowing to economic pressures that are forcing an ever-increasing proportion of students to take distance courses even when there are on-campus facilities near by [Hiltz and Turoff, 1994]
- Revitalising run down courses [Rossman, 1992]
- Making courses more student directed [Hiltz and Turoff, 1994]
- Improving the "quality" of education [Harasim, 1990] [Hiltz and Turoff, 1994]
- Linking exploded campuses
- On-the-job training, refresher courses, etc.

12.4 The Electronic Classroom

One of the first innovative electronic classrooms was the AT&T Teaching Theater at the University of Maryland [Shneiderman, 1993b]. Shneiderman reports using the classroom for:

- Student presentations
- Class exercises
- Homework projects
- Group programming
- Course reviews
- Brainstorming
- Hypercourseware
- On-campus database projects
- Off-campus database projects
- Graduate seminars
- Empirical studies research projects.

Shneiderman concludes, "Education by engagement and construction applies not just to computer science courses but to every discipline and at every age, from elementary school to continuing education" [Shneiderman, 1993b].

12.4.1 The "Virtual Classroom"

"Virtual Classroom" is the trademark for the New Jersey Institute of Technology's "Electronic Information Exchange System" [Hiltz, 1990, Hiltz and Turoff, 1994, Hiltz, 1995]. Although the term obviously has associations with virtual reality (VR) it has little to do with gadgetry. Here we are talking about *desktop VR* on a simple computer screen. Well over thirty courses are given in New Jersey's virtual classroom. Hiltz maintains that it is more effective than traditional teaching methods for many reasons, in particular because it supports active rather than passive group learning. Teams can make presentations and learn by being teachers. Although traditionally very few students answer questions, the anonymity provided by using pennames encourages participation and experimentation. Hiltz also points out that it removes space and time barriers (clashes with job or other classes) [Hiltz and Turoff, 1994, Hiltz, 1995].

12.5   Computer Mediated Communication (CMC)

Computer Mediated Communication (CMC) ranges from simple email to full conferencing systems, and each has a part to play:

- Electronic mail [Donath, 1993] [Hoffmann, 1993]
  [Weeks and Røyrvik, 1993]
- Bulletin boards [Lee and Tsang, 1994]
- News and interest group facilities
- Interactive broadcasts
- Audio graphics [Reynolds, 1994]
- Video conferencing – both synchronous and asynchronous.

Wells states, "CMC presents an instructor with many pedagogical opportunities, collaborative work, seminars, role plays, debates, to name but a few. Seminar discussions, for example, are often a powerful way to encourage peer learning and lessen the social and academic isolation experienced by many distance learners" [Wells, 1993].

12.5.1 Conferencing

We covered computer conferencing in Section 10.2.5. However, in the context of distributed learning, the term "conferencing" can be misleading. Conferencing systems are being used for much more than meeting support. They are a viable option for teaching modules "with specific aims and objectives" [Reynolds, 1994]. The amount of interactivity in conferencing systems can be varied from none at all to "free-for-all".

A recurring theme at today's educational conferences is the importance of group work to prepare students for life in the real world. Wayne Grant

(Human-Computer Interaction, Stanford University) stressed its utmost importance in the ED-MEDIA 94 invited address titled "Investigating Tomorrow's Technologies Today".

Conferencing technology ranges from the simplest (often just email) to full video conferencing, and what technology is appropriate is highly dependent on circumstances.

Asynchronous Conferencing. Although synchronous conferencing can solve some real-time problems [Harasim, 1990, Hiltz and Turoff, 1994], it can unfortunately cause delays in turn-around time for project completion.

Several interesting combinations of the above technology are evolving – such as using asynchronous communication at the beginning of a project and then switching to synchronous collaboration for the final stages.

12.6 Emerging Wide-Area Networked Learning Environments

The high level of interest in educational networked systems is illustrated by the fact that at the ED-MEDIA 94 conference in Vancouver half of the invited speakers addressed the topic. John Gage (Director, Sun Microsystems) talked about the net as a "social institution". J. M. Greenberg from the Open University, Walton Hall, UK, reported that their "home computing program includes 18 courses and supports over 20,000 students." Tony Bates from the Open Learning Agency, BC, Canada, stated that "Stentor, an alliance of Canadian telephone companies, announced an \$8 billion, 10 year initiative, called BEACON, that will bring broadband, multimedia services to 80–90% of all homes and businesses in Canada by the year 2004" [Bates, 1994]. And of course Ted Nelson's whole life has been a long crusade for his vision of such a system as hypertext.

Rossman gives a very good overview of emerging systems in his book titled *The Emerging Worldwide Electronic University: Information Age Global Higher Education* [Rossman, 1992]. Rossman is vice-president of the *Global Systems Analysis and Simulation* project (GLOSAS/USA) and Chair of the GLOSAS/Global University-Long-Range Planning Committee. Interestingly, the title of his book notwithstanding, Rossman argues that the days of "big is better" have gone. He and the groups he represents are convinced that although the future of higher education does lie with global networks, these networks will form from groups of sub-nets (hubs) that are composed of "safe professionally managed systems".

12.7 An Illustrative Survey of Distributed Learning Environments

12.7.1 The Open University at Walton Hall, UK

The Open University at Walton Hall, Milton Keynes, UK, claims to be a "world leader in distance education" [Greenberg, 1994]. It serves over 200,000 students per year. Its *Home Computing Program*, first started in 1988, includes more than 18 courses and serves over 20,000 students [Greenberg, 1994]. The university policy is to build on existing teaching material as far as is practical [Greenberg, 1994, Rumble, 1992]. The HOMER project, for example, integrated material (books, video, audio, and learning guides) from a previous course into a multimedia presentation. However some specialised software has been written, for example the graphical interface for computer conferencing [Jones et al., 1993].

The Open University first used computer conferencing systems back in 1988 [Mason, 1993], when it gave a distance learning course in Information Technology, to over 1300 students. Many courses, including an MBA program, have been given in the intervening years, and much has been learnt – for example the importance of keeping the conferencing system central to the course design. It was found that students still had to be kept focused by such methods as giving credit for time spent conferencing, otherwise (just as is the case with any assignment work) other commitments tended to crowd it out. It was also found that conferencing did increase the amount of work the students were required to do [Jones et al., 1993, Mason, 1993]. However, tutors and most students were positive about their experiences, one student going as far as to say "I think it has been one of the most worthwhile learning experiences I have undertaken for a long time. It requires you to develop all sorts of skills – technical, writing, communicating, discovering etc. Many thanks again for opening new doors" [Mason, 1993].

As part of the European COMETT project the Open University has run a graduate-level course for teachers and trainers interested in group work. Besides using the system for conferences and group work they use it for:

– Distributing introductory notes and messages
– Distributing assignments and grades
– On-line marking.

A survey entitled "Large scale conferencing for inexpert users" was carried out at the Open University [Mercer, 1993] It concludes, "The main finding was that large-scale computer conferencing may be well received and well used by inexpert users – even if they have no other direct membership links and are working in small groups."

Professor Kaye, professor of Information Management, Open Business School, has described an "Electronic Campus" and elaborated on both the advantages and disadvantages of CSCW [Kaye, 1993].

12.7.2 The Open Learning Agency, BC, Canada

The vision of the Open Learning Agency, BC, Canada [Bates, 1993] is: "Each person should be able to access high quality learning opportunities appropriate to their needs throughout their life. They should be able to do this from home, the work-place, local community-based centres, or through educational institutions". Bates notes that by 1992/93 "63% of all college enrolments in BC were part-time" [Bates, 1994].

The Open Learning Agency deals with a very large database of traditional distance-learning media: well over 20 tons of post mail, 120,000 video cassettes, 1 million audio cassettes, as well as 1.7 million floppy disks. It gives courses up to PhD level. It is involved with a consortium that is at the development stage for a system named VIEW (Virtual Interactive Environment for Workgroups). The system will provide tools for "multimedia conferences ... education and training ... home shopping, [and] financial services."

Bates [Bates, 1993] lists the following skills, defined by the Conference Board of Canada, that are needed in the workforce:

- Good communication skills (reading, writing, speaking, listening)
- Ability to learn independently
- Social skills: ethics, positive attitudes, responsibility
- Teamwork
- Ability to adapt to changing circumstances
- Thinking skills: problem-solving; critical, logical, numerical
- Knowledge navigation: where to get information and how to process it.

Skills such as these can be developed using interactive online environments.

12.7.3 Stanford University, California

Stanford University runs an Instructional Television Network (SITN) that delivers over 250 credit-based advanced engineering and science courses at over 200 sites to some 142 companies [DiPaolo, 1993]. Since 1991 it has run two-way compressed video transmissions throughout the United States. Using microwave links students participate in "lively discussions" [DiPaolo, 1993]. "The two-way technology is also used to offer advising sessions, tutorials, office hours and to support faculty/industry communications, especially around faculty consultative and research-related opportunities."

12.7.4 Europe

A comprehensive study of distance learning in Europe is provided in the paper "Existing and Future Technology for Teleteaching" [Rodruguez-Rosello, 1993].

The CO-LEARN project, according to the authors [Derycke and Kaye, 1993], is "concerned with a range of flexible and distance learning and training environments, and focuses particularly on access to human resources: tutors, experts, working colleagues, and peers." It provides a "first approach to the modelling of collaborative educational situations and learning activities."

As part of the DELTA programme (Development of European Learning through Technological Advance) Norway has initiated a "Just In Time Open Learning" project which has a wide list of international partners [Haugen, 1993].

12.7.5 The Open University of Thailand

Many Asian universities such as the Open University of Thailand – which has over one quarter of a million students – are looking for more cost-effective ways to reach students isolated by poor transport infrastructures. Rossman states, "New kinds and combinations of technologies for communication in education are being experimented with and developed each day and each 'new mix' brings the reality of the worldwide electronic university closer" [Rossman, 1992].

12.7.6 The Open Polytechnic of New Zealand

Swift states that the Open Polytechnic enables learners to "learn when they want (frequency, timing, duration), how they want (modes of learning), what they want (that is, learners can define what constitutes learning to them), and they can choose where they want to learn (at home, at an institution, at a training centre, etc.)" [Swift, 1994]. With this aim the Open Polytech has set up a network of resource centres to service the 35,000 student population. The staff is being trained in the use of distributed systems and electronic classrooms using synchronous conferencing systems.

In the paper "Moving from a Content Focus to a Learning Outcome Focus", Callaghan writes, "Courses are becoming more flexible with greater student choice, more openness in course organisation and with an increasingly wide variety of delivery media" [Callaghan, 1994].

12.7.7 The New Zealand Correspondence School

The New Zealand Correspondence School [Sutherland, 1994] has created interactive multimedia computer-assisted packages for mathematics and Japanese courses, with a project team consisting of:

- A project manager
- A subject writer for each course to storyboard existing text-based material
- A distance teaching adviser for each course
- An overall course material supervisor
- A quality controller responsible for collating and co-ordinating quality graphics for scanning, etc.

– A programmer for each course responsible for interpreting the storyboards and transferring the material into the authoring software.

In a section entitled "What for the future?" Sutherland concludes that "centres of learning are likely to become increasingly 'open' influencing what, how and where and when people learn", and that there is a "need for continuing lifelong education". The correspondence school has looked at both electronic mail and teleconferencing [Capper, 1994].

12.8 Online Learning: Lecture Rooms of the Future

In Chapter Eleven we described how high quality CAI material can be generated live during lectures and archived for later use. The lecturer is supported by an online hypermedia database such as Hyperwave [Kappe et al., 1993], and the students are encouraged to participate actively, using either portable computers or built-in signalling devices. Since there is no absolute need for the students to be physically present at the lecture we are really talking about distributed online learning. As we mentioned before, several projects have been initiated to implement this technology:

– Graz, Austria (see Section 12.8.1)
– Freiburg, Germany (see Section 12.8.2)
– Auckland, New Zealand (see Section 12.8.3)

12.8.1 The Learning And Teaching Environment: Graz University of Technology, Austria

The Learning And Teaching Environment is a project that integrates a number of current developments in information and communication technology, such as CAI, hypermedia, the World Wide Web, authoring systems, digital libraries, distance teaching systems, and CSCW [Maurer, 1996b]. Maurer has examined why CAI developments in the last three decades never achieved the expected breakthrough in education. He identified the major problems associated with learning and teaching systems in the past, and has designed the project to overcome them.

The project consists of a CAI nucleus built on Hyperwave and HM-Card (see Section 2.18). Hyperwave's communication facilities allow networked cooperation and collaboration between all users. HM-Card enables teachers to build powerful interactive multimedia presentations and courseware modules. Animation and rather complex question/answer dialogues can be prepared without programming or scripting. Material prepared with HM-Card can be used by itself or fully integrated into the Web environment. It is highly modular and can therefore easily be reused, reducing cost of authoring.

Keeping the authoring effort low is one of the main goals of the project. All modules are stored in Hyperwave servers to build a fully searchable digital library consisting of multimedia Web material, electronic versions of books and journals, etc. By customising pre-existing material, the work of creating electronic lessons is reduced, at least to a certain extent.

Modules can be used in the classroom to replace traditional lecturing aids such as the blackboard or overhead transparencies. Recording of the lecturer's voice and image is supported and it can be added to the lecture material, thus making "authoring on the fly" a reality. Modules can also be used by students for self-study and various features for interaction are provided, so that using a module becomes more than just "page turning in a multimedia enriched book".

Students can browse parts of the digital library related to their lecture material and they can activate simulation modules. They can interact with other students or teachers synchronously using chat and a whiteboard, or asynchronously using bulletin boards or structured discussions. They can test their knowledge by answering questions provided by HM-Card. If parts of a lecture are unclear, questions can be asked which will be answered by tutors or the lecturer, and the question/answer dialogues become part of the lecture and accessible to other users.

12.8.2 Authoring on the Fly: University of Freiburg, Germany

The Freiburg "Authoring on the Fly" project provides a range of tools for both capturing lectures and playing them back. In addition, lectures have been broadcast via the MBone (Multicast Backbone virtual network [Eriksson, 1994]) to multiple hosts around the world.

The captured material (audio, video, and whiteboard actions) is archived in Hyperwave collections. For playback a specialised Hyperwave viewer, SYNCVIEW, presents the material by synchronising the whiteboard actions with the video and sound.

12.8.3 A Distributed Learning Environment:
The University of Auckland, NZ

As in Graz and Freiburg, students at The University of Auckland have access to a the Hyperwave system. We aim to create an interactive distributed learning environment, using lecture material available from previous years, as described in the previous chapter.

Since there is a wide range of hardware that has to be supported, we have relied on common web browsers that support Java applets. Successful features of the Auckland project include:

1. The course outline, accessible to students from the beginning of the year, consists of lines which both describe the course, and also are links which point to further material automatically after each lecture is held.

2. As the course proceeds, additional lecture material, consisting of PowerPoint [PowerPoint, 1992] slides, are stored in Hyperwave, sequentially linked, and tables of contents generated.
3. For distant lectures to the university's satellite campus user feedback is of utmost importance. We have included, at the bottom of the browser screen, the simple button-controlled query menus that were described in Section 11.3.8 (see Figure 12.1), as well as text-based question-and-answer dialogue sessions.
4. Students can form text-based chat groups.
5. Both students and lecturers can annotate material, and restrict access to the annotations through Hyperwave's group access rights.
6. The system can be used in either asynchronous or synchronous modes.

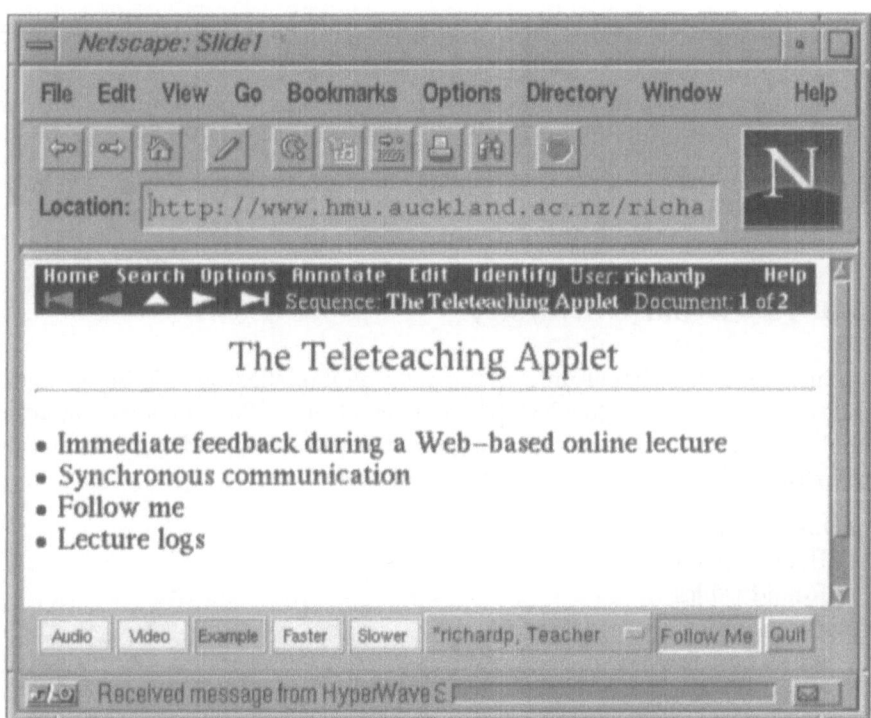

Fig. 12.1. Java Enhanced Screen Showing Feedback Buttons

12.8.4 Creating a Flexible Learning Environment

We believe that, ideally, an electronic learning environment should provide:

- Cross-platform access, via the Internet, to large hypermedia databases (such as Hyperwave), including:
  - Controlled access
  - Seamless integration of existing communication services such as email and bulletin boards
  - Home pages
  - Customisation of existing resources
- One-to-many broadcasting, including news and special interest group facilities
- A continuum of interactive broadcast options
- Computer mediated communication, including:
  - Text and graphical common workspace
  - Audio and video
- Video conferencing, both synchronous and asynchronous, including:
  - Shared spaces, both textual and graphical
  - A meeting scheduler
- Statistical reports, e.g., for keeping a log of student access.

To date no one system provides anywhere near all these features, but we believe that a carefully chosen combination of existing modules, when controlled by an interface such as that described in the next section, will go a long way to providing them.

12.9 A Virtual University

User interfaces for virtual universities may be modelled on existing physical structures, or abstract "locales" [Fitzpatrick et al., 1996] – or a combination of both. In all cases, students can be presented with tours and maps, including 3D fly-throughs, that guide them to facilities such as:

- Administration centres
  - Booking facilities
  - Round tables
- Notice boards
  - Important notices
  - Coffee room corners
- Supervisors' rooms
- Tutors' rooms
- Lecture/Presentation rooms
- Collaboration rooms (synchronous and asynchronous) with:
- Formal facilities such as full video conferencing with a moderator
- Informal facilities such as text-mail groups
- A technical assistance room with:
  - Faults report lists

- Help desks
- Electronic library stocked with:
  - General resources
  - Course-specific resources
  - Past lecture notes
  - Past test and exam papers
- Tutorial room equipped with:
  - CAI
  - Tutor
- Examination room
- Marking room

12.10 Afterword

We have to agree with Rossman [Rossman, 1992] that in many senses we are like Arthur C. Clarke's "fish trying to imagine fire". Even specialists are having difficulty keeping up to date in their own fields. However, as Rossman [Rossman, 1992] predicted, we are seeing the development of specialist hubs that other centres, worldwide, can hook into. Bates [Bates, 1993] states, "Teachers then will increasingly be advisers and managers and facilitators of learning, rather than providers of information." Systems such as Hyperwave will provide the information. "The teachers' role will concentrate more on developing skills, and in particular skills of navigating knowledge sources, and skills of processing and analysing information" [Bates, 1993]. We hope that the new technology may "empower our intellectual processes, to make us better thinkers, learners, and problem solvers" [Harasim, 1990].

13. Interactive and Annotated Movies[1]

13.1 Introduction

Free will is such a basic tenet of everyday belief that we assign it to the depths of our subconsciousness. Freedom of choice is assumed to be a basic human right. People expect choice – maximum choice, comprehensive choice. Computer technologists are compulsively answering the demand; and each answer raises further expectations. We have interactive TV, choice of TV programs from a multi-windowed screen display, and personal computers that can double as TVs and video recorders. Meanwhile on our computer screens more and more windows are appearing, with an increasing number of dialog boxes. Computer-controlled movies are developing such a range of options that, even at this stage, we must remember that more is not always best. Confusion, haste, inertia, and mental repetitive strain injury are only some of the human factors that will necessitate real research to optimise choice.

Interactive applications range from the partially interactive to the totally involving, from CD-ROM to virtual reality. Ironically it is the field between the extremes that has received the least attention to date. Yet that is an area inviting exploration. In this chapter we discuss progress and possibilities.

First we maintain that multimedia is much more than just a mix of new media in digitised form: it is virtually a new world (see Chapter 1).

Then in Section 13.2 we expand on the usual notion of "interactive". Certainly we expect to pause, rewind, fast-forward, jump to specific tracks or choose between various storylines as in the existing CD-I movies being promoted by commercial companies. However, current research in high-resolution digital technology provides many more interesting options. Users will be able to pause and gain all sorts of supportive features such as:

- User-controlled mapping of parts of a scene (see Section 13.3.1)
- High-resolution zooming – gaining detail (see Section 13.3.2)
- Annotated movies with hypermedia support in a range of forms: text, diagram, digitised speech, encyclopedia entries, etc.
- Simultaneous Movies (see Section 13.6.3)

---

[1] A previous version of part of this chapter was published in the proceedings of Ed-Media'95 [Jayasinha et al., 1995].

In Section 13.4.1 we give examples of the new interactive technology as it could be used in education.

13.2 A New Definition of Multimedia

The term "multimedia" is frequently used with too narrow a meaning. It must be generalised to mean much more than just a mix of linked text, graphics, pictures, animations, video and sound. Any definition of multimedia must now incorporate, diagrams, maps, CAD drawings, 3D objects, 3D models of scenes of arbitrary complexity – and much more [Lennon and Maurer, 1994d]. The term "multimedia" also includes an entire range of interactive technology (see next section).

"Real" Interactivity. Maurer states, "Real computer-based multimedia means applying the power of the computer to achieve interactivity beyond just being able to choose, at time to time, from a number of alternatives selected" [Maurer, 1994b]. Such "real" interactivity includes interactive video, video games, and powerful new educational techniques such as the *interactive* and *annotated* movies (see Sections 13.3 and 13.4) that are based on new techniques in high-resolution graphics. And in its most general form it must include virtual reality as it is described in Section 5.3.1.

Interactive CD (CD-I). Some years ago, interactive CD technology was widely promoted. Many movies exist that let the user jump from one scene to another, fast forward, play, and jump back again. A few have keyword searches. But in most we have seen so far the actions available to the user are very limited and we are left with doubts as to whether this form of technology will ever really take off.

However, techniques that do provide useful options are those that efficiently interleave several different languages among video frames. For example, documentaries can be played in French, German, English, or Italian, as selected by the user. Since digital technology is improving steadily we hope that before long even more innovative techniques will be discovered.

13.3 Telescopic Movies

We are looking for new ways for users to control what they see on their screens. Modern research is steadily pushing the limits in high-resolution movie making and this is opening the way for exciting new developments. The idea of super-wide movies has been pursued in the field of public entertainment, producing wide-screen epics first, then circular screen productions. These may be spectacular, but it is almost in the nature of them that their content is more than any one person can even see, let alone take in. In cases like these more information is provided than can be processed by any one person at one time, and most viewers are left with a niggling feeling that they may have missed something by looking at the wrong place at the wrong time. We need to increase the user's involvement without introducing mutually exclusive three-ring circuses.

13.3.1 User-Controlled Mapping of Parts of a Scene

Current research is working towards resolutions of much better than TV quality. This factor alone will add a new dimension to movie making as for example when a high-resolution film is mapped down to TV quality in a computer window. We can map a selected part of the high resolution movie and let the user determine which part. It will be as if the user is looking through a telescope that, within limits, can be moved (see Figure 13.1).

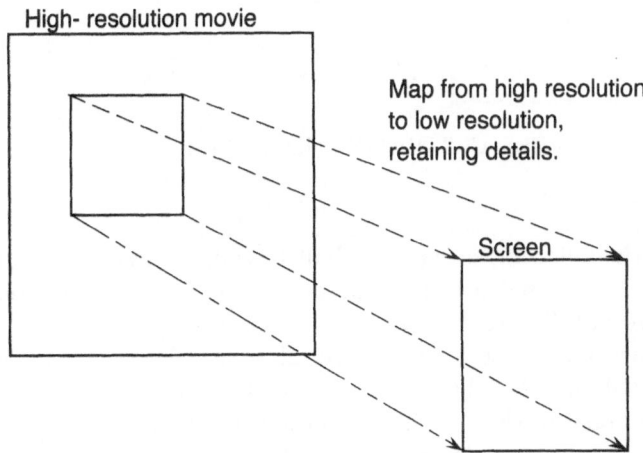

Fig. 13.1. Telescopic Movies

Users will be able to pan across a scene at will, but they may also be provided with acoustic clues pointing them to important sections that are currently out of sight: the viewer may hear a waterfall, or see a puff of smoke appear at an edge. Or, rather more mundanely, they may be provided with coloured indicators, or icons, at relevant places in the document's margins.

Interesting non-sequential options can arise in interactive movies. Consider, for example, a scene in a cowboy movie showing the characters discussing the coming of the Indians. If a cloud of dust appears, the viewer may be able to zoom directly into the heart of the action. Or if a rider is seen disappearing into the distance the viewer may be able to pause the current action and follow the new path of action.

13.3.2 High-Resolution Zooming

We shall now look at an equally fascinating alternative: viewing a high-resolution movie as if through a telescope with powerful zoom control. We shall be able to zoom into any section to reveal hidden detail, with no loss of quality!

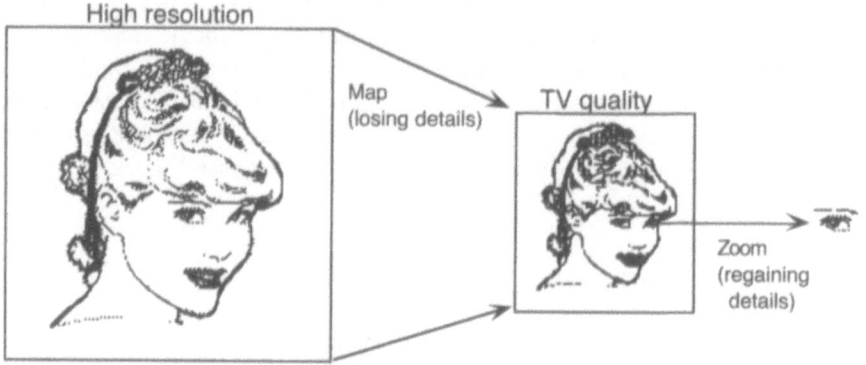

Fig. 13.2. High-Resolution Zooming

Consider the following scenario. A ballet or an orchestral performance is filmed, using a wide-angled lens, and stored as a high-resolution document. It is then shown at TV resolution on the viewer's screen:

Since we assume that users will have full video-player options, including pause, they will then be able to zoom onto any particular performer and have them enlarged to show additional detail. In an orchestral performance the instruments can be enlarged and, just as modern video cameras can localise and magnify sound, it will be possible to have the sound adjusted to correspond to the pictorial zooming. Metaphorically it will place the viewer at the performer's feet.

Another important possibility is interactive "signposting". To take another scenario, the viewer of a ballet may wish to follow the principal dancers, zooming in at times to look at costume detail. There will be times, however, when they wish to pay attention to particular supporting dancers. The interactive placement of markers will enable the viewer to efficiently return to a signpost in order to follow another character in more detail. That is something we all wish we could do at live performances!

We are sure that highly creative interactions, combining both zooming and panning, await innovative developers.

13.4 Annotated Movies

Commercial technology, incorporating video coding procedures such as Motion JPEG or MPEG compression, is making use of movies of video quality. These movies frequently use only one quarter of the screen. If they are enlarged to full screen they use tricks such as multiplying each pixel by four. We suggest that such movies could lend themselves to much more ingenious and promising strategies than this.

Let us divide the screen into four quadrants, with the movie taking up only the top left (see Figure 13.3). All four quadrants may be used interactively. The top right may show enlargements. The bottom left may show key words from the currently playing section of the movie and support powerful modern key-word searches. The bottom right section may show any related item such as relevant diagrams or maps:

Again we assume that users will have all the usual video options including the ability to freeze the movie. Obviously it is highly desirable that the enlargements show additional information – not just more of the same. One method to achieve this is to interleave high-resolution frames. If (say) every twentieth frame is high resolution, then the user can pause the movie and zoom into a selection displayed from the closest high-resolution frame. Assuming a one-hour movie, where some 10% of the frames are critical, we would need to add 450 pictures, each 1200×1000 pixels with 24 colour bits (about 3.6 MB each). Modern compression techniques such as JPEG will reduce each picture to 150 KB, so we would be adding approximately 68 MB – an amount that can easily be coped with using modern storage techniques.

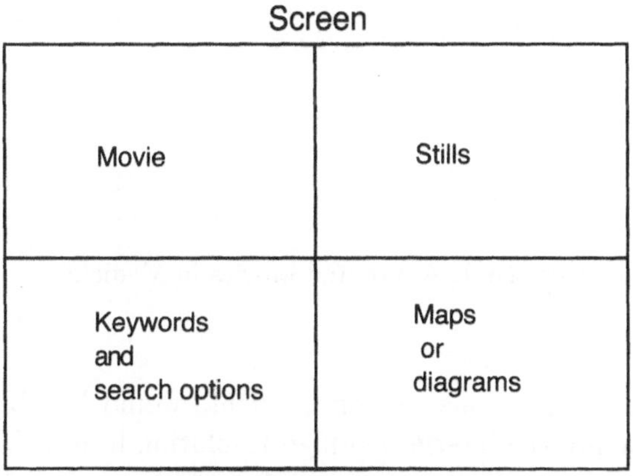

Screen

Movie	Stills
Keywords and search options	Maps or diagrams

Fig. 13.3. Annotated Movies

Of great advantage would be a computer program that could "analyse" video (in black and white, with intensified contrast, and taking extreme points) and produce a sequence of diagrams that could run as an animated version of the video. This could well provide an area of very profitable research.

13.4.1 Annotated Movies in Education

We can imagine many uses for annotated movies in education and we have chosen but two illustrative examples. As a first example consider a teaching movie for medical students: an interactive one showing an ear operation. The annotated movie (see Figure 13.4) could show:

1. A movie of an actual operation by a skilled surgeon.
2. Close-up pictures of the instruments being used.
3. Diagrams of parts of the ear.
4. A useful list of keywords taken from a transcript of the surgeon's explanations. If students did not understand any term they heard spoken, they would be able to pause the movie and have it looked up in the electronic medical dictionary.

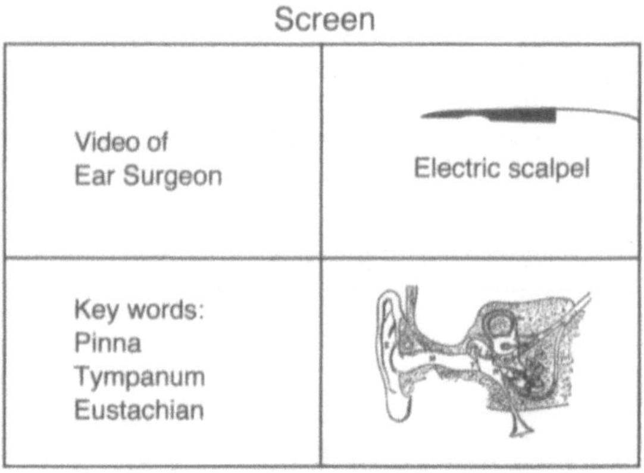

Fig. 13.4. Annotated Movies in Medicine

As described in the previous section, students would be able to freeze the movie and zoom into the interleaved high-resolution frames. They would also be able to link into other related movies for additional information. At this point we add that we are very aware of potential overload problems. Any system utilising four screen partitions would have to be interactive enough to let users have full control over what they watch when.

Obviously, many fields would benefit by the opportunities offered. If, for example, an annotated movie were made about Lawrence of Arabia, it could satisfy viewer interest in questions from a great range of background topics: the geography of the region, desert warfare, history ancient and modern, archaeology, and political, ethnic, and cultural information.

13.4.2 Annotated Movies as Entertainment

From the most highbrow of entertainment to adventure games there is obviously unlimited scope for annotated movies. A movie supporting an art exhibition might show the life of the artist, offer a commentary incorporating stills of related works (which could easily be displayed side by side), and give a study of the period with its philosophy and expression, illustrated with artefacts in forms both visual and auditory, from architecture and clothing to music and poetry.

For the reader of a Russian novel, query options could give valuable character and family tree information as well as a plot summary if the story became too complex. Whodunits would show wonderfully detailed maps and models of arsenals. And certainly there should be opportunities for interaction from the reader as we described in Section 13.3. And perhaps showing re-takes of various scenes, i.e., showing rejected clips, might add humour as well as insight to the movie.

13.5 Movies Where the Reader Influences the Action

Movies in which the viewer can influence the plot, at least to a limited extent, have been around for many years. The Czechoslovakian pavilion at the Montreal Expo (1966) had a movie with ten decision points, i.e., theoretically 2^{10} different endings!

In practice, of course, most paths merge to common points: ——◇——, and the user is forced to view whole sections more than once as well as being presented with many duplicate endings – a frustrating activity. The user needs to know how to avoid paths that will lead to unacceptable overlap. Perhaps films could provide guided tours of, say, the six most important scenes. It would be an interesting problem to apply work done on graphs. For example, determining the shortest path covering all scenes is a minimal

routing problem: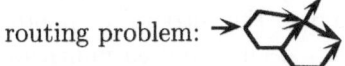

Of course we are aware that this may defeat the purpose of many movies. However in other cases it may well provide a very valuable tool – for example, when a lecturer wishes to preview material before giving it to students to explore.

Video games are often classified as interactive movies, but again the basic flow of action and scenes is predefined. The player has relatively little control over the basic contents of the game.

13.6 New Ways of Using Old Media

It could be said that until now the achievement of computerised multimedia has been essentially to make the use of existing multimedia material more flexible and convenient. But we contend that there are still many untapped ways of using old media in new ways, yielding entirely new techniques and communication facilities. One reason why such techniques have not been employed before is that they were impossible: only the advent of powerful multimedia computers has placed them at our disposal.

13.6.1 Invoking Our Natural Parallel Processing Ability

The human brain is amazingly good at parallel processing – making telephone calls while driving the car, reading a book while watching television, keeping an ear on several conversations at once, etc. This suggests that we may be able to do more simultaneous processing of computer information than we do at present. Before going further it must be made clear that we are not referring to super-humans. We do not expect to concentrate on parallel streams of information for prolonged periods – any more than we do in everyday life. We know from watching simultaneous translators that such work can be very exhausting, since we have seen them covered in sweat after just twenty minutes. But it may be that just as sometimes we choose to make a fast ascent of a mountain rather than maintain a customary plod, we can similarly pace ourselves while data processing. If we need to find some particular piece of information urgently, we may be prepared to expend additional mental energy on the problem even if we do emerge exhausted.

We are also aware of problems of overload. Next time you are waiting in line for the fifth time in a day at a place like Disney World, comfort yourself with the reflection that it has been "proved" by Professor Maurer [Maurer, 1994c] that if there were no such lines you would be a zombie well before the end of the day and need to sleep a full sixteen hours to make up for it!

13.6.2 Picture Galleries

Applications such as CDWriter are making extremely effective use of the idea of displaying sets of miniaturised pictures to aid in the retrieval of photos from a CD. We have seen anything from twenty to one hundred miniature photos on the screen at once and it is surprising how easily we can locate the ones we want, particularly when we are familiar with the originals. We can imagine a particularly useful real-estate system based on ideas such as this. Demonstration catalogues could be set up which include multiple shots of the same house. We would have a particularly attractive system if it were coupled with graphical query and visualisation programs such as one developed at the University of Maryland [Williamson and Shneiderman, 1993].

13.6.3 Simultaneous Movies

Suppose that for a biology course we have three movies each depicting a bird flying: for example, an albatross, a fantail, and a sparrow. Displaying the three movies simultaneously will make a very effective demonstration for comparing and contrasting different methods of flight. It will be still more effective if we can resize the windows, zooming into specific ones, and better still if we can replay all three clips simultaneously in slow motion. With the advent of Quicktime movies demonstrations such as this should become much easier to develop.

One well known package for simulating sorts is the Balsa program [Brown, 1988]. This application makes very good use of multiple windows for showing different views of each simulation run. Its use of sound is captivating and it is altogether a very good illustration of what can be done using parallel displays.

Since the preparation of demonstrations containing video clips is such a time-consuming task we should look at alternative ways of doing it more efficiently. Simply finding the sections we wish to use can be a major problem, while frequently we need to look at more than one video to find the best clip. This is one circumstance where we may choose to expend more mental energy than usual in order to get the job finished before the deadline. If we know what we are looking for we should be able to save precious minutes by scanning two (or maybe more) movies at the same time.

13.7 Total Immersion Learning Environments

Winn [Winn, 1994] makes the point that using virtual reality supports a "natural" style of learning. Students who interact directly with either the real world or a virtual one gain knowledge from their own perspective. Also, since worlds have "rules", discovery learning allows students to benefit by experience gained learning from their mistakes.

As mentioned in Chapter 5, several virtual learning environments already exist using video disks. One such project is the Athena project developed at Massachusetts Institute of Technology [Murray and Malone, 1992] that includes, for example, a total-immersion environment for learning French. However, excellent as some of these projects may be, the potential of interactive multimedia lies in digital, not analog, technology. One very good reason for this follows from a simple calculation on the minimum number of pictures that must be stored to provide users with panoramic views. A 360-degree two-dimensional panorama can be obtained, using overlapping techniques, from only six digital photos (one picture per 60 degrees) – as compared to 360 analog frames (one picture per degree). Then, to provide a reasonable amount of three-dimensional panning, with digital technology we need to multiply by only a factor of three, compared with more than 100 for video. All in all, a complete panorama using digital technology needs only 18 pictures, whereas the analog equivalent needs at least 36,000. Factors such as this, together with the low resolution of video, strongly suggest that high-quality virtual learning environments will rely on progressively more digital technology.

We believe that it is environments such as those described in Section 5.3.1, which simulate real world domains that cannot be explored visually in any other way, that will provide exciting prospects for lifelong learning.

13.8 Afterword

We have shown how the very definition of "multimedia" must be changed to include a wide range of new applications ranging from interactive and annotated movies to virtual realities.

There is no doubt that, all too often, leading-edge multimedia technology is driven by Hollywood dollars, and we cannot expect that interactive and annotated movies, regardless of the form they evolve into, will be blessed with natural immunity. However we believe they can provide important, and exciting, opportunities for education in universities, museums, and hospitals as well as for pure entertainment.

14. Hypermedia and the Notion of a Personal Assistant[1]

14.1 Introduction

Evolution in human-computer interface design has brought us a long way from the days when computers were all but dictators, when users obeyed enigmatic rules or risked ignominious crashes! Years of research and many trials involving users (willingly and unwillingly) have steadily improved computer interfaces to the point where today's operators are much more in control. However, we believe that the next few years will see another quiet revolution as the computer becomes more of a versatile supportive ally – a true Personal Assistant (PA for short).

The idea of an electronic assistant has already been promoted with much hype by major computer companies. The impression given is that computers may eventually dominate our lives, relaying frantic messages between offices and homes, frustrating even our rest and relaxation. This is certainly not our vision: we look to the computer to help us, not discombobulate us.

A PA, as we use the term in this book, is not to be confused with the devices that several companies are developing as PDAs (*Personal Digital Assistants*) or *message pads*. Those are still extremely limited in the applications they support. We believe that a PA system should – and can – do a great deal more.

We consider the assistance we might expect from a PA in a few workaday activities:

- Making literature searches (see Section 14.2.1)
- Improving spelling checkers and grammar checkers (see Section 14.2.2)
- Tasks using the computer's ears, eyes and voice (see Section 14.8)
- Helping with transaction processing (see Section 14.9)
- Being a secretary, tutor, or even a parent (see Section 14.11)

---

[1] A previous version of this chapter was published in J.UCS [Lennon and Vermeer, 1995].

14.2 Personal Assistance in Writing Documents

There are probably countless ways in which a PA can aid us in the exacting labour of writing documents. Certainly, as we shall see in Section 14.7, PAs will relieve us of a large amount of repetitive editing by making predictions based on our personal work patterns. As we shall see in this section, they can do a great deal more than this.

14.2.1 Making Literature Searches

Making a literature search is a frequent necessity, a time-consuming, exacting chore, yet vital whether our need is to find information or to check our work. In particular, a PA should help us set up and manage a filter system so that our searches are as effective as possible. This is particularly important when searching in large hypermedia systems. The PA will learn what filters we prefer to have set under various conditions and apply them. It will provide intelligent cross-links so that better use can be made of databases. Obviously everything we write should be open to verification. One such system, Ways 2, produced by the Swiss researcher Keller, has been marketed by Vobis in Germany with considerable success. In a PA system, data in wordprocessing text will be checked against data in our spreadsheets and databases. Running as a background processor, it can make continuous searches for relevant references, aiding us in the verification of both our own work and the reference material we are reading. Having such checking done automatically, or semi-automatically, is possibly the only way of ensuring that the increasing amount of archived work taken to be authoritative is at least relatively free of errors.

14.2.2 Improving Spelling and Grammar Checkers

Spelling and grammar checkers are often inefficient and cumbrous. Most spelling checkers are not even context driven; grammar checkers are clumsy, throwing up too many red herrings. Users should be able to tailor grammar checkers to their personal requirements. An intelligent editor should also be able to learn rules of style appropriate to the particular type of document being edited – such as appropriate levels of word difficulty, or suitable sentence length. The system should be flexible enough to allow the user a choice between flash mode checking, and checking only on a File Save or Quit command.

Programs such as these need to be able to learn from their mistakes. For example, in a mathematics paper the second occurrence of the word "group" probably should not be replaced by "collection"! If a user has to override the second occurrence, an intelligent editor will query whether it is a technical term and act accordingly.

We need to refer to a whole range of dictionaries – maybe at just the click of a button. And using techniques such as those described in Section 4.4.1, we look forward to much better success rates in our searches.

An interesting application applies to natural language translation. Obviously we are not referring to full natural language translation – a complex and subtle specialty still struggling for success. But word-for-word translations are practical and this opens up several rather thought-provoking possibilities. For example, a researcher trying to read foreign journal articles with only a smattering of the language would be greatly helped by a handy translation option. Similarly, if correspondents restrict their sentences to grammatically simple ones, translation programs will have a better success rate. The qualified success of existing style-checking programs suggests that certain types of document may be amenable to automatic rewriting in simplified words and phrases – a facility of great use to new immigrants, for example.

14.3 Personal Assistance While Reading Documents

Browsing electronic text consumes so much of our time that all personalised assistance with it will be welcome. For example, since most of us have neither time nor motivation to wade through the extensive manuals that come with every new software package, the principle of Just-in-Time Learning has become essential to our work and sanity. We would value a PA that could control the electronic Help tools, a PA which could take into account our previous experience – or lack of it!

Many people find reading from the screen more tiring than reading print, particularly when windows are densely packed with text. The displayed text is either too small for comfort or too clumsily large. One solution may be to indicate the particular line we are reading by moving the cursor up and down manually (or by methods mentioned in Section 14.8) so that the editor can enlarge it. It may also be desirable that a line or two above or below the current line be enlarged to some degree as well. This will obviously be dependent on personal preferences, but each user should be able to individually "train" their text windows.

Since reading is so much faster than writing, any referencing facility that is provided needs to be very efficient for us not to feel unnecessarily held up by it. Hence, though aids for referencing and checking are just as vital for reading as for writing, they will have to be uninhibiting to be really useful. Perhaps in Browse mode a single click on a word could initiate a dictionary look-up or a reference check. Each person will decide which dictionaries or databases are to be filtered and used.

Yet another desirable feature is a date computation routine. For example, if I read that a colleague is arriving on 18th May my immediate question will probably be "What day of the week is that?" I should be able to click on the "18" and "May" and have a formula (such as Snell's) calculate the day

– given any particular year. Or maybe I need to know what date Easter falls on. Even more important, when making travel arrangements I must know which days are public holidays in the countries I am visiting, so that I can either avoid them or make sure I see any special festivities.

14.4 Managing Email

We all agree that there must be better ways of managing email than keeping our names off mailing lists [Denning, 1982]. MIT has made considerable progress with its Information Lens and Object Lens projects [Malone et al., 1987, Robinson, 1991]. Ideally, we should be able to set up our own preferential filtering systems so that a PA, perhaps working as a background processor, can search all incoming mail for names and keywords. It will search the body of each item, as well as the subject line, and classify the mail according to our own prescriptions. Furthermore, we need additional options such as ranking and grouping by author. Answering mail from your boss may be more urgent than attending to personal matters; and if he has mailed more than one item it is important that they appear together so that we do not waste time answering the first item only to find that it was superseded by a later item!

As more and more correspondence is sent by email, we are looking forward to additional electronic assistance with all the chores associated with daily avalanches of mail. A personal assistant will serve us by keeping address lists up to date. It will assist us in writing form-letters (see Section 14.8) and help with addresses. It can manage certain housekeeping tasks such as archiving necessary information before deleting messages. Notices in template format can enable the system to use the advertised dates to generate expiry dates – these may, of course, be overridden by the user. Ideally the user should also be able to define what is to be done with the notice once the expiry date has passed: delete it, or place it in a Past Events list to be maintained by the system. This list will be invaluable for compiling such things as end-of-year reports, although decisions will have to be made on how to maintain it. Email must also support structured discussions and systematic collaboration between two or more participants, i.e., conferencing. Furthermore, we should have the option of attaching notes to individual letters in group dispatches. In fact, as information proliferates in all systems, the ability to annotate at all levels of the system becomes increasingly important.

It is intriguing to ponder the consequences of having email answered automatically. For example, we may wish to generate replies that indicate we are unavailable. Of course we would avoid being naive and publicising to all and sundry that a house or office is unattended and hence is a good burglary risk! We could, however, have different responses to different people.

14.5 Intelligent Calendars

Electronic diaries will become much more useful when they are more widely linked into electronic mail systems. Calendars should also be capable of generating mail for us – either mail to ourselves or mail to others. On a personal level, they should be able to send us reminder notices that contain much more than just bald statements of events and dates. Perhaps, when we are prompted that next week is an important anniversary, we also need to be reminded that last year's bright idea for a gift wasn't a success!

On a more workaday note, an intelligent PA could set up some of our appointments for us. Incoming email about meetings will be searched, our calendar checked and updated, and outgoing email messages generated. The PA system should be intelligent enough to be capable of adaptive behaviour. Conceivably, it could even learn when one person in a group is being unreasonably difficult about the times they are available and it could take a tough negotiating line! On the other hand, although I may wish my system to negotiate for me I may also not want all my timetable to be known!

The logical extension of this is, of course, that we shall eventually have networks of PAs communicating with each other and the user will, at best, only be required to approve the final result.

14.6 Information Retrieval

As elaborated in Section 9.10, journals such as the Journal of Universal Computer Science (J.UCS) [Calude et al., 1994, URLz1] have many significant advantages over traditional and existing electronic journals. Furthermore since it is based on Hyperwave [Kappe et al., 1994] the structure of J.UCS lends itself to user-controlled filtering and automatic notification of new material and updates, necessary components of any PA.

14.6.1 Retrieving Information from Libraries

A big step forward for all researchers will be a PA giving us easier access to library information. As described in Section 9.9 we believe that in the foreseeable future it will become standard practice for librarians to insert the table of contents and/or a brief summary into the hypermedia database so that researchers can rapidly access the new information. This much at least can be done without infringing copyright laws. With a system such as this, a PA can constantly check all new books and journals and, using our own categorisation system, notify us of those that are relevant.

14.6.2 Hypermedia Document Searches

When hypermedia systems were just growing like Topsy it was not surprising there were problems. In large hypermedia systems users still lose their sense of orientation within the environment. Recent research has seen interesting developments, particularly in the design of hypermedia structures [Maurer et al., 1993a, Maurer et al., 1993b] with links, and even without links [Maurer et al., 1994c]. At the very least we should be to be able to signal "Help!" and have the system help us backtrack. However a good PA system will help us avoid disorientation in the first place by indicating our current position on a graphical map of our environment. Furthermore the system will remember from day to day, and week to week, which paths we have used, and how often, so that by making predictions it can help us navigate much more efficiently than we can now.

14.6.3 Webs and Guided Tours

A large amount of work has been done on webs, paths, and electronic guided tours, helping users navigate complex hypermedia structures [Yankelovich et al., 1988, Haan et al., 1992, Kappe et al., 1993]. Features such as these will be utilised by an all-embracing electronic assistant.

Another move in the right direction is the increasing use of the guided task paradigm [Tuck and Olsen, 1990], where users are introduced to new applications by interactively participating in guided demonstrations.

14.6.4 Sending Electronic Agents Through the Networks

As we have elaborated in Section 6.9, programs that search for information in wide-area networks are proliferating [Communications, 1994b]. Under the best of circumstances, a PA could be trained to control the electronic *agents* that are sent through the Web, so that information relevant to our current needs is gathered – and summarised into their own personal newsletter.

A detailed description of collaborative agents in computer conferencing environments is given in "A framework for controlling cooperative agents" [Lee et al., 1993].

14.7 Observing and Predicting: Electronic Assistance

During the past twenty years many papers have been written describing specific applications that incorporate forms of intelligent electronic assistance under various titles: intelligent editors, cooperative agents, programming by example, programming by rehearsal, to list just a few. An exceptionally well presented overview is given in the book *Watch What I Do: Programming by*

Demonstration [Cypher, 1993]. In 1985 Zissos and Witten described a "computer coach" that helps users avoid repetitive formatting tasks in a wordprocessing environment [Zissos and Witten, 1985]. It "unobtrusively monitors interaction with a system and offers individualised advice." The work has been greatly extended and several such systems have now been developed [Mo and Witten, 1992, Witten and Mo, 1993]. A more generalised personal assistant has been proposed by Maurer [Maurer, 1993b].

Several major computer companies are committed to developing what they are terming *electronic agents.* As mentioned in Section 1.5, Apple Macintosh has demonstrated the prototype version of an electronic agent that can learn from simple, mouse-controlled, repetitive actions. For example, as the user steps through each stage of a process, each selection and menu choice may be highlighted with a colour. This indicates to the user that his actions are being shadowed by the agent. If all actions are shadowed correctly the user has the option of letting the electronic agent help from then on: for example, selected pieces of text may be copied from one document and tabulated into another automatically.

Producing animated graphical sequences is a very repetitive task and this must surely be one area that will greatly benefit from having an electronic personal assistant or agent to help. In fact some of the earliest work done in the field of programming by example was done using graphics programs. In the paper "Metamouse: specifying graphical procedures by example" [Maulsby et al., 1989] the authors describe a system that "induces picture-editing procedures from execution traces". It incorporates a very likeable icon called Basil – a turtle in the best LOGO tradition [Papert, 1980]. The work has been significantly extended [Maulsby and Witten, 1993, Maulsby et al., 1992]. Recently, Apple Macintosh have released a program designed for use by children, that lets them create animations by demonstration [URLp3].

A unique visual programming environment is described in the paper "Programming by rehearsal" [Finzer and Gould, 1984], where a "stage" is set and peopled with "performers". In the book *Creating User Interfaces by Demonstration* [Myers, 1988] the author describes PERIOT (Programming by Example for Real-time Interface design Obviating Typing). Graphical menus and windows are created by example. MARQUISE is another interesting example of an interactive tool that creates graphical user interfaces by demonstration [Myers et al., 1993].

Considered all together, applications such as these suggest that there is a wealth of experience waiting to be pooled into an all-embracing and indispensable interface [Piernot and Yvon, 1993].

14.8 Making Use of the Computer's Ears, Eyes, and Voice

Now that microphones and video cameras are almost standard computer attachments, dramatic innovations may stem from their use. For example, when a significant number of PCs are connected to law enforcement networks then automatic reporting of break-ins will surely result in a proportional reduction in the number of unsolved burglaries!

With the addition of "eyes" and "ears", our PC will be capable of a wide variety of new functions. It will be able to inform us if someone is at the door when our back is turned. As we work it will adjust the screen brightness when the room brightness changes, or boost the volume of our headsets when background noises increase. We shall be able to dictate our email, and have voice prompt and help systems. It is no longer inconceivable that an intelligent PA could even note our mood when we first enter the office in the morning and give appropriate responses – perhaps we might appreciate an occasional joke or even some artificial intelligence doctoring in the style of the Eliza program [Weizenbaum, 1966]. Certainly a very practical welcome would be for the machine to open the document we last worked on and have the cursor sitting ready where we left off – surely not too much to ask, considering that there is at least one lap-top already on the market that leaves files open when re-booted.

The ability of the machine to recognise simple gestures such as a nod or shake of the head opens up many possibilities. Work on eye tracking, such as that done by MIT's Media Lab [Starker and Bolt, 1990] and the Washington Naval Research Laboratory [Jacob, 1990], suggests that in the future we shall be able to look at a section of the screen, and, perhaps with only a simple nod, have that particular section enlarge automatically. These techniques may also help us in many types of searching tasks. Imagine, for example, scanning miniaturised photos from CDs, or thumbnail pictures, and having an object of interest automatically expand as we pause and look at it.

If we would like to have lines of text enlarged for working on in a word-processing task, eye movements may prove to give us better control than the cursor method explained in Section 14.3. Even if eye tracking proves to be too imprecise, then perhaps finger tracking may still be a better alternative. Text scroll bars as well as computer movie options could also be controlled by eye movements. And when presented with choices in a dialogue box we may prefer to focus on an option and then simply nod.

Computers that can carry out a whole range of voice commands are no longer fiction – a fact that has been widely demonstrated recently:

- "Computer open Word file" – the word processing package is opened.
- "Computer write letter to John Jones" – the letter is headed with the sender's and receiver's addresses, plus opening and closing sentences.

– "Computer include thankyou message" – a whole paragraph is generated
....

And, of course, this leads us to speculate how widespread computer-generated speech will become and how long it will be before we can actually converse with our personal assistant.

14.9 Help with Transaction Processing

Electronic shopping is here to stay, and the next question we must address is how we are going to make the best use of yet another barrage of information. Newsgroups have already advertised software that can send electronic agents through the networks to find best buys. as well as making and changing hotel, restaurant or airline reservations for us. Of course, as with any new technology, we can expect problems both small and large – cases of electronic agents running amok in the networks have already been reported.

In many European countries *telebanking* has become a routine aspect of life due to the continuing spread of VideoTex [Maurer and Sebestyen, 1982]. In a perfect world, our PA could help us with our banking and paying of bills via our computer. Gone would be paper invoices, checks and forms. The conversation with my computer might go something like this:

"Computer please pay 400 dollars to Mike".
"Mike who?"
"Computer, to Mike Melon of course."
"PIN no?" (I type in my PIN number.)
"Transaction number?" (I type in the correct transaction number
    from the current block.)

Of course, some security mechanism will be necessary to guard against impersonators (see Section 4.6). The computer will encrypt messages for security, and use a different transaction number with each message to ensure that any electronic eavesdropper cannot simply copy previous messages to repeat transactions.

Although jokes are still made about the "paperless office", with the advent of electronic funds transferral we have made significant steps in that direction, and indications are that the current expansion of the home computing market will lead to further advances.

14.10 The Individualisation Process

There is a rather interesting inference to be made from the current vogue of having personalised emblems put on everything from coffee mugs to designer jeans. With PA assistance in mastering intricacies of design, we shall be design our own emblems, embellishments, and even, if we are so inspired, our own works of art. We can then let our PA scan the networks to find the "best" supplier and have our specifications emailed directly to them!

14.11 Secretary? Tutor? Or even Parent??

From all that we have discussed, it is obvious that when we use the term Personal Assistant the emphasis remains on the word "Personal". A good PA system will be trainable so that after a few weeks my PA will act in a very different way from yours – even if we purchased identical software to begin with.

Ideally, it will also be desirable to have alternative sets of characteristics built into a PA that modify it for specific tasks. At the office I shall expect my PA to act as my own personal secretary – it will help me with all my correspondence, arrange meetings (see Section 14.5), help with time management, and so on. Of significant assistance will be a My Archive program that helps classify and archive all types of information: text, graphics, video and audio clips, important documents and interesting little snippets. All archived material will be amenable to retrieval by powerful search techniques such as those described in Section 4.4.1.

At university or school, the PA will become my personal tutor, helping me organise work and make the most of opportunities that are offered. However, when I lend my PC to my six-year-old child I hope my PA will not only protect all my work from sabotage but will transact on quite a different level. It could act as a "parent" – even to pulling the plug on games and bringing up some homework!

Thus when designing a PA we shall need to ask ourselves what the characteristics are of a manager's best secretary, a student's favourite lecturer, and even more elusively a "good" parent, to see if we can simulate at least some of their attributes. A challenge indeed!

14.12 Looking to the Future

As small gets smaller, and more powerful still, we can expect that computers the size of notebooks will support more PA functions than we have described. The initial interest created by pen-based electronic notebooks such as Apple Macintosh's Newton or Casio's Zoomer suggests that users enjoy that environment, limited as it still is. Users particularly enjoy sketching in environments that help them work more efficiently by neatening up their work, letting them work with constraints, and supporting incompleteness [Kimura, 1989] [Zhao, 1993]. There is even a certain perverse satisfaction in erasing errors by scribbling over them! All this is certainly an indication of things to come.

In the article "To forecast information technology is impossible yet necessary" [Maurer and Lennon, 1994], we argue that future advances in information technology are quite unpredictable. However we go on to surmise: "In ten or fifteen years from now everyone will carry small but powerful Notebook computers around with them. PDAs, such as the much heralded Newton, are certainly first steps in this direction. You will be able to talk into your notebook and have more commands, programs, and facilities available than we can imagine. For example, if you go to a foreign country and talk into your notebook in English out will come Greek or French. A global positioning system will display maps for you and show you at any time exactly where you are located on the surface of the earth. And of course a mobile telephone will be integrated into your notebook, giving access to all the databases of the world – so you can look up theatre programmes and bus and train connections. It will be your digital photo camera, and it will replace your wallet and credit cards. It will be indispensable."

14.13 Summary

Our definition of a true personal assistant obviously bears little relation to any currently available commercial product. It is not just a glorified Newton. It is part background processor (continuously scanning the networks), part consistent graphical interface (across all applications), and part special routines integrated into application programs. It thus supports the user at all levels of activity. By making predictions from repetitive tasks it saves us both time and frustration. It manages our email, classifies and archives our work, and employs powerful fuzzy search algorithms to retrieve documents from complex hypermedia systems. It is much more than a generalised help system. It can be a model secretary, tutor and baby-sitter, a police officer who patrols our surroundings while simultaneously ensuring that we do not inadvertently break copyright laws or lose ourselves in hyperspace. It will be our augmented eyes and ears, an alter ego we create for ourselves.

15. Hypermedia and a New Symbolism for Improved Communication[1]

15.1 Introduction

This chapter introduces MUSLI[2] – a MUlti Sensory Language Interface.

Our current MUSLI work has two main thrusts: facilitating the use of abstract moving symbols (abstract movies), and exploring new ways of using old media to create a true multi-sensory environment. New ways of incorporating old media into a MUSLI environment is the subject of the next chapter.

This chapter introduces the idea of dynamic abstract symbols which have associated attributes and states (see Section 15.6.3). We make a first attempt at describing a dynamic abstract visual language. Of course we realise that an artificial language, consisting of abstract symbols with attributes, is certainly not a new idea [Lodowyck, 1652]; but what is new is our ability to modify and animate the symbols – and animate them with comparative ease.

In Section 15.8 we describe how a MUSLI editor/player will provide such a highly simplified graphical editing environment, that we may at last look forward to spontaneous graphical communication.

In Section 15.6.5 we describe one of the most important features of the MUSLI editor, the ability to condense (and expand) abstract symbols. We believe that this feature alone could enhance traditional help and browsing facilities, letting the user determine the level of abstraction and the amount of detail showing on the screen.

We know that hypertext systems are available which offer certain solutions to the problem of efficient information processing [Maurer et al., 1993a, Nielsen, 1990]. Unfortunately we are still severely limited by the lack of tools

---

[1] A previous version of this chapter was published in Proceedings Ed-Media'94 [Lennon and Maurer, 1994c].

[2] The name MUSLI evolved from MUSIL – MUlti Sensory Information Language. The original choice was apt since it is also the name of the famous Austrian poet and novelist Robert Musil (1880–1942), who was not only a master of that abstract communication device, language, but employed language on a notably abstract level in inner monologues or streams of consciousness – the technique familiar to readers of James Joyce's novels. The new name, MUSLI: A MUlti-Sensory Language Interface, is equally appropriate in another sense – it is food for thought consisting of good ingredients which when mixed properly give something still better.

for efficiently producing documents that involve all the senses. Thus the aim of our MUSLI research is to investigate new ways of using multimedia, including dynamic abstract symbols (*abstract movies*), to allow the efficient expression of ideas difficult to communicate otherwise. We shall introduce new ways of "writing" multimedia material in forms that will aid "reading". We shall expand the idea of browsing and take the first steps toward introducing a more flexible system for conveying information.

15.2 The Environment

MUSLI is an abstract visual language which uses dynamic abstract symbols with associated attributes and states to represent and animate computer-displayed productions. Instead of animating concrete objects, MUSLI authors deal with abstract symbolic representations. Thus a MUSLI movie may abstractly represent a sociological situation without requiring concrete interpretations to be made of the "players" involved. Thus MUSLI does not aim at "programming as a vehicle to reach mathland", but rather aims to provide a new medium of expression.

As will be elaborated further in the next chapter, MUSLI assumes a rich multimedia environment with the full range of video, graphics, sound, signs, and symbols. The distinction between signs, symbols, ideograms, and icons can become very blurred, but all have a place in MUSLI movies. A telling treatise in favour of ideograms can be found in *Tao: The Watercourse Way* [Watts and Huang, 1976].

The design of iconic systems, particularly of iconic systems intended specifically for computer interfaces, has received attention in many books and papers. We have selected just a token few of these [Fujii and Korfhage, 1989, Kaneko et al., 1989, Shu, 1988, Wood and Wood, 1990]. In most contexts ambiguity is regarded as an undesirable feature. In the paper "Iconic Interfacing" [Lodding, 1983] there is a photo of an icon which supposedly represents airport arrivals but could also be read as graphically depicting a plane crashing! It is interesting to note however that in MUSLI movies we may well wish to introduce ambiguity – consider the power of poetry and puns. Unlike graphical parsing languages [Lakin, 1987], MUSLI movies are not tied down to any formal grammar. We can be as creatively abstract as we like!

15.3 Alternative Forms of Communication

Computers are giving us yet another method of communication. Humanity has evolved so many ingenious systems of communication since civilisation first dawned that it makes sense to look briefly at a few of these before we propose a new one.

One of the most striking features about communication using signs and symbols is the tremendous variety in medium and form – from the simplest runes on clay or parchment to the most intricate designs on human flesh. Prehistorians believe that many of the ancient cave drawings found in France can be considered as forms of writing: they have discovered groups of drawings which taken together form codes [Jean, 1989]. Paintings in the Renaissance were richly redolent with emotionally charged symbolism. Carvings on wood, stone and metal range from concrete signs to abstract symbolism. Signalling devices range from smoke signals to systems of bells, mirrors and musical instruments, to semaphore and electric morse-code – and in the future we are bound to discover new options using digitised sound. Cistercian monks who practise vows of silence have developed highly refined systems of gestures [Umiker-Sebeok and Sebeok, 1987]. Many signs used by deaf people today [Jeanes, 1982] are based on these and it is significant that in many respects signing can convey meaning more quickly than spoken language. Dramatic gestures are to be found in theatre all over the world: western mime and dance, Japanese Kabuki theatre, Chinese processions, Tibetan dance, etc. With the advent of tools like Geographic Information Systems (GIS), the field of cartography is evolving its use of signs rapidly – we find military operations planning, in conjunction with GIS [Zaidah et al., 1993], giving a new dimension to semiotics.

15.4 The Basic Idea

Any new language demands dedication to learn, and since the system we propose includes abstract symbols it is certain to be no exception.

In the article "Why Hypermedia Systems are Important" [Maurer, 1992b] the author states, "Much research and experimentation will be necessary before we are able to exploit the potential of abstract movies beyond the trivial level of diagrams and slightly stylised (cartoon-like) movies. However, there is also much promise.... a scene of a flower gingerly embracing the sun, but cordially embracing shadow and water may be a much better way of showing the preferred habitat of that flower than a verbal description".

Good readers are often disappointed when they see the film version of a book they have read. The problem is often that while books leave room for personal interpretation and imagination, movies do not. The "beautiful mountain" of the book will look different in the minds of different readers, but all viewers of a movie see, inevitably, the same beautiful mountain. What has happened is that there has been a shift in the level of abstraction – the abstract notion "beautiful mountain" has been replaced by a concrete version of a mountain. In MUSLI the proportion and level of abstraction can be chosen to fit the situation, varying from abstract to very concrete as the movie producer feels is appropriate to communicate exactly what is desired.

It is an interesting observation that a mountain can be an analogy for an idea [Maurer, 1992a] and it is significant that we talk about having a "point of view" on a topic. As an example of looking at something in more than one way consider the well-known problem in first-year computer science courses of calculating the Fibonacci series. Many books use this example to teach recursion and then almost apologise for mentioning that it can be solved better using iteration. Very few lecturers indeed show a third way of looking at the problem using dynamic programming. Yet each of the three methods provides insights that are valid and complementary views of the problem. In an interactive multimedia system students can compare ideas to an even greater extent than ever before.

In any multimedia presentation readers should certainly be able to stop and start at will, rewind, review, and then resume. The system should also enable readers to master new material by building up additional skills as they go. In a MUSLI movie (i.e., a hypermedia document that includes special moving abstract symbols) users can stop and display additional information – at any time they feel ready for it.

As explained in Sections 15.6.5 and 15.6.6, any group of symbols can be condensed to a single *short-form*, and double-clicking on the composite symbol will decompose it again. This gives the user significant control over the amount of data on the screen at any particular time. The user will be able to obtain additional detailed information about scenes, characters, ideas, etc., when it is relevant to them, as well as readily refreshing their memory if they have forgotten the meaning of a symbol. This reference facility in itself will give MUSLI documents significant advantages over traditional books.

More significantly, users will be able to skim condensed versions of a document, searching for relevant sections, before decomposing the symbols to display pertinent information. With facilities such as these, it will be possible to speed-read MUSLI documents faster than printed text.

15.5 What MUSLI is Not

MUSLI is not simply a system of cartoons – cartoons are designed to be understood without any investment in learning and are quite close to a simplified reality. MUSLI is not a silent movie or some system of signs. It will make appropriate use of computer graphics (2D and 3D), cartoons, audio clips (music and speech both analogue and digital), video clips (analogue and digital), photographs (digitised), animation including 3D modelling; and of course text. Naturally there will still be movies – we delight in the work on human animation being done by scientists and artists such as those at the MIRALab at the University of Geneva [Magnenat-Thalmann and Thalmann, 1991b]. Visualisation will continue to be an important means of communication [IEEE, 1993] and we watch with interest the work being done in the field of virtual reality.

It is our hope that all of these achievements will be eventually integrated into a single grand design: MUSLI.

15.6 A First Tentative Proposal

In our move towards a theory of dynamic abstract symbolism, we explored research in semiotics in an attempt to choose a grammar. Several alternatives such as the grammar of Conceptual Dependency Theory [Schank, 1975, Schank and Abelson, 1977] remain to be explored. However as an anchor point for our first proposal we quote from An Introduction to Functional Grammar [Halliday, 1985]: "Our most powerful conception of reality is that it consists of 'goings-on': of doing, happening, feeling, being". Halliday identifies the three most common types of processes: material processes, mental processes and relational processes. These categories seem amenable to representation. We shall begin by symbolising examples of the three processes, considering each process in turn.

1. Material processes: processes of doing. Here we have the common "Actor, Process and Goal" construct that suggests animation. We can animate actions for walk, run, jump, dance, break, make, give, take, etc.

2. Mental processes: processes of sensing. Since these can be regarded as directed actions we shall indicate them by dynamic lines or arrows. For example, love can be a golden shaft directed towards the object. Liking will be represented by a less intense yellow while hate will be brown or black. Directed fear and worry will be jagged shafts.

3. Relational processes: processes of being. Here we shall consider two classes: those that are attributes of the object, and those which can be considered as states of the object. Attributes we shall assign as associated symbols (see Section 15.6.2). States we can indicate by colouring objects, for example, pink for happy and blue for sad.

15.6.1 Using Abstract Symbols

The basic symbols we introduce will need to be simple – yet be beautiful in their own right. The more frequently a symbol is used the simpler it should be. Additional characteristics will be added by association and only when needed. Obviously we shall not have to introduce new symbols for all words: we shall include accepted signs [Liungman, 1991], such as an X for "forbidden", and we can have dictionaries of known shapes and symbols to call on. We shall try to avoid using shapes that are too lifelike, partly because this limits the reader's imagination and partly because using abstract symbols gives us more freedom to add attributes without contravening our built-in sense of appropriateness. For example, while it may be quite inappropriate to paint a lifelike symbol of a beautiful woman a golden yellow colour, a golden circle definitely transmits the idea of beauty.

There are two distinct facets to abstraction: abstraction of appearance and abstraction of senses (feeling, thinking and emotion). As described above, a golden circle may represent beauty of appearance. But beauty applies just as significantly to the abstract, and it is qualities such as feelings, thoughts and emotions that have proved difficult for existing visual forms of communication. Abstract symbols can take on additional attributes with no conflict. Beautiful feelings, beautiful thoughts, beautiful emotions: all can be abstractly displayed as golden states. Even speech (or thought) balloons which look clumsy on lifelike characters may be attached to symbols artistically.

We shall begin by introducing basic symbols using the classification system shown in Figure 15.1.

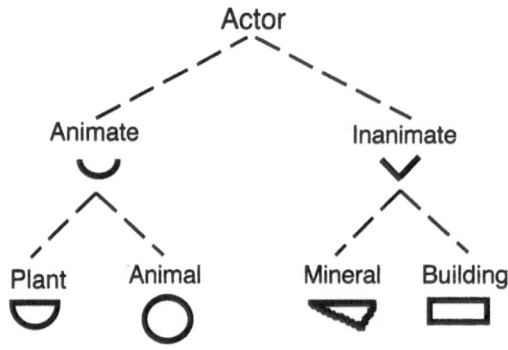

Fig. 15.1. Basic Symbols

15.6.2 The Addition of Attributes

We shall be able to modify basic symbols by associating attributes. These modifiers may be either one or more associated symbols, or an integral part of the basic symbol, such as colour. Let us for example, introduce the following common biological symbols:

Then we have symbolic representations for:

Female animal   Male animal

Using the symbol ˜ to represent "intelligent" (for "brain waves") these can be further modified to represent:

Woman   Man

15.6.3 Extending the Language by the Addition of States

Since so much work has been done in natural language parsing by people working in artificial intelligence and/or system design, it does make sense to keep an eye on that for anything which could be incorporated into MUSLI. For example, it could in theory help us develop natural language control of our movies. The work on Conceptual Dependency Theory done at Stanford University [Schank, 1975, Schank and Abelson, 1977] suggests a logical extension to our work.

We have already suggested that states such as fear, anger, hunger, disgust and surprise may be represented by colour or pattern. In Conceptual Dependency Theory [Schank, 1975] the authors suggest scales for each state. Scales such as these lend themselves particularly easily to visualisation techniques: we can allocate intensity values to the colours of auras surrounding actors.

If, as in Schank's examples, shocked = surprise(6) AND disgust(-5), then a shocked man might be represented:

With a system such as this we can create dynamically varying states.

15.6.4 Applying the Principle of Orthogonality

The term "orthogonality" was introduced by Aad van Wijngaarden in the design of programming languages, to mean features that carry across from one context to another [Wijngaarden, 1965]. To ease learning we shall build into MUSLI as much orthogonality as possible.

For example, we can define:

Female plant   Male plant   Bisexual plant

If we now introduce the additional attributes:

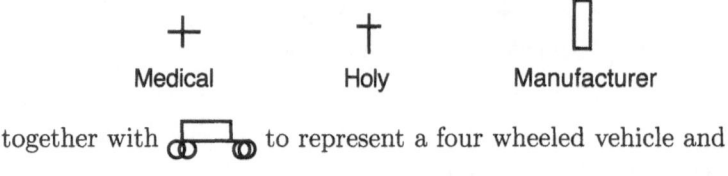

together with 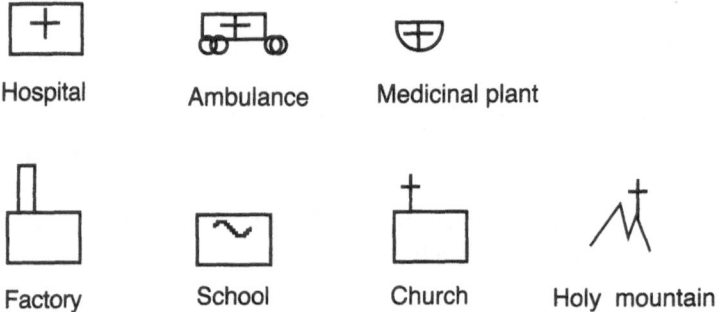 to represent a four wheeled vehicle and

to represent a mountain,

we can now form the following definitions:

(Note the high level of abstraction by leaving the gender open).

Doctor

Hospital   Ambulance   Medicinal plant

Factory   School   Church   Holy mountain

We can introduce additional conventions which will communicate variations in such attributes as:

1. Age. Old, older ...

2. Height. Tall, taller ...

3. Health. We can represent a sick person or animal or plant by showing
   symbols with jagged outlines. A small amount of jaggedness could imply
   only slightly sick, a large amount very sick; and of course as the movie
   progresses the state will change. We can introduce additional conventions
   that will communicate variations in such attributes as age (an increasingly thick outline) or dying (a cracking or breaking symbol).

15.6.5 Condensing a Group of Symbols

If the attributes in a group are relatively constant then the original symbol plus attributes can be replaced by a condensed short-form. We shall use a frame to group primitives and $>$ to represent condensation.

A wise old solitary man (i.e., a hermit) condenses to

A working (manufacturing) intelligent woman:

Compound symbols can be condensed at any stage either by the reader pausing and clicking on them or by the system converting them. Usually the reader will need warning before a symbol condenses and this can be achieved in a variety of ways. Perhaps the compound symbol will have its border change colour before the change or both symbols may be displayed at once with the compound one gradually decreasing in size while the condensed symbol increases. Interesting possibilities of letting an electronic personal assistant control the degree and timing of the condensations remain to be explored.

The condensed symbols will be animated just as groups of primitives can be. For example, a working (manufacturing) woman carrying water may be

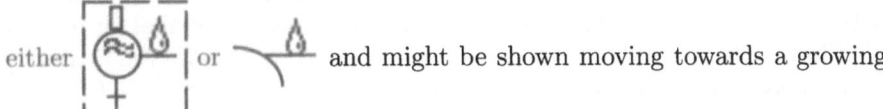 and might be shown moving towards a growing

(manufacturing) plant . We would then, of course, see the attribute for growing increase in size!

Again we emphasise that we are not producing cartoons: the symbols, like those shown above, will have to be learnt. They are not intended to be immediately obvious, but to carry meanings that will not be forgotten once learnt.

15.6.6 Expanding Condensed Symbols

Expanding symbols is the reverse process to condensing symbols. Readers will be able to freeze the display at any point in time and then, for example, by double-clicking on a compound symbol display the original primitives. Thus double-clicking on the symbol for a vehicle , may expand it back to: where >> is the symbol for motion (since a vehicle is an inanimate object moving people).

15.7 Bringing It All Alive with Dynamic Symbols

At this point the reader may be forgiven for wondering whether we are not simply reinventing a system of hieroglyphics. The difference is that people such as the Egyptians did not have ways to animate their written symbols! People who have played Pictionary[3] will appreciate how even a small amount of dynamic action added to static drawings can aid understanding immensely.

In a MUSLI document objects can move and change with time, and hence we frequently refer to it as a movie. Describing dynamic processes is not easy, and of course we look forward to the day when we shall be writing a MUSLI movie instead of static text!

We shall begin by very briefly indicating how we might dynamically represent each of the processes introduced in Section 15.6. First of all it is easy to see how we can animate the material processes of doing. Symbols can be made to move on the screen in ways that suggest walking, running, jumping, dancing, breaking, and making – for "making" we can show the parts coming together to form a whole. For the cases of giving and taking we suggest introducing a dynamic shaft with an arc at the end of it. On object is "given" by letting the shaft extend and push the object away. An object is "taken" when it is drawn in closer to the subject as the shaft shortens.

Secondly, mental processes of sensing, which we represent by dynamic lines, will continuously change in position, length, width, colour and intensity. The golden shaft of love, reaching out towards its object, may become more or less intense in colour as the movie continues. A child's initial fear of a doctor will be palpably obvious when shown by a pulsating black jagged arrow and with time the fear may fade (literally) and morph into the symbol for respect.

Thirdly there are the relational processes of being. Besides the attributes that are assigned as associated symbols, as described in Section 15.6.2, there are the emotions, which we can indicate by shading the object different colours. Here again the dynamic nature of our medium allows emotions to change in a continuous spectrum – as of course they do in real life. Conflicting emotions can be beautifully depicted by showing an animated interplay between the colours representing the rival emotions – both colours and intensities can interact.

Attributes can also be dynamic. A symbol that depicts an animal slowly ascending a mountain can certainly suggest a very high mountain.

Going one step further, symbols themselves may be formed from animated sequences. A simple circle representing an animal "flying" off a base line can represent a bird flying,

---

[3] Pictionary is a game, published by Parker Bros, in which one member of a team must use drawings to convey a randomly chosen word or phrase to the rest of the team.

Of course this can be condensed:

And again, the condensed symbol can be animated – in this case by letting the wings move. And so on.

Certain abstract classes, difficult to represent statically, can be represented dynamically. For example, consider the following frequently quoted abstraction:

```
[red car] ---> [cars]  ---> [vehicles]
```

One way of representing the class [vehicles] is to show a little "thumbnail movie" of a succession of vehicles.

The modifiers may also change with time. The symbol representing "immature" may morph into the symbol for "sophisticated" as the character in a story gains experience.

At this point we would like to change our point of view to the "other side of the mountain" and make a brief reference to the language for cosmic intercommunication: LINCOS [Freudenthal, 1960]. The author hypothesises that the "reader" can deduce meaning from the given graded series of examples. New words are introduced one at a time and the hypothesis is that if the number of examples read is large enough then the reader will deduce from its context the intended meaning for each newly introduced "word" (in this case a word is a pattern of radio pulses). This principle can obviously be applied to MUSLI movies, particularly those that contain symbols for abstract ideas. Although LINCOS deliberately avoids "showing" as a means for illustrating meaning, MUSLI can use dynamic symbols to represent abstract concepts such as number. We can successively display two plants, two animals, two vehicles, and so on, before condensing the dynamic symbol down to a static one. Once the numeric symbols have been introduced we can then dynamically introduce the symbol for the set of natural numbers, etc. The LINCOS exercises introducing the rules of number would in themselves make appropriate MUSLI movies for introducing algebra.

We can also use dynamic symbols for other abstract ideas such as "human". In this case the dynamic symbol would show various subsets of the set [man, woman, child] before condensing to the symbol for human. An idea like "medical" can be formed by demonstrating its adjectives.

We are very aware of how much we have left undone but we look forward to delving deeper. We refer the reader to the paper "DynamIcons as dynamic graphic interfaces: interpreting the meaning of a visual representation" [Jonassen et al., 1993] for an exposition on moving icons.

15.8   Creating MUSLI Movies

Two conflicting demands will be made on the MUSLI system since it should support:

1. Professional quality movies, such as those produced by applications like Macromind Director [MacroMind, 1991], which can incorporate video clips and support animation to any level of sophistication. Unfortunately these are very time consuming to create.
2. Quickly drawn movies that employ simple symbols and have a user-friendly interface.

Some easy-to-use movie systems have already been developed, for example the PLAY (Pictorial Language for Animation by Youngsters) system, an iconic programming language and animation environment for children [Tanimoto and Runyan, 1986].

15.8.1 Real-Time Communication Using Dynamic Abstract Symbols

There are two distinct aspects of electronic communication to be considered. To use terminology from computer-supported collaborative work, they are:

1. Synchronous: In a synchronous system the participants are logged on to the computer system at the same time and although they are not necessarily all in the same room together they may be involved in real-time information interchange.
2. Asynchronous: In an asynchronous system authors archive material which is later retrieved and used.

Thus far we have concentrated on asynchronous communication, i.e., writing documents that are read only when complete – the length of time spent authoring being no more relevant to the reader than it customarily is when reading a communication.

However one very important observation, which has been made before, should be included here. Our second most important sensory organ, the ear, has a counterpart – the mouth. But our eyes have no such counterpart. We cannot project mental images for other people to capture. In the paper "Computer visualization, a missing organ, and a cyber-equivalency" [Maurer and Carlson, 1992] the authors suggest that multimedia systems may develop to a stage where they will provide us with a prosthesis to make up for this deficiency. We may be able to produce concrete and abstract projections of our mental images, by computer, so easily and naturally that they will provide us with a new dimension in communication that may well transform our lives. As TV is enhanced by interactive TV we shall inevitably discover more opportunities for user-controlled learning. However even this will fall short as a medium for expressing and recalling ideas with precise, dramatic clarity. As wide-area and broad-band networks expand we have an increasingly powerful medium for communication and collaboration. This, coupled with the fact that multimedia machines are becoming increasingly powerful and affordable, implies that we have the mechanics for truly inter-active hypermedia communication systems.

In the next section of this chapter we take the very first steps towards synchronous communication, in the sense of letting more than one person build up a document containing animations – without too much waiting for each other.

15.8.2 Creating Real-Time Animations

Applications with shared graphical workspaces are becoming commonplace. But thus far, animation has been out of the question since it has been too complex. However, since the basic "actors" in a MUSLI system are abstract symbols and the primitive actions are a comparatively restricted set, pro-duction is dramatically simplified. Factors such as this suggest that MUSLI movies can be created much more efficiently than is currently possible. We are moving towards spontaneous graphical communication.

15.8.3 Requirements for a MUSLI Editor

Many additional, and highly desirable, features are needed for any MUSLI application, only a few of which are mentioned here:

- The program should support easy access to databases of background pic-tures, symbols and signs as well as text. A well structured database should support both graphical and textual searches. Research concerning graph-ical queries on pictorial data is still in its infancy, but since many ab-stract symbols can be considered as icons we can capitalise on work be-ing done on iconic queries [Bordogna et al., 1989]. A graphical thesaurus would be an added bonus! The system must also support graphical brows-ing [Batini et al., 1991]. And of course users must be able to add their own pictures and symbols to the collections.
- Obviously we shall require that actors can be bit-maps, and that they can be placed in their initial positions either by importing pictures from a database (either internal or external) or by copying user-drawn actors from a Drawing window. External bit-map actors should be accessible to editing in the Drawing window.
- Users should have the option of defining states either by giving starting and ending values (or colours), as implemented, or by interactively using sliders. For example, we should be able to show the varying intensity of an emotion such as love by first selecting the particular state we wish to animate and then moving an intensity slider while "re-taking" the scene, or scenes, in slow motion. The latter alternative is particularly attractive

in view of our desire to create a language that will flow like a rippling stream.

- Full graphical painting and drawing should be supported, including assisted and constrained sketching. The appeal of pen-based electronic notebooks such as Apple Macintosh's Newton or Casio's Zoomer suggests that users enjoy sketching in environments that neaten up their work and support incompleteness [Kimura, 1989, Zhao, 1993]. We note that Sketchpad [Sutherland, 1990] uses a light pen to make animated sketches.
- The program should be capable of smoothing the animation paths.
- The user should have the option of building up the dynamics of each scene by successively "recording" each actor in turn as it is dragged by the user along any path.
- We shall need the ability to morph one actor into another. For example if someone sickens and ages we will want to see the symbol representing the person gradually change into a jagged and thickened form.

It is tempting to speculate about software powerful enough to enable us to produce MUSLI movies using a voice-controlled command language coupled with a gesturing system. With such a system we would truly be able to "dance" with our language!

15.9 Examples

It is very difficult in a printed document such as this to describe what are essentially highly dynamic processes. We shall outline just a few examples here.

Our first abstract document, produced in Macromind Director, was an exceedingly simple yet surprisingly convincing movie of a sick child's visit to hospital. The animated symbols show clearly the bonding between the mother and child. The trip into the hospital and the child's recovery were also easily animated.

Our second project was a little more ambitious: we produced a MUSLI movie that depicted a city plagued by smog. The interactions between citizens and administrators lent themselves well to dynamic representations. At the beginning the interactions are overtly hostile but they change dramatically with time. The solution to the crisis is a novel one as it neither bans personalised transport nor enforces public systems.[4]

---

[4] The small low-powered individualised units which are used for short trips can be coupled together, as required, with the rightmost vehicle assuming control. For longer journeys the various units, together with their passengers, are driven onto high speed public transportation vehicles. Individual drivers and passengers relax in their own seats or take advantage of on-board facilities such as dining cars and boutiques and may even find time and opportunity for an overdue haircut!

We would like to see a hypermedia system implemented where the user can be provided with interactive MUSLI movies corresponding to alternative search paths through the network – complete with symbols indicating the type of links that are used and what kind of data is available on the way.

And imagine how much more enjoyable it would be coping with email presented in a MUSLI setting with dynamic symbols – particularly if we had an electronic personal assistant to help us!

An interesting extension of the ideas presented here would be to combine MUSLI with inferencing programs, such as those described by Schank and Abelson [Schank and Abelson, 1977], to allow a user to "explore the consequences" of a plan, or to "check the reality" in some sense. There are two examples from work on belief systems in the early 1970s that we feel could well be revisited in this form. The first example [Colby, 1973] concerns the simulation of paranoia. Colby developed a computer program to simulate a person in a paranoiac state that was sufficiently life-like to pass a form of the Turing test. Different "intensities" of paranoia could be pre-set. If one of the states available in MUSLI was "degree of paranoia", then MUSLI movies could be set up and checked for reality, or possibly let run to show the future consequences. Stress factors such as work, money, age, etc., could be added and perhaps interactively varied so that optimum solutions could be visualised.

The second example [Abelson, 1973] concerns the simulation of the belief system of a "cold warrior" (typically, a Vietnam War supporter circa 1972). The checking of MUSLI movies against belief systems of this type, to give a measure of the degree of likelihood of the scenario presented, as for example in power struggles such as those in the Middle East or Bosnia, opens all sorts of intriguing possibilities for the understanding of others' points of view.

A more down-to-earth application for MUSLI may well follow from the increasing presence of laptop computers at conferences. Some conference organizers are already advising presenters that they "are strongly encouraged to bring portable computers to use with LCD panels and in discussions". Delegates will be able to link directly into the conference database and obtain electronic information about the sessions. During talks, quick notes and even small abstract movies to illustrate dynamic points can be added to their resource material by the individual delegate, and condensed as each wishes. Once delegates will have electronic cameras coupled to their laptops they will be able to add pictures directly to their documents. By the end of the conference each delegate have an almost complete presentation practically ready to show at the inevitable post-conference debriefing sessions.

It is interesting to speculate on how a system such as MUSLI will benefit students in lecture rooms of the future [Lennon and Maurer, 1994b] when a significant proportion of students will have their own portable computers. It will be dynamic notetaking, lecturing, and distance teaching at its best.

15.9.1 Our Own Shorthands

The MUSLI system lends itself particularly well to all sorts of shorthand systems – from chemical symbols to dance notations. Once dictionaries of symbol abbreviations are widely available, documents written in abbreviated form will be open to expansion by other readers. Perhaps authors can be given the option of saving additional special symbols along with their documents.

And wouldn't it be great to be able to use our own shorthand hieroglyphics in our text and then to be able to expand them if it is necessary to print out the document or email it to a colleague. One classics scholar we know has an abbreviation system that includes: c (approximately), ti (something), tis (somebody), v (against), as well as a variety of penstrokes such as / (the). For example, the code ``If tis > ti then ^^ gets it \" might replace "If somebody condenses something then double-clicking gets it back".

And the beauty of it all is that if at any time we cannot remember what a symbol means (whether someone else's or our own!) we can get the full description back with just the click (or double click) of a mouse.

15.10   Afterword

Even a superficial survey of signs and symbols shows the richness of our semiotic heritage. The system we have proposed will be flexible enough to blend traditional forms of documentation into modern multimedia information retrieval systems while gradually becoming enriched with its own symbolic language. MUSLI allows reading at different levels using an extended version of a reference system, and makes maximal use of the principle of orthogonality to aid learning. We discussed the necessary general requirements for a symbolic language before making a first concrete proposal based on the principles of functional grammar. We are aware that the mastery of any new language involves effort, but we take heart from the success of other interactive activities such as video games.

The system we have described is a first step towards mastering the art of electronic communication involving all our senses, so that we can reap the real benefits associated with a new age of hypermedia. It seems appropriate to close this chapter with a quotation from a Gary Larson cartoon. The medieval soldiers are fighting to grim death on the battlements of the castle. Arrows and spears are flying thick as rain. Then one soldier turns to another and remarks that it doesn't really matter whether they win or lose: it's fun! This is how we feel about MUSLI: it is not yet clear whether the eventual outcome will be a revolution in communication and language, or a modest addition to the theory of semiotics. However there is enormous fun both in developing it, and in exploring its potential, as we go on to do in Chapter 16.

16. Hypermedia and a New Multi-Sensory Environment[1]

16.1 Introduction

In the previous sections we described the current version of the MUSLI editor/player prototype and we made a first attempt at describing a dynamic abstract visual language. However, we hope MUSLI will develop into not just a language but a whole multi-sensory environment. This hope is reflected in the name change from MUSIL (MUlti Sensory Information Language) to MUSLI (MUlti Sensory Language Interface). For example, as explained in Section 16.11, interactive, annotated and simultaneous movies should all be part of the environment. In Section 16.6.2 we also consider possible ways of "speed-reading" the wave forms of digitised speech.

16.1.1 New Ideas Described in This Chapter

In this chapter we describe several possible extensions to the MUSLI editor. For example, by introducing the notion of alternative representations of objects (see Section 16.5) we shall create interactive documents that will let readers determine their own preferred levels of abstraction, adjust the proportion of verbal and nonverbal material, and enhance their own natural abilities in visual imagery. We shall let users select the transactional style, thus realising Umberto Eco's "revolutionary" dream where "the addressee rediscovers his freedom of decoding" (Eco, 1976).

Since the new interactive documents correspond, to a rather amazing degree, to new cognitive science models about how our visual and imagery systems work (see Section 16.4.1), they may offer a more natural and holistic method of communication, enhancing all our leisure and lifelong learning experiences.

We also posit several new applications of MUSLI: a tool to help people with disabilities (see Section 16.8), a learning-to-read tool (see Section 16.9), and a story-boarding tool (see Section 16.10).

---

[1] A previous version of part of this chapter was published in the proceedings of Ed-Media'95 [Lennon, 1995b].

16.1.2 Motivation

In 1986 Joseph Weizenbaum said, "I think that children have a power to imagine that is almost magical when compared to the adult imagination, and there is something irrecoverable that a child loses when he or she becomes bound by logic" [Brady, 1986]. Now that computers are used so widely we must keep on asking whether too much exposure to educational films, video, pictures, etc., may indeed encourage our children to be too dependent on "realism".

In this chapter we consider new ways of using multimedia that encourage imagination and creativity rather than restricting it. We describe documents that avoid the extremes of either too much passive realism (fact or fantasy) or too much cold, irrelevant data – documents that encourage imagination and creativity rather than restricting it.

16.2   Retaining Our Power to Imagine

Hollywood, television and advertising dollars have fed the trend towards an ever increasing proportion of pictorial images in information material. New multimedia technology is adding fuel to the fire. However, as the authors of the book *Reading Images* [Kress and van Leeuwen, 1990] point out, there has still been little analysis of visual communication compared with the amount of work done on textual languages – e.g., on written grammars. They suggest that academic research into visual semantics is in effect being discouraged. Since literate societies are inevitably seen as more "advanced" than illiterate ones, textual literacy has enjoyed a very long history of social esteem, and at school children are exposed to a high proportion of pictorial content only during their first few years.

Yet what a loss this represents! In *Reading Images* [Kress and van Leeuwen, 1990] the authors also state that "children very early on .... develop a surprising ability to use elements of the visual 'grammar' – an ability that, we feel, should be understood better and developed further, rather than being cut off prematurely as is, too often, the case at present".

We see the need to go even further: we suggest that not only children but adults need to be empowered to make better use of multimedia documents.

It is interesting to note that in the thought-provoking book *Tao: The Watercourse Way* [Watts and Huang, 1976] describes the writing of Chinese (the oldest and most widely used graphical symbolic language) as "dancing with brush and ink" and creating "the same beauty we recognise in moving water, in foam, spray, eddies, and waves, as well as in clouds, flames and weavings of smoke in sunlight". A well-designed dynamic symbolic language should flow so beautifully that it will create comparable effects.

16.3 Hints and Flashes

The title of the paper "Mental imagery and visualisation: from the mind's machine to the computer screen" [Lennon, 1995a] evolved from the popular but illuminating book *Ghosts in the Mind's Machine; Creating and Using Images in the Brain* where "images – ghosts – flit through the physical machinery that is our brain" [Kosslyn, 1983]. It is important to note from the outset that in contrast to the photographic "snapshots" of eidetic memory the images we are referring to are more complex and abstract – and thus difficult to describe in words. They are Tichener's "hints" and "flashes" [Arnheim, 1970], that he compares to Impressionists' notes. They have a quality "invaluable of abstract thought ... reducing a theme visually to a skeleton of essential dynamic features" [Arnheim, 1970]. For example a "humble suitor" may give a dynamic "flash of a bent back".

Both Arnheim and Kosslyn argue that, whether we are conscious of it or not, we all practise this type of dynamic visual thinking. But for centuries education has been dependent on an unnatural, one-sided form of communication consisting of sequential, narrowly defined, and rigidly controlled natural-language "hardcopy" texts – pages of words.

16.4 The Imagery Debate

The debate that has been waged over the relationships between imaging and language-based concepts is an interesting one [Tye, 1991]. Alan Paivio may be thought of as the grandfather of what he called a "dual coding approach" to human mind and memory [Paivio, 1971], and in the book *Mental Representations: A Dual Coding Approach* [Paivio, 1986] he notes that "Human cognition is unique in that it has become specialised for dealing simultaneously with language and with nonverbal objects and events". Each of the two systems supports the other, in ways highly specialised to each individual person. Paivio's work has since been greatly extended [Kosslyn, 1994]. For example, which process "wins" (i.e., returns a result) is now thought to depend both on our own particular inbuilt abilities and on the type of problem.

Now new advances in computer technology are providing certain user options which are exciting because they correspond to a rather amazing degree to new psychological discoveries (models) about how our visual and imagery systems work.

16.4.1 A Cognitive Science Model

Kosslyn, in the book *Image and Brain: The Resolution of the Imagery Debate* [Kosslyn, 1994] describes studies that show how imagery "plays a key role in normal perception". It appears that either consciously or unconsciously we all use imagery to various degrees. From a computer science point of view it is interesting that cognitive scientists have hypothesised theories of "data compression", "parallel processing" and, most of all, sets of functions. We have the ability to "scan" images recalled from memory, "zoom" into them acquiring more detail, and "transform" them in multiple ways [Kosslyn, 1980] and [Kosslyn, 1994].

Interestingly, each and every one of the imagery functions listed by Kosslyn in Table 11.2 of Image and Brain [Kosslyn, 1994] is capable of being simulated in a MUSLI environment. A small subset of the table is reproduced here:

Table 16.1 A subset of a table in *Image and Brain* [Kosslyn, 1994]

FIND	Looks up description; looks up procedures specified in description; executes procedures on surface matrix.	Passes back Locate/ Not Locate; if Located, passes back Cartesian coordinates of part.
PUT	Looks up name of image file, location relation, and foundation part; ... calls FIND to locate foundation part; adjusts mapping function; calls PICTURE.	Part integrated into image (produces new content).
SCAN	Moves all points in surface matrix along vector; fills in new material at leading edge via inverse mapping function.	Image repositioned (alters content).
ZOOM	Moves all points in surface matrix out from the center; fills in new material via inverse mapping function; calls RESOLUTION; calls PUT to insert new parts as resolution allows.	Scale change in image, higher resolution, and new parts (alters content).
PAN	Moves all points in surface matrix in from the center.	Scale change in image, lower resolution (alters content).
ROTATE	Moves all points in bounded region in specified direction around a pivot.	Reorients image (alters content).

16.4.2 Simulating the Visual Processes

We shall now look at the processes listed in the table above to see how they can be simulated in a MUSLI environment.

- FIND. Ideally, just as our brains parallel-process requests, the Find system in a MUSLI environment should be able to search both textually and graphically. Perhaps, if notated graphics are used, simultaneous searches can be made.
- PUT. The PUT function places an object, located by FIND, into the movie. It is important to note that most of the time our brains only call up some sort of symbolic representation of any subject, containing just enough detail for the current job on hand. For example, if we are asked to visualise an elephant we usually do so diagrammatically. Only when asked whether the tusks are straight or curved do we call up the required additional detail. It is just this sort of flexibility that a MUSLI environment can provide (see Section 16.5).
- SCAN. This function is almost exactly reproduced in interactive and annotated movies using the techniques described in Chapter Thirteen. We suggested the function could be likened to panning with a telescope.
- ZOOM. This function is already commonly simulated in interactive movies. In chapter Thirteen we described how it can be done without loss of resolution – a function which in nature is performed automatically by the eyes.
- PAN. The PAN function controls our ability to scale images. We recognise objects almost regardless of size. The ability to scale objects in MUSLI is so important that it will be given high priority in the next version of the MUSLI Editor.
- ROTATE. Since ROTATE is a common option in graphical drawing packages we assume that it will be available in any generalised MUSLI Editor.

In summary, since the processes of scanning, zooming, transforming, and distorting images are all natural features of our brain's visual system we can hope that integrating them, together with natural language, into MUSLI documents will lead to a much more natural and holistic environment for communication than we have ever had before.

16.5 Multiple Representations and User-Determined Levels of Abstraction

It is important to note that in a MUSLI document each element may have multiple representations – not just one or two (see Figure 16.1). These alternatives may be stored as linked resource files. By invoking a Preferences option, users may define the order in which they wish the alternatives to be presented. For example, a document may give the following alternative views:

1. Symbolic – condensed
2. Symbolic – expanded
3. Iconic

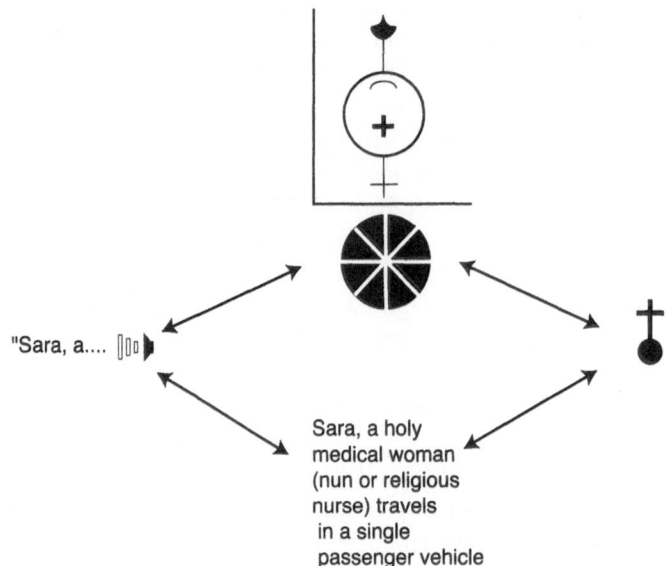

Fig. 16.1. Alternative Representations of a Single MUSLI Element

4. Pictorial and/or graphical
5. Natural language text
6. Digitised speech.

These options can be condensed and expanded iteratively. Thus if a user prefers the ordering shown above, (1) will be displayed first, and double clicking on it will expand it to (2). Double clicking on (2) will get (3), and so on. However, since readers obviously have different preferences, another user may choose to have the more verbal options (5) or (6) presented before any of the visual options.

There is no doubt that there is a wide variety of preferences among readers for both the level of abstraction they like, the amount of detail they feel ready for, and the amount of redundancy they need [Allen, 1975]. Using options such as we have described above, users can control the choice of media to suit their own preferences and natural learning styles. As we discuss in Section 16.9, systems such as we propose may at last resolve the war that has been waged among the learning-to-read experts concerning "Look-and-Say" versus phonics.

16.5.1 Making the Concrete More Abstract and the Abstract More Concrete

Winn [Winn, 1989] states, "Designers have frequently found that realistic pictures may carry too much information for effective instruction. Some students, particularly the less able, may be overwhelmed by irrelevant detail and there may be a need to replace them by more abstract equivalents.... The instructional advantages of graphics lie in their simplifying complex illustrations in which there is a lot of unnecessary detail, and particularly in presenting abstract ideas more concretely through a variety of formats that involve the analogical use of space, lines, arrows and so on" [Winn, 1989].

On the other hand abstract concepts such as "predation" and "transfer of energy in a food chain" can be better depicted in a much more concrete manner as dynamic diagrams [Winn, 1989]. Also, the more able students need "procedures that are perceptually rich in information, concepts and sensory information ... [and] place a requirement on learners to organize, hypothesize, abstract and manipulate symbolic meaning" [Allen, 1975].

In a MUSLI document there is no longer such a conflict between the abstractness and concreteness since we can always have alternative views.

The views may also be continually adapted to match users' increasing levels of sophistication.

16.5.2 New Ways of Coping with Individual Differences

Individual differences! Differences in the way we "see" things, in the way we transact, in the way we communicate – they are a source of endless frustration for educators. A workshop entitled "Coping with Heterogeneous Classes" that was held at a recent educational conference ended in despair. Certainly we are already seeing moves away from *teacher centred* learning environments to *student centred* ones [Petruk, 1992], and the development of electronic classrooms offers certain solutions. However we believe that the problem goes much deeper than this. As we pointed out in Section 16.3, for too long education has been straitjacketed by being dependent on the printed word.

Now, for the very first time, we are in a position where we can create dynamic "texts" that "readers" can tailor to suit their own individual differences in learning styles.

16.5.3 The Importance of Alternative Views

As educators, it is not so much that we underestimate the importance of alternative views, but that until now we have not been provided with the technology to implement them. In the previous chapter we elaborated on the importance of looking at the "other side of a mountain" in detail. In-depth research by Gick [Gick, 1989] and Gick and Holyoak [Gick and Holyoak, 1980, Gick and Holyoak, 1983] also confirms that students often seem to need more than one example before they can usefully generalise or apply their knowledge to analogous situations.

In another interesting case study performed by Winn students were presented with a circuit diagram [Winn, 1989]. It was found that if components were represented in labelled iconic form the students learnt them but frequently failed to comprehend the pattern of the overall circuit design. However, when the detailed components were replaced by abstract symbolic representations they learnt the pattern more easily than they remembered the components. They concluded: "It appears, therefore, that different types of graphic are appropriate to the teaching of patterns and sequences. The amount of detail in the elements in the graphics, and their familiarity to students, appear to be related to whether they help serial or parallel [mental processing]".

In a MUSLI environment we have documents where the degree of abstraction is initiated by the author but can be controlled by the user.

16.6 Making Better Use of Sound

We look forward to making much better use of sound than we do at present. There is hardly a better way of setting moods for scenes and indicating such things as a really good thunderstorm than by using appropriate sounds. An interesting point made by Alty [Alty, 1993] is that peripheral or parallel streams of information containing redundant information can be of importance in helping students understand complex ideas.

16.6.1 Using Digitised Speech

In many situations recorded speech is an added dimension that we welcome. Consider the freedom to add annotations to documents by simply picking up a microphone (see Section 16.10).

Furthermore, as teleteaching and distance learning become more computerised, the use of digitised sound must inevitably increase. This will put pressure on us to provide more efficient information retrieval systems – we shall need to be able to "search" digitised speech more efficiently than we can do at present. We note that it is now possible for computers to play back speech at twice the recorded speed and still maintain an acceptable level of pitch and clarity. This is certainly a first step in the right direction.

Another interesting alternative to traditional search techniques is to divide a recording into (say) four parts and to play all four sections simultaneously. If, for example, we know that the recording of a twenty-minute lecture contains a section on ozone holes that is of particular interest to us, we can divide the speech up into four five-minute sections and play them simultaneously. The word "ozone" will stand out prominently just as names jump out at us from a crowd at a noisy party.

16.6.2 Picturising Sound

If the waveform patterns corresponding to speech are displayed on the screen then, in some sense, it may be possible to "read" them.

Let us suppose that the waveforms associated with a lecture are displayed in "lines".

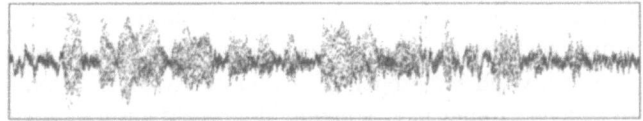

Fig. 16.2. Picturising Sound

We may, for example, be able to find significant passages by noting changes in volume. If the wave patterns are expanded and the amplitude is displayed in (say) red while the pitch is displayed in blue, additional information can be gained. Alternating passages of high and low pitch may well mark dialogue. Exciting passages will stand out. Sentences will be seen marked off from one another and other information will be visible such as the occurrence of a question. We may learn to recognise our own characteristics and to differentiate them from a colleague's patterns so that we can see certain demarcations in conversations. However, in order to make detailed searches we shall obviously need the additional help that is described in the next section.

16.6.3 Adding Signposts

If the author of the document provides signposts in the form of icons alongside key passages users will be further aided in their searches. The signposts can be inserted at key intervals such as the beginning of new paragraphs and sections. The symbols can be text or icons and can, of course, be edited at any stage. Like any MUSLI symbol they can be expanded, as explained in the previous chapter, to provide additional information which can include text, graphics and movie clips, as well speech and other types of sound.

It should also be possible for specialised computer programs to scan the material in greater detail. With methods such as these, authors will be able to produce documents allowing readers to understand ideas more readily.

16.7 Creative Thinking

Many of the greatest of our creative thinkers, from the Greek poet Simonides to Coleridge and Einstein, were high visualisers. To quote Einstein, "The words or the language, as they are written or spoken, do not seem to play any role in my mechanism of thought. The psychical entities which seem to serve as elements in thought are certain signs and more or less clear images which can be 'voluntarily' reproduced and combined" [Hadamard, 1945]. Almost certainly freedom to associate ideas visually has a large part to play in the creative act [Rugg, 1963]. In fact, the playful practice of taking an idea into a radically different context and exploring the new relationships for humour or creativity relies on metaphorical, often visual comparisons.

But, you may well be asking, is there any hope for people gifted with neither genius nor a vivid imagination? To quote Kosslyn, "Comfortingly, ... in most of our imagery experiments people definitely improved with practice. .... Although we may never be in a position to fit glasses to myopic mind's eyes, however metaphorically, we may be able to prescribe exercises to help people improve their inner vision" [Kosslyn, 1983]. In the MUSLI environment even those of us without a vivid visual imagination will enjoy the ability to transform, distort, and otherwise morph images.

Using imagery, whether mental or computer-generated, we can exploit our inbuilt capacity for constructing dynamic processes and foreseeing new consequences [Paivio, 1971, Paivio, 1986]. To quote from Paivio, "Images appear to be effective modes of representing static situations as well as changes in situations. Indeed, subjective reports of their role in creative thinking (surely the ultimate in transformation thought) suggest that imagery is the very basis of swift creative leaps of imagination" [Paivio, 1971].

16.8 Helping People with Disabilities

The usefulness of computers for the disabled has been widely recognised, to the extent that even the government purse has opened to ensure that as many as possible have access to them. The provision of good interactive material to suit their needs has not yet caught up with this market. Many commercial applications are frequently little more than dictionaries of static symbols.

However considerable research has been undertaken. In the mid-1970s a system called VIC (A Visual Communication System) was developed for aphasics [Lakin, 1986]. Techniques for semantic compaction, in the interest of speech-impaired people, are discussed in the paper "Using images to generate speech" [Baker, 1986]. In the paper "Visual tools and languages: directions for the '90s" [Glinert et al., 1989] the authors propose that "members of the visual programming community should play a central and leading role in developing languages and systems that are accessible to people with disabilities." They describe the Blissymbolics ideographic language [Dreyfuss, 1972] that is still under development.

Also, while surveying existing systems of nonverbal signs [Dreyfuss, 1972, Jeanes, 1982, Liungman, 1991, Umiker-Sebeok and Sebeok, 1987], we saw many examples of cases where dynamic attributes were obviously needed; for example, the signs for "push" and "pull" are particularly difficult to make unambiguous. Many static iconic signs corresponding to verbs are cripples.

Even in natural language there is a temptation to use expressions such as "increasingly more" in an effort to explain a dynamic process!

Teachers and therapists who already use the computer as a learning medium for people with disabilities are showing considerable interest in the possibilities MUSLI can offer. Once dictionaries and encyclopedias, taken from hypermedia databases, can be displayed as clickable palettes by the MUSLI editor, then all the many advantages of animation will become available.

16.9 MUSLI as a Learning-to-Read Tool

To our initial surprise, remedial reading teachers have also expressed great interest in MUSLI. Traditionally we have associated the use of symbols with the more academically able. However, symbols are already widely used in remedial work. For example, if students have (laboriously) read a passage of text, they often enjoy drawing the story line or an alternative ending, using a series of symbolic diagrams. Children are encouraged to develop their own symbols – an oval in an arc may represent a whale in a small pool. Within the MUSLI environment the children will be able to use a controlled "vocabulary" of existing signs, modifying them at will – or scale their own drawings down to fine-looking symbols!

These activities may generalise into a new approach to reading suitable for all youngsters. It is encouraging to note there is evidence that even pre-school children can effortlessly learn to "read" text with a very high proportion of symbolic drawings – a fact that is illustrated by the great success of Dick Bruna's books without words [Kress and van Leeuwen, 1990].

16.10 MUSLI as a Story-Boarding Tool

As multimedia becomes more widely used there will be an increasing amount of in-house or in-school video production [Mackay and Davenport, 1989, Mathews et al., 1994]. There is obvious potential for MUSLI as a story-boarding tool. Traditionally video producers have used cardboard cards on which they sketched characters. Now, within MUSLI, each card can be replaced by an animated sequence – an abstract movie (see Figure 16.3). Double-clicking on the symbol for an actor will bring up additional information such as notes and sketches of costume detail or set design.

– Actors may be represented by easily reproducible symbols or icons.
– Expanding the actors will reveal additional details such as wardrobe sketches, descriptions and pictures.
– There will be easy-to-use animation paths for the actors on each "card".
– Background props can be expanded to give structural details.

Most important, annotations in the form of digitised speech can be associated with each actor. A prototype story-board program with speech annotation facilities was developed as a student project at the University of Auckland. It had a very good interactive path-summary feature using thumbnail miniatures of each scene. We would very much like to see MUSLI incorporating features such as these. And, of course, where a storyboard ends and a creative MUSLI movie begins is just a matter of definition.

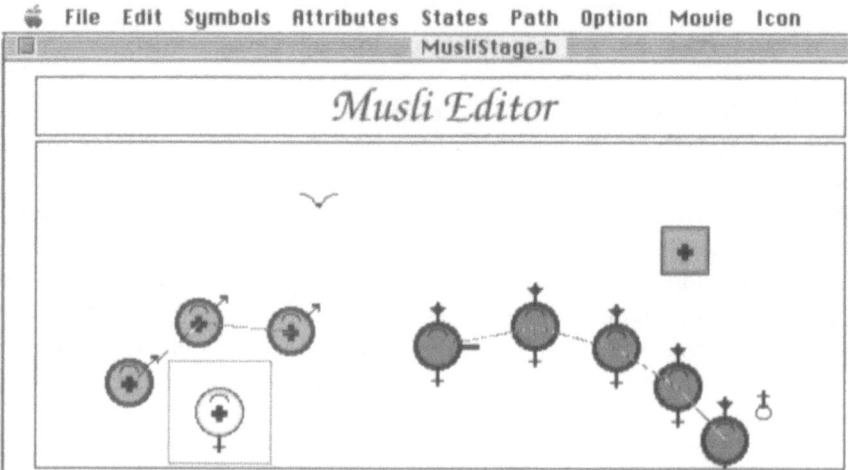

Fig. 16.3. A MUSLI Stage

16.11 Mastering the New Media

At the First Congress of the International Association for Semiotic Studies in Milan back in June 1974, Umberto Eco gave a concluding address in which he stated, "As a matter of fact in the Congress people have simply dealt with everything – and nothing else" [Eco, 1979]. The question we must ask is a similar one. Are we introducing documents that contain just about "everything – and nothing else"? We must now consider whether the new documents can be "read" effectively.

We might, of course, simply proceed in hope, taking heart from a quote in *A Theory of Semiotics* [Eco, 1976]: "Curiously enough, this assumption carries speculation about languages back to the position adopted by Giambattista Vico, who proposed that languages arise as poetic inventions and are only accepted by convention afterward".

16.11.1 New Types of Document

"All my notions are too narrow. Instead of 'Sign,' ought I not to say Medium?" (Charles S. Peirce in 1906)

Semioticians such as Umberto Eco have long since generalised the theory of semiotic codes to the point where it embraces representations of "semantic universes" corresponding to the one we live in [Eco, 1976]. We believe that we are now approaching the point where we must look at electronic computer networks in a similar light. For example, a complete paper could be written on semiotics in networked communities. Specific cultures are evolving on Internet, each with their own communication mores. We also look forward to seeing the results of merging electronic networking techniques with successful human networks such as those described in the book *Learning Networks in Adult Education: Non-formal Education on a Housing Estate* [Fordham et al., 1979]. Developments such as this could, in itself, revolutionise lifelong learning practices.

We now summarise features that may be included in the next generation of interactive documents. We use a presentation method which illustrates how a new freedom will be provided for writers and readers, a freedom which may have far-reaching effects for communication, education, and creative learning experiences.

– Hypertext links:

– In-line video clips:

– In-line audio clips:

Thumbnail pictures expandable in place:

– Bookmarks (textual):

– Bookmarks (pictorial):

- Interactive and/or annotated movies (Chapter 13) including zooming, panning and MUSLI movies (see Figure 16.4).
- Simultaneous movies as described in Section 13.6.3.
- User-controlled levels of abstraction.

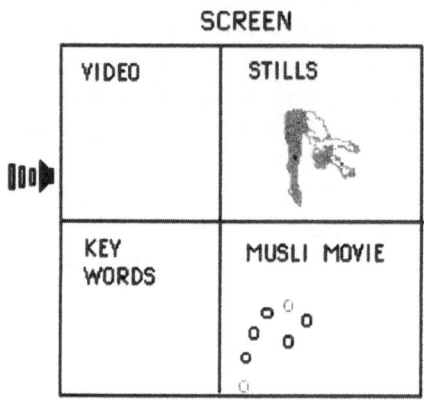

Fig. 16.4. Interactive and Annotated MUSLI Movie

16.12 Regaining our Power to Imagine

MUSLI movies can be used to express ideas difficult to express otherwise. For example, we have considered the viability of making a MUSLI movie of Leonard Cohen's "Light as a Breeze" lyric. As an explicit movie it probably would not pass a censor's rating – but it would lend itself to a highly artistic and creative MUSLI movie (see Figure 16.5).

Moreover, since it was deliberately written with ambiguous meanings, alternative versions of the movie could perhaps be shown in adjacent quadrants. It would be fascinating to survey viewers' comprehension of the different movie versions. Almost certainly different people would "click" onto different versions at different times. And ideally, in a true multi-sensory environment, viewers should then be able to make their own changes and creative additions!

16.13 Afterword

Whether consciously or unconsciously, in our dealings with the real world we use a wide range of nonverbal skills such as inspecting, zooming, panning, and

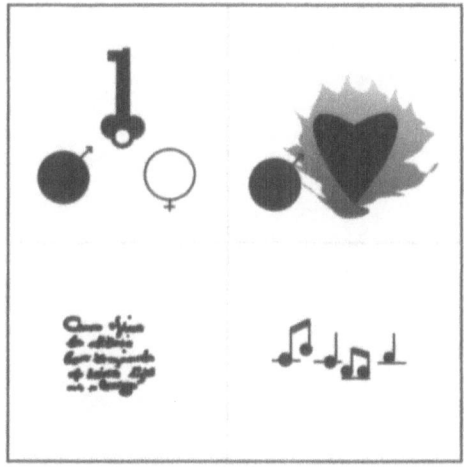

Fig. 16.5. Simultaneous MUSLI Movies

transforming images. Abilities such as these are obviously highly individual, and undoubtedly account for much of the frustration seen when learners are faced with traditional "one-size-fits-all" documents.

Although modern multimedia systems are being developed that let us create documents that incorporate zooming and panning, very few are designed to let users "play with animation" in an easy-to-use environment. We suggested that dictionaries of shapes and symbols, that can be easily modified, distorted, morphed, and animated in real-time, should be associated with the encyclopedic material that is now being widely distributed. Once we can "write" documents that let "readers" use both verbal techniques and this wealth of nonverbal techniques, we shall at last free ourselves from the relatively narrow "unnatural" world of text-based communication and rediscover a new "freedom of decoding" [Eco, 1976].

"Readers" will be encouraged to develop their imaginative skills rather than becoming "bound by logic" [Brady, 1986].

Most important, fresh perspectives developed by any individual working or playing can be shared with other individuals anywhere on the globe! We believe that, as distributed hypermedia systems are used increasingly for communication and collaboration, their impact will not only tie information together but, even more significantly, "tie people together" [Maurer, 1993a]. Surely, we can have hope for its liberating and liberalising influence.

List of URLs

URLf3   http://hypatia.dcs.qmw.ac.uk/

URLg1   http://home.mcom.com/home/how-to-give-feedback.html

URLg2   http://www.ManGlobe.com

URLg3   http://www.cs.waikato.ac.nz/nzdl/

URLh2   http://www.ncsa.uiuc.edu/General/Internet/WWW/
HTMLPrimer.html

URLh3   http://nii.nist.gov/nii.html

URLi2   http://werbach.com/barebones/

URLi3   http://www.iconbazaar.com/

URLj1   http://www.amazon.com/

URLj2   http://www.mit.edu/afs/athena/user/w/s/wsmart/WEB/
HTMLtutor.html

URLj3   http://www.microsoft.com/ie/

URLk1   http://www.uky.edu/Artsource/artsourcehome.html

URLk2   http://www.altavista.digital.com/

URLk3   http://www.aeiou.at/aeiou

URLl1   http://ausarts.anu.edu.au/ITA/AusArts/www/
exhibition.html

URLl2   http://www.mat.sbg.ac.at/uhl/wav.html

URLl3   http://www.iicm.edu/hmcard/

URLm1   http://www.primenet.com/art-rom/museumweb/

URLm2   http://www.lib-online.com/

URLm3   http://www.hyperwave.com/

URLn1   http://etext.virginia.edu/TEI.html

URLn2   http://www.swets.nl/index.html

URLn3   http://www.iicm.edu/liberation

URLo2   http://pathfinder.com/@@GL5*6gYAUkVOWnST/Netly/
daily/nnhome.html

URLp1   http://www.infoanalytic.com/cdrw/catalog-text.html

URLp2   http://www.metacrawler.com/

URLp3   http://www.cocoa.apple.com

URLq1   http://digiplanet.com/DP/index.html

URLq2   http://www.oracle.com/products/websystem/intranet/
index.html

URLq3   http://catless.ncl.ac.uk/Risks

URLr1   http://www.oracle.com/

URLr3   http://ganges.cs.tcd.ie/mepeirce/Project/oninternet.html

URLs2   http://www.cs.unca.edu/davidson/indexes.html

URLs3   http://csrc.ncsl.nist.gov/nistbul/csl95-02.txt

URLt2   http://www.excite.com/

URLt3   http://www.is.co.za/mikev/cia–hack/

URLu2   http://www.w3.org/pub/WWW/

URLv2   http://www.w3.org/pub/WWW/Press/Backgrounder.html

URLw2   http://www.yahoo.com/

URLw3   http://www.cs.indiana.edu/ripem/dir.html

URLx2   http://www.infoseek.com/

URLx3   http://web.mit.edu/network/pgp.html

URLy2   http://www.lycos.com/

URLy3   http://www.ifi.uio.no/staalesc/PGP/

URLz1   http://www.iicm.edu/jucs

URLz2   http://www.forteinc.com/forte/agent/freagent.htm

URLz3   http://www.visa.com/cgi-bin/vee/sf/set/intro.html

Bibliography

[Abelson, 1973] Abelson, R. The structure of belief systems. In Schank, R. and
   Colby, K., editors, *Computer Models of Thought and Language*, pages 287–339.
   W. H. Freeman and Co., San Francisco, CA.

[Aboba, 1993] Aboba, B. *The Online User's Encyclopedia: Bulletin Boards and
   Beyond.* Addison-Wesley, Reading, MA.

[Akscyn et al., 1988] Akscyn, R. M., McCracken, K. L., and Yoder, E. A. KMS:
   A distributed hypermedia system for managing knowledge in organizations.
   Communications of the ACM, 31(7):820–835.

[Alberti et al., 1994] Alberti, B., Anklesaria, F., Lindner, P., McCahill, M., and
   Torrey, D. The Internet Gopher User's Guide. Available by anonymous ftp
   from boombox.micro.umn.edu in directory `pub/gopher/gopher\_protocol`.

[Allen, 1975] Allen, W. H. Intellectual abilities and instructional media design. *AV
   Communication Review*, 23(2):139–170.

[Alty, 1993] Alty, J. L. Multimedia: We have the technology but do we have a
   methodology? In Maurer, H., editor, *Proc. ED-MEDIA 93 – World Conference
   on Educational Multimedia and Hypermedia*, pages 3–10. Association for the
   Advancement of Computing in Education (AACE).

[Anderson et al., 1996] Anderson, C., Burns, C., and Klemme, M. Watermarking
   for the hyperwave hypermedia system. In Maurer, H., editor, *WebNet 96 —
   World Conference of the Web Society*, San Francisco. The Web Society and the
   Association for the Advancement of Computing in Education (AACE), part of
   the electronic proceedings.

[Andreessen, 1993] Andreessen, M. NCSA Mosaic technical summary 2.1. Available by anonymous ftp from ftp.ncsa.uiuc.edu as file /Web/Mosaic.ps.Z.

[Andreessen, 1996] Andreessen, M. The netscape intranet vision and product
   roadmap.
   http://home.netscape.com/comprod/at_work/white_paper/intranet/
   vision.html.

[Andrews et al., 1994a] Andrews, K., Kappe, F., and Maurer, H. Hyper-G and
   Harmony: Towards the next generation of networked information technology.
   Technical report, IICM.

[Andrews et al., 1994b] Andrews, K., Kappe, F., and Maurer, H. The Hyper-G
   network information system. In *Special issue: proceedings of the Workshop on
   Distributed Multimedia Systems*, Graz, Austria.

[Andrews et al., 1995] Andrews, K., Maurer, H., and Scherbakov, N. Semantic
   modeling of object-oriented hypermedia databases. In Blumenthal, B., Gornos-
   taev, J., and Unger, C., editors, *Human-Computer Interaction, EWHCI'95*,
   pages 121–134. LNCS 1015, Springer, Berlin Heidelberg New York.

[Arnheim, 1970] Arnheim, R., editor. *Visual Thinking.* Faber and Faber, London.

[Augenstein et al., 1993] Augenstein, F., Ottmann, T., and Schoning, J. Logical markup for hypermedia documents: The TRAIN-system. In Maurer, H., editor, *Proc. ED-MEDIA 93 – World Conference on Educational Multimedia and Hypermedia*, pages 17–25. Association for the Advancement of Computing in Education (AACE).

[Authorware, 1991] Authorware. *Authorware Professional Reference Manual.* Authorware Inc., Minneapolis, MN.

[Badre et al., 1992] Badre, A., Beranek, M., Morris, J., and Stasko, J. Assessing program visualization systems as instructional aids. In Tomek, I., editor, *Proc. ICCAL92*, pages 87–99. LNCS 602, Springer, Berlin Heidelberg New York.

[Baeza-Yates and Gonnet, 1992] Baeza-Yates, R. and Gonnet, G. A new approach to text searching. *Communications of the ACM*, 35(10):74–82.

[Baker, 1986] Baker, B. R. Using images to generate speech. *Byte*, 11(3):160–168.

[Balkovich et al., 1985] Balkovich, E., Lerman, S., and Parmelee, R. Computing in higher education: The Athena experience. *IEEE Computer*, 18(11):112–125.

[Barker et al., 1993] Barker, P., Giller, S., Richards, S., and King, T. The evaluation of interactive multimedia courseware. In Maurer, H., editor, *Proc. ED-MEDIA 93 – World Conference on Educational Multimedia and Hypermedia*, pages 32–38. Association for the Advancement of Computing in Education (AACE).

[Bates, 1993] Bates, A. W. Educational aspects of the telecommunications revolution. In *Proc. IFIP TC3 Third Teleteaching Conference Teleteaching 93*, pages 1–10.

[Bates, 1994] Bates, A. W. Educational multi-media in a networked society. In Ottmann, T. and Tomek, I., editors, *Proc. ED-MEDIA 94*, pages 3–8. Association for the Advancement of Computing in Education (AACE).

[Batini et al., 1991] Batini, C., Catarci, T., Costabile, M. F., and Levialdi, S. Visual strategies for querying databases. In *Proc. 1991 IEEE Workshop on Visual Languages*, pages 183–189, Kobe, Japan. IEEE Computer Society Press.

[Bauer, 1997] Bauer, F. L. *Decrypted Secrets. Methods and Maxims of Cryptology.* Springer, Berlin Heidelberg New York.

[Berends, 1993] Berends, T. Screen magic for travellers. *New Zealand Herald*, August 10th(Section 4):7.

[Berners-Lee et al., 1992] Berners-Lee, T., Cailliau, R., Groff, J., and Pollermann, B. World Wide Web: The information universe. *Electronic Networking: Research, Applications and Policy*, 1(2):52–58.

[Berners-Lee et al., 1994a] Berners-Lee, T., Cailliau, R., Luotonen, A., Nielsen, H. F., and Secret, A. The World Wide Web. *Communications of the ACM*, 37(8):76–82.

[Berners-Lee et al., 1994b] Berners-Lee, T., Masinter, L., and McCahill, M. Uniform Resource Locators (URL). ftp://ds.internic.net/rfc/ rfc1738.txt.

[Blum et al., 1986] Blum, L., Blum, M., and Shub, M. A simple unpredictable pseudo-random number generator. *SIAM Journal on Computing*, 15:364–383.

[Bordogna et al., 1989] Bordogna, G., Gagliardi, I., Merelli, D., Mussio, P., Padula, M., and Protti, M. Iconic queries on pictorial data. In *Proc. 1989 IEEE Workshop on Visual Languages*, pages 38–42. IEEE Computer Society Press.

[Bowman et al., 1994] Bowman, C., Danzig, P., Hardy, D., Manber, U., Schwartz, M., and Wessels, D. Harvest: A scalable, customizable discovery and access system. Technical Report CU-CS-732-94, Department of Computer Science, University of Colorado, Boulder. Available by ftp from ftp.cs.colorado.edu in /pub/techreports/schwartz.Harvest.ps.

[Brady, 1986] Brady, H. Hold on to the power to imagine: an interview with Joseph Weizenbaum. In *Computers in Education*, pages 266–268. Dushkin, Guildford, CT.

[Brennecke and Keil-Slawik, 1995] Brennecke, A. and Keil-Slawik, R. Notes on the Alltagspraxis of hypermedia design. In Maurer, H., editor, *Educational Multimedia and Hypermedia Annual (Proc. of ED-MEDIA 95, Graz)*, pages 115–120. Association for the Advancement of Computing in Education (AACE).

[Brickell, 1984] Brickell, E. F. Breaking iterated knapsacks. In Blakely, G. R. and Chaum, D., editors, *Advances in Cryptology. Proc. CRYPTO 84*, pages 342–358. LNCS 196, Springer, Berlin Heidelberg New York.

[Brown, 1988] Brown, M. Exploring algorithms using Balsa-II. *IEEE Computer*, 21(5):14–36.

[Bush, 1945] Bush, V. As we may think. *Atlantic Monthly*, 176(1):101–108.

[Callaghan, 1994] Callaghan, R. Moving from a content focus to a learning outcome focus. In *Proc. Distance Education: Windows on the Future*, pages 45–49. The Correspondence School, Wellington, NZ.

[Calude et al., 1994] Calude, C., Maurer, H., and Salomaa, A. J.UCS: The Journal of Universal Computer Science and its applications to science and engineering teaching. Computer Science Report Report 91, University of Auckland, Auckland, NZ.

[Capper, 1994] Capper, H. The new technology – what works best. In *Proc. Distance Education: Windows on the Future*, pages 537–543. The Correspondence School, Wellington, NZ.

[Carmody et al., 1969] Carmody, S., Gross, T., Nelson, T., Rice, D., and van Dam, A. Hypertext editing system for the /360. In *Proc. Conference in Computer Graphics*, University of Illinois.

[Catlin et al., 1989] Catlin, T., Bush, P., and Yankelovich, N. Internote: Extending a hypermedia framework to support annotative collaboration. In *Proc. Hypertext'89*, pages 365–378. ACM.

[Cerf and Kahn, 1974] Cerf, V. and Kahn, R. A protocol for packet network intercommunication. *IEEE Transactions on Communications*, com-22(5):637–648.

[Chaum et al., 1988] Chaum, D., Fiat, A., and Naor, M. Untraceable electronic cash. In Goldwasser, S., editor, *Advances in Cryptology. Proc. CRYPTO 88*, pages 319–327. LNCS 403, Springer, Berlin Heidelberg New York.

[Cheyney et al., 1994] Cheyney, M., Gloor, P., Johnson, D. B., Makedon, F., Matthews, J., and Metaxas, P. Conference on a disk: A successful experiment in hypermedia publishing. In Ottmann, T. and Tomek, I., editors, *Proc. ED-MEDIA 94*, pages 129–134. Association for the Advancement of Computing in Education (AACE).

[Colby, 1973] Colby, K. Simulations of belief systems. In Schank, R. and Colby, K., editors, *Computer Models of Thought and Language*, pages 251–286. W. H. Freeman and Co., San Francisco, CA.

[Communications, 1994a] Communications. Special issue on hypermedia. *Communications of the ACM*, 37(2).

[Communications, 1994b] Communications. Special issue on intelligent agents. *Communications of the ACM*, 37(7).

[Communications, 1995] Communications. Special issue on digital libraries. *Communications of the ACM*, 35(4).

[Computer, 1989] Computer. Special issue on visualization: Bringing data into focus. *IEEE Computer*, 22(8).

[Conklin, 1987] Conklin, J. Hypertext: An introduction and survey. *IEEE Computer*, 20(9):17–41.

[Conklin and Begeman, 1988] Conklin, J. and Begeman, M. L. gIBIS: A hypertext tool for exploratory policy discussion. *ACM Transactions on Office Information Systems*, 6(4):303–331.

[CorelDraw, 1992] CorelDraw. *CorelDraw Users Manual*. Corel Corporation, Canada.

[Cushman et al., 1990] Cushman, W., Ojha, P., and Daniels, C. Usable OCR: What are the minimum performance requirements? In *Proc. CHI'90: Empowering People*, pages 145–151. ACM.

[Cypher, 1993] Cypher, A., editor. *Watch What I Do: Programming by Demonstration*. MIT Press, Cambridge, MA.

[Daniel, 1994] Daniel, J. Twenty-five candles on the cake: Reflections on the silver jubilee of the Open University. In *Proc. Distance Education: Windows on the Future*, pages 544–551. The Correspondence School, Wellington, NZ.

[Davies, 1994] Davies, D. Learning network design: A methodology for the construction of co-operative distance learning environments. In Ottmann, T. and Tomek, I., editors, *Proc. ED-MEDIA 94*, pages 147–152. Association for the Advancement of Computing in Education (AACE).

[Davies et al., 1991] Davies, G., Maurer, H., and Preece, J. Presentation metaphors for very large hypermedia systems. *Journal of Microcomputer Applications*, 14(2):105–116.

[Denning, 1982] Denning, P. Electronic junk. *Communications of the ACM*, 25(3):163–165.

[Derycke et al., 1993] Derycke, A., Croisy, P., and Vilers, P. Computer supported cooperative learning: A real-time multimedia approach. In Maurer, H., editor, *Proc. ED-MEDIA 93 – World Conference on Educational Multimedia and Hypermedia*, pages 131–138. Association for the Advancement of Computing in Education (AACE).

[Derycke and Kaye, 1993] Derycke, A. C. and Kaye, A. R. Participative modelling and design of collaborative distance learning tools in the CO-LEARN project. In *Proc. IFIP TC3 Third Teleteaching Conference Teleteaching 93*, pages 191–200.

[Deutsch, 1992] Deutsch, P. Resource discovery in an internet environment-the archie approach. *Electronic Networking: Research, Applications and Policy*, 2(1):45–51.

[Dewan, 1993] Dewan, P. A survey of applications of CSCW including some in educational settings. In Maurer, H., editor, *Proc. ED-MEDIA 93 – World Conference on Educational Multimedia and Hypermedia*, pages 147–152. Association for the Advancement of Computing in Education (AACE).

[Diffie and Hellman, 1976] Diffie, W. and Hellman, M. New directions in cryptography. *IEEE Trans. Inform. Theory*, 22:644–654.

[Diffie and Hellman, 1977] Diffie, W. and Hellman, M. Exhaustive cryptanalysis of the NBS data encryption standard. *Computer*, 10:74–84.

[DiPaolo, 1993] DiPaolo, A. Educational aspects of the telecommunications revolution. In *Proc. IFIP TC3 Third Teleteaching Conference Teleteaching 93*, pages 23–26.

[Domik, 1993] Domik, G. Scientific visualization. In Maurer, H., editor, *Proc. ED-MEDIA 93 – World Conference on Educational Multimedia and Hypermedia*, pages 153–160. Association for the Advancement of Computing in Education (AACE).

[Donath, 1993] Donath, R. Intercultural learning with the AT&T learning network: An electronic-mail journey of a German class. In *Proc. IFIP TC3 Third Teleteaching Conference Teleteaching 93*, pages 201–209.

[Dreyfuss, 1972] Dreyfuss, H. *Symbol Sourcebook*. McGraw-Hill, New York.

[Eco, 1976] Eco, U. *A Theory of Semiotics*. Indiana University Press, London.

[Eco, 1979] Eco, U. Concluding remarks. In *Proc. First Congress of the International Association for Semiotic Studies*, pages 246–251. Mouton Publishers, The Hague.

[Ellis et al., 1991] Ellis, C., Gibbs, S., and Rein, G. Groupware: Some issues and experiences. *Communications of the ACM*, 34(1):38–58.

[Elrod et al., 1992] Elrod, S., Bruce, R., Gold, R., Goldberg, D., Halasz, F., Janssen, W., Lee, D., McCall, K., Pedersen, E., Pier, K., Tang, J., and Welch, B. Liveboard: A large interactive display supporting group meetings, presentations and remote collaboration. In *Proc. CHI 92*, pages 599–607. ACM.

[Engbring et al., 1995] Engbring, E., Keil-Slawik, R., and Selke, H. Neue Qualitäten in der Hochschulausbildung – Lehren und Lernen mit interaktiven Medien. Technischer Bericht 95, Heinz Nixdorf Institut.

[Engelbart, 1962] Engelbart, D. C. Letter to Vannevar Bush and program on human effectiveness. In Nyce, J. M. and Kahn, P., editors, *From Memex to Hypertext: Vannevar Bush and the Mind's Machine*, pages 235–244. Academic Press, Boston, MA.

[Engelbart, 1963] Engelbart, D. C. A conceptual framework for the augmentation of man's intellect. In *Vistas in Information Handling*, volume 1, pages 1–29. Spartan Books, London.

[Engelbart and English, 1968] Engelbart, D. C. and English, W. K. A research center for augmenting human intellect. In *Proc. AFIPS/ Fall Joint Computer Conference*, volume 33, Part I, pages 395–410.

[Eriksson, 1994] Eriksson, H. MBONE: The multicast backbone. *Communications of the ACM*, 37(8):54–60.

[Feistel, 1970] Feistel, H. Cryptographic coding for data-bank privacy. Technical report, IBM Report RC2827, 18 March.

[Feistel, 1973] Feistel, H. Cryptography and computer privacy. *Scientific American*, 228(May):15–23.

[Fenn and Maurer, 1994] Fenn, B. and Maurer, H. Harmony on an expanding net. *ACM Interactions*, 1(4):26–38.

[Fernandez, 1994] Fernandez, D. S. Intellectual property protection for multimedia technology. In *Proc. Distributed Multimedia Systems and Applications Conference*, pages 299–301. ISMM-ACTA Press.

[Finzer and Gould, 1984] Finzer, W. and Gould, L. Programming by rehearsal. *Byte*, 9(6):187–210.

[Fisher, 1993] Fisher, M. The IBM 'Advanced technology classroom' project: A report on an experimental multimedia, interactive instructional system. In Maurer, H., editor, *Proc. ED-MEDIA 93 – World Conference on Educational Multimedia and Hypermedia*, pages 193–196. Association for the Advancement of Computing in Education (AACE).

[Fitzpatrick et al., 1996] Fitzpatrick, G., Mansfield, T., and Kaplan, S. Locales framework: Exploring foundations for collaboration support. In Grundy, J. and Apperley, M., editors, *Proc. Sixth Australian Conference on Computer-Human interaction*, pages 34–41. IEEE.

[Flohr, 1995] Flohr, U. Hyper-G organizes the web. *Byte*, pages 59–64.

[Fordham et al., 1979] Fordham, P., Poulton, G., and Randle, L. *Learning Networks in Adult Education: Non-formal Education on a Housing Estate.* Routledge and Kegan Paul, London.

[Freudenthal, 1960] Freudenthal, H. *LINCOS: Design of a Language for Cosmic Intercourse.* North-Holland, Amsterdam.

[Fujii and Korfhage, 1989] Fujii, H. and Korfhage, R. R. Features and a model for icon morphological transformation. In *Proc. 1989 IEEE Workshop on Visual Languages*, pages 240–245. IEEE Computer Society Press.

[Gaisbauer et al., 1995] Gaisbauer, M., Leitner, H., and Steiner, H. HyGen: Architectural design document. Internal report, Siemens, Austria.

[Garzotto et al., 1993] Garzotto, F., Paolini, P., and Schwabe, D. HDM: A model-based approach to hypertext application design. *ACM Transactions on Information Systems*, 11(1):1–26.

[Gick, 1989] Gick, M. L. Two functions of diagrams in problem solving by analogy. In Mandl, H. and Levin, J., editors, *Knowledge Acquisition from Text and Pictures*, pages 215–231. North-Holland, Amsterdam.

[Gick and Holyoak, 1980] Gick, M. L. and Holyoak, K. J. Analogical problem solving. *Cognitive Psychology*, 12:306–355.

[Gick and Holyoak, 1983] Gick, M. L. and Holyoak, K. J. Schema induction and analogical transfer. *Cognitive Psychology*, 15:1–38.

[Gilbert, 1993] Gilbert, W. The AT&T teaching theatre at the University of Maryland at College Park. In Maurer, H., editor, *Proc. ED-MEDIA 93 – World Conference on Educational Multimedia and Hypermedia*, pages 210–214. Association for the Advancement of Computing in Education (AACE).

[Gilster, 1994] Gilster, P. *Finding it on the Internet: The Essential Guide to Archie, Veronica, WAIS, WWW (Including Mosaic), and Other Search and Browsing Tools*. John Wiley & Sons, New York.

[Glinert et al., 1989] Glinert, E. P., Blattner, M. M., and Frerking, C. J. Visual tools and languages: Directions for the '90s. In *Proc. 1989 IEEE Workshop on Visual Languages*, pages 89–95. IEEE Computer Society Press.

[Goodman, 1988] Goodman, D. *The Complete Hypercard Handbook (Second edition)*. Bantam Books, Toronto.

[Greenberg, 1994] Greenberg, J. M. Integrated multimedia in distance education. In Ottmann, T. and Tomek, I., editors, *Proc. ED-MEDIA 94*, pages 21–25. Association for the Advancement of Computing in Education (AACE).

[Grønbæk and Trigg, 1994] Grønbæk, K. and Trigg, R. H. Editorial. *Communications of the ACM*, 37(2):28–29.

[Haan et al., 1992] Haan, B. J., Kahn, P., Riley, V. A., Coombs, J. H., and Meyrowitz, N. K. IRIS hypermedia services. *Communications of the ACM*, 35(1):36–51.

[Hadamard, 1945] Hadamard, J. *An Essay on the Psychology of Invention in the Mathematical Field*. Dover Publications, New York.

[Hahn and Stout, 1994] Hahn, J. and Stout, R. *The Internet Complete Reference*. Osborne, McGraw-Hill, New York.

[Halasz, 1988] Halasz, F. Reflections on notecards: Seven issues for the next generation of hypermedia systems. *Communications of the ACM*, 31(7):836–852.

[Halasz, 1991] Halasz, F. Keynote address transcript. http://www. parc. xerox.com/spl/projects/halasz-keynote/transcript.html.

[Halasz and Schwartz, 1994] Halasz, F. and Schwartz, M. The Dexter hypertext reference model. *Communications of the ACM*, 37(2):30–39.

[Halliday, 1985] Halliday, M. A. K. *An Introduction to Functional Grammar*. Arnold Ltd, Baltimore.

[Hanson and Heng, 1992] Hanson, A. and Heng, P. Illuminating the fourth dimension. *IEEE Computer Graphics and Applications*, 12(4):54–62.

[Harasim, 1990] Harasim, L. M. *Online Education: Perspectives on a New Environment*. Praeger, New York.

[Hardman et al., 1993] Hardman, L., Bulterman, D. C., and van Rossum, G. The Amsterdam hypermedia model: Extending hypertext to support real multimedia. *Hypermedia*, 5(1):47–69.

[Hardman et al., 1994] Hardman, L., Bulterman, D. C., and van Rossum, G. The Amsterdam hypermedia model: Adding time and context to the Dexter model. *Communications of the ACM*, 37(2):50–62.

[Haugen, 1993] Haugen, H. Just in time open learning – a European project from a Norwegian point of view. In *Proc. IFIP TC3 Third Teleteaching Conference Teleteaching 93*, pages 345–351.

[Herz, 1995] Herz, J. *Surfing on the Internet: a Nethead's Adventures On-line*. Little Brown, Boston, MA.

[Hewitt, 1993] Hewitt, L. Interactive multimedia in a distance education milieu. In Maurer, H., editor, *Proc. ED-MEDIA 93 – World Conference on Educational Multimedia and Hypermedia*, pages 247–254. Association for the Advancement of Computing in Education (AACE).

[Hiltz, 1986] Hiltz, S. R. The 'virtual classroom': Using computer-mediated communication for university teaching. *Journal of Communication*, 36:95–104.

[Hiltz, 1990] Hiltz, S. R. Evaluating the virtual classroom. In Harasim, L. M., editor, *Online education: Perspectives on a new environment*, pages 133–169. Praeger, New York.

[Hiltz, 1995] Hiltz, S. R. *The Virtual Classroom: Learning Without Limits via Computer Networks*. Ablex, Norwood, NJ.

[Hiltz and Turoff, 1994] Hiltz, S. R. and Turoff, M. Virtual classroom plus video: Technology for educational excellence. In Ottmann, T. and Tomek, I., editors, *Proc. ED-MEDIA 94*, pages 26–31. Association for the Advancement of Computing in Education (AACE).

[Hoffman, 1990] Hoffman, L. *Rogue Programs: Viruses, Worms, and Trojan Horses*. van Nostrand Reinhold, New York.

[Hoffman, 1995] Hoffman, L., editor. *Building in Big Brother. The Cryptology Policy Debate*. Springer, Berlin Heidelberg New York.

[Hoffmann, 1993] Hoffmann, R. The distance brings us closer: Electronic mail, ESL learner writers, and teachers. In *Proc. IFIP TC3 Third Teleteaching Conference Teleteaching 93*, pages 391–399.

[Huber et al., 1989] Huber, F., Makedon, F., and Maurer, H. HyperCOSTOC: A comprehensive computer-based teaching support system. *Journal of Microcomputer Applications*, 12:293–317.

[Hypercard, 1989] Hypercard. *Hypercard Reference Manual*. Apple Computer Inc., Cupertino, CA.

[Hypermedia Unit, 1994] Hypermedia Unit, U. A. Unimedia – an experimental guide to the University of Auckland. CD-ROM.

[IEEE, 1993] IEEE. Special issue on visualization. *IEEE Computer Graphics and Applications*, 13(4).

[Jacob, 1990] Jacob, R. What you look at is what you get: Eye movement-based interaction techniques. In *Proc. CHI'90: Empowering People*, pages 11–18. ACM.

[Jayasinha et al., 1995] Jayasinha, C., Lennon, J., and Maurer, H. Interactive and annotated movies. In Maurer, H., editor, *Proc. ED-MEDIA 95 – World Conference on Educational Multimedia and Hypermedia, Graz)*, pages 366–371. Association for the Advancement of Computing in Education (AACE).

[Jean, 1989] Jean, G. *Langage de Signes, L'écriture et son Double*. Gallimard.

[Jeanes, 1982] Jeanes, R., editor. *Dictionary of Australasian Signs for Communication With the Deaf*. Victorian School for Deaf Children, Melbourne.

[Johnson and Shneiderman, 1993] Johnson, B. and Shneiderman, B. Treemaps: A space-filling approach to the visualization of hierarchical information structures. In Shneiderman, B., editor, *Sparks of Innovation in Human-Computer Interaction*, pages 309–325. Ablex Publishing, Norwood, NJ.

[Johnson and Johnson, 1975] Johnson, D. W. and Johnson, R. T. *Learning To-gether and Alone: Cooperation, Competition, and Individualization.* Prentice-Hall, Englewood Cliffs, NJ.

[Jonassen et al., 1993] Jonassen, D. H., Goldmann-Segal, R., and Maurer, H. Dy-namicons as dynamic graphic interfaces: Interpreting the meaning of a visual representation. Report 376, Institutes for Information Proc., Graz, Austria.

[Jones et al., 1993] Jones, A., Kirkup, G., and Kirkwood, A. *Personal Computers for Distance Education: The Study of an Educational Innovation.* St. Martin's Press, New York.

[Kahn, 1967] Kahn, D. *The Codebreakers: The Story of Secret Writing.* Macmillan, New York.

[Kaneko et al., 1989] Kaneko, S., Ikemoto, H., and Kusui, Y. Approach to de-signing easy-to-understand icons. In *Proc. 1989 IEEE Workshop on Visual Languages*, pages 246–253. IEEE Computer Society Press.

[Kappe, 1995] Kappe, F. A scalable architecture for maintaining referential in-tegrity in distributed information systems. *Journal of Universal Computer Sci-ence*, 1(2):84–104.

[Kappe et al., 1994] Kappe, F., Andrews, K., Faschingbauer, J., Gaisbauer, M., Maurer, H., Pichler, M., and Schipflinger, J. Hyper-G: A new tool for dis-tributed hypermedia. In *Proc. Distributed Multimedia Systems and Applications Conference*, pages 209–214. ISMM-ACTA Press.

[Kappe and Maurer, 1994] Kappe, F. and Maurer, H. From hypertext to active communication/information systems. *Journal of Microcomputer Applications*, 17:333–344.

[Kappe et al., 1993] Kappe, F., Maurer, H., and Sherbakov, N. Hyper-G – a uni-versal hypermedia system. *Journal of Educational Multimedia and Hypermedia*, 2(1):39–66.

[Kay and Goldberg, 1977] Kay, A. and Goldberg, A. Personal dynamic media. *Computer*, 10(3):31–41.

[Kaye, 1993] Kaye, G. R. Electronic campus – UK. In *Proc. IFIP TC3 Third Teleteaching Conference Teleteaching 93*, pages 487–502.

[Kimura, 1989] Kimura, T. D. Pen-based user interface (Panel Session). In *Proc. 1989 IEEE Workshop on Visual Languages*, pages 168–173. IEEE Computer Society Press.

[Klemme, 1996] Klemme, M. Tools for an electronic learning and teaching environ-ment. Technical Report 135, University of Auckland Department of Computer Science.

[Koegel-Buford, 1994] Koegel-Buford, J., editor. *Multimedia Systems, SIGGRAPH Series.* ACM Press, New York.

[Kosslyn, 1980] Kosslyn, S. M. *Image and Mind.* Harvard University Press, Cam-bridge, MA.

[Kosslyn, 1983] Kosslyn, S. M. *Ghosts in the Mind's Machine.* W. W. Norton, New York.

[Kosslyn, 1994] Kosslyn, S. M. *Image and Brain: The Resolution of the Imagery Debate.* MIT Press, Cambridge, MA.

[Kress and van Leeuwen, 1990] Kress, G. and van Leeuwen, T. *Reading Images.* Deakin University, Victoria.

[Lai et al., 1988] Lai, K., Malone, T., and Yu, K. Object lens: A 'spreadsheet' for cooperative work. *ACM Transactions on Office Information Systems*, 6(4):332–353.

[Lai et al., 1991] Lai, X., Massey, J. L., and Murphy, S. Markov ciphers and differ-ential cryptanalysis. In Davies, D. W., editor, *Advances in Cryptology: EURO-CRYPT '91*, pages 17–38. LNCS 547, Springer, Berlin Heidelberg New York.

[Lakin, 1986] Lakin, F. Spacial parsing for visual languages. In Chang, S., Ichikawa, T., and Ligomenides, P., editors, *Visual Languages*, pages 35–85. Plenum Press, New York.

[Lakin, 1987] Lakin, F. Visual grammars for visual languages. In *Proc. Sixth National Conference on Artificial Intelligence*, Seattle, WA. Morgan Kaufmann.

[Le Gall, 1991] Le Gall, D. MPEG: A video compression standard for multimedia applications. *Communications of the ACM*, 34(4):46–58.

[Lee et al., 1993] Lee, K., Mansfield, W., and Sheth, A. A framework for controlling cooperative agents. *Computer*, 26(7):8–16.

[Lee and Tsang, 1994] Lee, V. and Tsang, E. Student electronic bulletin board for distance education. In *Proc. Distance Education: Windows on the Future*, pages 608–613. The Correspondence School, Wellington, NZ.

[Lennon, 1995a] Lennon, J. Distributed learning environments: A future with hypermedia. Computer Science Report 108, University of Auckland, NZ.

[Lennon, 1995b] Lennon, J. Mental imagery and visualization: From the mind's machine to the computer screen. In Maurer, H., editor, *Proc. ED-MEDIA 95 – World Conference on Educational Multimedia and Hypermedia*, pages 27–32, Graz, Austria. Association for the Advancement of Computing in Education (AACE).

[Lennon and Maurer, 1994a] Lennon, J. and Maurer, H. From personal computer to personal assistant. Technical Report 386, Institutes for Information Proc., Graz, Austria.

[Lennon and Maurer, 1994b] Lennon, J. and Maurer, H. Lecturing technology: A future with hypermedia. *Educational Technology*, 34:5–14.

[Lennon and Maurer, 1994c] Lennon, J. and Maurer, H. MUSLI: A MUlti-Sensory Language Interface. In Ottmann, T. and Tomek, I., editors, *Proc. ED-MEDIA 94*, pages 341–348. Association for the Advancement of Computing in Education (AACE).

[Lennon and Maurer, 1994d] Lennon, J. and Maurer, H. You believe you know what multimedia is? and what internet will do for you? well think again! *J.UCS (Journal of Universal Computer Science)*, 0(0):54–108.

[Lennon and Maurer, 1995] Lennon, J. and Maurer, H. New ways of using old media. *NZ Science Monthly*, 6(7):10–11.

[Lennon and Vermeer, 1995] Lennon, J. and Vermeer, A. From personal computer to personal assistant. *J.UCS (Journal of Universal Computer Science)*, 1(6):406–418.

[Lennon, 1993] Lennon, M. A paperless EDI system allowing secure contracts. In Hosking, J., editor, *Proc. 13th New Zealand Computer Society Conference*, pages 110–116, Wellington, NZ. NZCS.

[Liu et al., 1994] Liu, C., Peek, J., Jones, R., Buus, B., and Nye, A. *Managing Internet Information Services*. O'Reilly & Assocs., Sebastopol, CA.

[Liungman, 1991] Liungman, C. G. *Dictionary of Symbols*. ABC-CLIO, Santa Barbara, CA.

[Lodding, 1983] Lodding, K. Iconic interfacing. *IEEE Computer Graphics and Applications*, 3(2):11–20.

[Lodowyck, 1652] Lodowyck, F. *The Ground-work of a New Perfect Language*. The Scolar Press, Menston, England. Reprinted 1968.

[Lupton and Rushby, 1994] Lupton, P. and Rushby, L. Open up learning: Teleconferencing and the professional development of teachers. In *Proc. Distance Education: Windows on the Future*, pages 614–619. The Correspondence School, Wellington, NZ.

[Lynch, 1992] Lynch, C. A. The Z39.50 protocol in plain English. http://www.research.att.com/~wald/pe-doc.txt.

[Mackay and Davenport, 1989] Mackay, W. and Davenport, G. Virtual video editing in interactive multimedia applications. *Communications of the ACM*, 32(7):802–810.

[MacroMind, 1991] MacroMind. *MacroMind Director 3.0 Reference Manual.* MacroMind Inc., San Francisco, CA.

[Magnenat-Thalmann, 1994] Magnenat-Thalmann, N. The Seventh International-Conference on Computer Animation, advanced program.

[Magnenat-Thalmann and Thalmann, 1991a] Magnenat-Thalmann, N. and Thalmann, D. Complex models for animating synthetic actors. *IEEE Computer Graphics and Applications*, 11(5):32–44.

[Magnenat-Thalmann and Thalmann, 1991b] Magnenat-Thalmann, N. and Thalmann, D. *Computer Animation '91.* Springer, Berlin Heidelberg New York.

[Malone et al., 1987] Malone, T. W., Grant, K. R., Turbak, F. A., Brobst, S. A., and Cohen, M. D. Intelligent information-sharing systems. *Communications of the ACM*, 30(5):309–402.

[Maly et al., 1994] Maly, K., Overstreet, C. M., Abdell-Wahab, H., and Gupta, A. K. Melding television, networking, and computing for interactive remote instruction: Exploiting potentials. In Ottmann, T. and Tomek, I., editors, *Proc. ED-MEDIA 94*, pages 367–372. Association for the Advancement of Computing in Education (AACE).

[Marchionini and Maurer, 1995a] Marchionini, G. and Maurer, H. Digital libraries as components of modern computer supported learning. In *Proc. ED-MEDIA 95*, pages 413–417. Association for the Advancement of Computing in Education (AACE).

[Marchionini and Maurer, 1995b] Marchionini, G. and Maurer, H. The roles of digital libraries in teaching and learning. *Communications of the ACM*, 38(4):67–75.

[Mason, 1993] Mason, R. Designing collaborative work for online courses. In *Proc. IFIP TC3 Third Teleteaching Conference Teleteaching 93*, pages 569–577.

[Mathews et al., 1994] Mathews, J., Makedon, F., and Gloor, P. VideoScheme: A research, authoring, and teaching tool for multimedia. In Ottmann, T. and Tomek, I., editors, *Proc. ED-MEDIA 94*, pages 385–390. Association for the Advancement of Computing in Education (AACE).

[Maulsby and Witten, 1993] Maulsby, D. and Witten, I. Metamouse: An instructible agent for programming by demonstration. In Cypher, A., editor, *Watch What I Do: Programming by Demonstration*, pages 155–181. MIT Press, Cambridge, MA.

[Maulsby et al., 1989] Maulsby, D., Witten, I., and Kittlitz, K. Metamouse: Specifying graphical procedures by example. *Computer Graphics*, 23(3):127–136.

[Maulsby et al., 1992] Maulsby, D. L., Witten, I. H., Kittlitz, K. A., and Franceschin, V. G. Inferring graphical procedures: The compleat metamouse. *Human-Computer Interaction*, 7(1):47–89.

[Maurer, 1992a] Maurer, H. Die andere Seite des Berges. Essay 142, Maurers Meinung, Austrian BTX.

[Maurer, 1992b] Maurer, H. Why hypermedia systems are important. In Tomek, I., editor, *Proc. ICCAL92*, pages 1–15. LNCS 602, Springer, Berlin Heidelberg New York.

[Maurer, 1993a] Maurer, H. From multimedia to hypermedia. In Hosking, J., editor, *Proc. 13th New Zealand Computer Society Conference*, pages 2–9, Wellington, NZ. NZCS.

[Maurer, 1993b] Maurer, H. *Spekulationen Über die Multimediale Zukunft.* CAP, Debis.

[Maurer, 1994a] Maurer, H. The A.E.I.O.U. hypermedia project. In *Computer Animation*. IEEE Computer Society Press, Los Alamitos, CA.

[Maurer, 1994b] Maurer, H. Internet and electronic publishing. Invited presentation for STM Innovations Seminar.

[Maurer, 1994c] Maurer, H. Private communication.

[Maurer, 1995a] Maurer, H. Hypermedia in a gambling casino setting. In *Proc. Hypertext, Information Retrieval and Multimedia*, Constance. German Society of Computer Science.

[Maurer, 1995b] Maurer, H. On some new aspects of networked multimedia systems. In Bartosek, M., Staudek, J., and Wiedermann, J., editors, *SOFSEM'95: Theory and Practice of Informatics*, pages 315–333. LNCS 1012, Springer, Berlin Heidelberg New York.

[Maurer, 1996a] Maurer, H. *HyperWave: The Next Generation Web Solution*. Addison-Wesley, UK.

[Maurer, 1996b] Maurer, H. LATE: A unified concept for a learning and teaching environment. *J.UCS (Journal for Universal Computer Science)*, 2(8):580–595.

[Maurer and Carlson, 1992] Maurer, H. and Carlson, P. Computer visualization, a missing organ, and a cyber-equivalency. *Collegiate Microcomputers*, 10(2):110–116.

[Maurer and Flinn, 1994] Maurer, H. and Flinn, B. On levels of anonymity. Technical report, Institute for Information Proc., Graz, Austria.

[Maurer et al., 1993a] Maurer, H., Kappe, F., Scherbakov, N., and Srinivasan, P. Structured browsing of hypermedia databases. In *Proc. VCHCI'93*, pages 51–62, Vienna, Austria. LNCS 733, Springer, Berlin Heidelberg New York.

[Maurer et al., 1994a] Maurer, H., Kappe, N., and Scherbakov, N. Authoring a large distributed hypermedia system: Document linking and embedding (DLE) concept. In Herzner and Kappe, editors, *Multimedia/Hypermedia in Open Distributed Environments: Proc. Eurographics Symposium 1994*, pages 230–243, Graz, Austria. Springer, Berlin Heidelberg New York.

[Maurer and Lennon, 1994] Maurer, H. and Lennon, J. Forecasting: An impossible necessity. *NZ Science Monthly*, 5(1):12–13.

[Maurer et al., 1994b] Maurer, H., Muelner, H., and Schneider, A. An electronic library and its ramifications. Technical Report 382, Institute for Information Proc., Graz, Austria.

[Maurer et al., 1994c] Maurer, H., Philpott, A., and Scherbakov, N. Hypermedia systems without links. *Journal of Microcomputer Applications*, 17:321–332.

[Maurer et al., 1994d] Maurer, H., Rajasingham, L., and Tiffin, J. New Zealand heritage: Sold! *NZ Science Monthly*, 5(2):6–7.

[Maurer et al., 1994e] Maurer, H., Sammer, P., and Schneider, A. Multimedia systems for the general public: Experiences at world expositions and lessons learned. In *Proc. International Interactive Multimedia Symposium*, pages 333–341, Perth.

[Maurer and Scherbakov, 1996] Maurer, H. and Scherbakov, N. *Multimedia Authoring for Presentation and Education*. Addison-Wesley, Bonn.

[Maurer et al., 1995] Maurer, H., Scherbakov, N., and Schneider, A. HM-Card: A new hypermedia authoring system. *Journal for Multimedia Tools and Applications*, 1(3).

[Maurer et al., 1993b] Maurer, H., Scherbakov, N., and Srinivasan, P. A new hypermedia data model. In *Proc. DEXA'93*, pages 685–696, Prague, Czech Republic. LNCS 720, Springer, Berlin Heidelberg New York.

[Maurer and Schmaranz, 1994] Maurer, H. and Schmaranz, K. J.UCS – the next generation in electronic publishing. *J.UCS (Journal of Universal Computer Science)*, 0(0):117–126.

[Maurer and Schneider, 1994] Maurer, H. and Schneider, A. Conferencing – do it the hypermedia way! Computer Science Report 101, University of Auckland.

[Maurer and Sebestyen, 1982] Maurer, H. and Sebestyen, I. 'Unorthodox' videotex applications: Teleplaying, telegambling, telesoftware and telecomputing. *Information Services & Use*, 2:19–34.

[Maurer et al., 1991] Maurer, H., Stone, M., Stubenrauch, R., and Gillard, P. Question/answer specification in CAL tutorials (automatic problem generation does not work). *Schriftenreihe Didaktik der Mathematik*, 21:191–197.

[McLuhan, 1964] McLuhan, M. *Understanding Media: The Extensions of Man*. Hazel Watson and Viney Ltd, UK.

[McLuhan, 1989] McLuhan, M. *The Global Village*. Oxford University Press, Oxford.

[McLuhan and Fiore, 1968] McLuhan, M. and Fiore, Q. *War and Peace in the Global Village*. McGraw-Hill, New York.

[McQueen, 1993] McQueen, R. Groupware: Experience in New Zealand. In Hosking, J., editor, *Proc. 13th New Zealand Computer Society Conference*, pages 10–20, Wellington, NZ. NZCS.

[Medina-Mora et al., 1992] Medina-Mora, R., Winograd, T., Flores, R., and Flores, F. The action workflow approach to workflow management technology. In *Proc. CSCW'92*, pages 281–288, Toronto. ACM.

[Mercer, 1993] Mercer, D. S. Large scale conferencing for inexpert users. In *Proc. IFIP TC3 Third Teleteaching Conference Teleteaching 93*, pages 601–609.

[Merkle, 1978] Merkle, R. Secure communications over insecure channels. *Communications of the ACM*, 21(4):294–299.

[Merkle and Hellman, 1978] Merkle, R. and Hellman, M. E. Hiding information and signatures in trap door knapsacks. *IEEE Trans. Inform. Theory*, 24:525–530.

[Miller, 1971] Miller, J. *McLuhan*. Fontana, UK.

[Mo and Witten, 1992] Mo, D. and Witten, I. Learning text editing tasks from examples: a procedural approach. *Behaviour and Information Technology*, 11(1):32–45.

[Murray and Malone, 1992] Murray, J. and Malone, S. The structures of advanced multimedia learning environments: Reconfiguring space, time, story and text. In Tomek, I., editor, *Proc. ICCAL92*, pages 21–33. LNCS 602, Springer, Berlin Heidelberg New York.

[Myers, 1988] Myers, B. *Creating User Interfaces by Demonstration*. Academic Press, Boston, MA.

[Myers et al., 1993] Myers, B. A., McDaniel, R. G., and Kosbie, D. S. Marquise: Creating complete user interfaces by demonstration. In *Proc. INTERCHI'93: Human Factors in Computing Systems*, pages 293–300, Amsterdam. ACM.

[Nelson, 1965] Nelson, T. H. A file structure for the complex, the changing, and the indeterminate. In *Proc. ACM 20th National Conference*, pages 84–100. ACM.

[Nelson, 1972] Nelson, T. H. As we will think. In *Online 72, Proc. Intl. Conf. on Online Interactive Computing*, pages 439–454. Brunel University, Uxbridge, UK.

[Nelson, 1987] Nelson, T. H. *Literary Machines*. Mindful Press, Sausalito CA, 87.1 edition.

[Neuwirth et al., 1992] Neuwirth, C., Chandhok, R., Kaufer, D., Erion, P., Morris, J., and Miller, D. Flexible diff-ing in a collaborative writing system. In *Proc. CSCW'92*, pages 147–154, Toronto. ACM.

[Newcomb et al., 1991] Newcomb, S. R., Kipp, H. A., and Newcomb, V. T. HyTime: The hypermedia/time-based document structuring language. *Communications of the ACM*, 34(11):67–83.

[Nielsen, 1990] Nielsen, J. *Hypertext and Hypermedia*. Academic Press, Boston, MA.

[Norman, 1993] Norman, K. The electronic teaching theatre: Interactive hypermedia and mental models of the classroom. In [Shneiderman, 1993d], pages 133–154. Ablex Publishing, Norwood, NJ.

[Nunamaker et al., 1991] Nunamaker, J., Dennis, A., Valacich, J., Vogel, D., and George, J. Electronic meeting systems to support group work. *Communications of the ACM*, 34(7):40–61.

[Nyce and Kahn, 1991] Nyce, J. M. and Kahn, P., editors. *From Memex to Hypertext: Vannevar Bush and the Mind's Machine*. Academic Press, Boston MA.

[Odlyzko, 1994] Odlyzko, A. M. Tragic loss or good riddance? The impending demise of traditional scholarly journals. *J.UCS (Journal for Universal Computer Science)*, 0(0):3–53.

[Odlyzko, 1995] Odlyzko, A. M. Tragic loss or good riddance? The impending demise of traditional scholarly journals. In Peek, R. and Newby, G., editors, *Electronic Publishing Confronts Academia: The Agenda for the Year 2000*. MIT Press, Cambridge, MA. ASIS monograph.

[Paivio, 1971] Paivio, A. *Imagery and Verbal Processes*. Holt, Rinehart and Winston, New York.

[Paivio, 1986] Paivio, A. *Mental Representation: A Dual Coding Approach*. Oxford University Press, New York.

[Paouri et al., 1991] Paouri, A., Magnenat-Thalmann, N., and Thalmann, D. Creating realistic three-dimensional human shape characters for computer-generated films. In *Computer Animation '91*, pages 89–99. Springer, Berlin Heidelberg New York.

[Papert, 1980] Papert, S. *Mindstorms: Children, Computers, and Powerful Ideas*. Harvester Press, Brighton, UK.

[Petruk, 1992] Petruk, M. W. Adjusting to the paradigm shift in teaching and learning or: What do I do now? In Tomek, I., editor, *Proc. ICCAL92*, pages 34–38. LNCS 602, Springer, Berlin Heidelberg New York.

[Piernot and Yvon, 1993] Piernot, P. P. and Yvon, M. P. The AIDE project: An application-independent demonstrational environment. In [Cypher, 1993], pages 383–401. MIT Press, Cambridge, MA.

[PowerPoint, 1992] PowerPoint. *Microsoft PowerPoint Handbook*. Microsoft Corp., Redmond, WA.

[Press, 1994] Press, L. Tomorrow's campus. *Communications of the ACM*, 37(7):13–17.

[Price, 1993] Price, R. MHEG: An introduction to the future international standard for hypermedia object interchange. *ACM Multimedia 93*, pages 121–128.

[Qualtrough and Schneider, 1994] Qualtrough, P. and Schneider, A. Let's see what's happening in Auckland! Interactive telewatching in a networked hypermedia environment. Computer Science Report Report 100, University of Auckland, NZ.

[Rajasingham, 1988] Rajasingham, L. *Distance Education and New Communications Technologies*. Victoria University of Wellington, NZ.

[Reynolds, 1994] Reynolds, J. Videoconferencing: The practical realities. In *Proc. Distance Education: Windows on the Future*, pages 649–656. The Correspondence School, Wellington, NZ.

[Rivest et al., 1978] Rivest, R., Shamir, A., and Adleman, L. A method for obtaining digital signatures and public-key cryptosystem. *Communications of the ACM*, 21(2):120–126.

[Robinson, 1991] Robinson, M. Through a lens smartly. *Byte*, 16(5):177–187.

[Rodruguez-Rosello, 1993] Rodruguez-Rosello, L. Existing and future technology for teleteaching. In *Proc. IFIP TC3 Third Teleteaching Conference Teleteaching 93*, pages 61–70.

[Rossman, 1992] Rossman, P. *The Emerging Worldwide Electronic University: Information Age Global Higher Education.* Greenwood Press, Westport, CT.

[Rugg, 1963] Rugg, H. *Imagination.* Harper & Row, New York.

[Rumble, 1992] Rumble, G. *The Management of Distance Learning Systems.* UNESCO: International Institute for Educational Planning.

[Salomaa, 1990] Salomaa, A. Public-key cryptography. *EATCS Monographs*, 23. 2nd ed. 1996, Texts in Theoretical Computer Science. An EATCS Series. Springer, Berlin Heidelberg New York.

[Sanderson, 1993] Sanderson, D. *Smileys.* O'Reilly & Assocs., Sebastopol, CA.

[Schank, 1975] Schank, R. C. *Conceptual Information Processing.* North-Holland, Amsterdam.

[Schank and Abelson, 1977] Schank, R. C. and Abelson, R. *Scripts, Plans, Goals and Understanding.* Lawrence Erlbaum Associates, Hillsdale, NJ.

[Schneider, 1995] Schneider, A. Hypermedia authoring with HM-Card. In *Proc. ED-MEDIA 95.* Association for the Advancement of Computing in Education (AACE).

[Schneier, 1994] Schneier, B. *Applied Cryptography: Protocols, Algorithms and Source Code in C.* John Wiley & Sons, New York. 2nd ed. 1995.

[Sen, 1994] Sen, P. Multimedia services over the public network: Requirements, architectures, and protocols. In Buford, J. F. K., editor, *Multimedia Systems*, pages 305–322. ACM Press, New York.

[Shannon, 1949] Shannon, C. Communication theory of secrecy systems. *Bell System Technical Journal*, 28:656–715.

[Sheffield, 1993] Sheffield, J. The impact of electronic meeting systems on New Zealand organisations. In Hosking, J., editor, *Proc. 13th New Zealand Computer Society Conference*, pages 21–40, Wellington, NZ. NZCS.

[Sheffield and Gallupe, 1993] Sheffield, J. and Gallupe, B. Using electronic meeting technology to support economic policy development in New Zealand Part II: Follow-up results. In Hosking, J., editor, *Proc. 13th New Zealand Computer Society Conference*, pages 41–60, Wellington, NZ. NZCS.

[Shneiderman, 1993a] Shneiderman, B. Direct manipulation: A step beyond programming languages. In [Shneiderman, 1993d], pages 17–37. Ablex Publishing, Norwood, NJ.

[Shneiderman, 1993b] Shneiderman, B. Education by engagement and construction: Experiences in the AT&T teaching theater. In Maurer, H., editor, *Proc. ED-MEDIA 93 – World Conference on Educational Multimedia and Hypermedia*, pages 471–479. Association for the Advancement of Computing in Education (AACE).

[Shneiderman, 1993c] Shneiderman, B. Information visualization: Dynamic queries, treemaps, and the filter/flow metaphor. In [Shneiderman, 1993d], pages 275–279. Ablex Publishing, Norwood, NJ.

[Shneiderman, 1993d] Shneiderman, B., editor. *Sparks of Innovation in Human-Computer Interaction.* Ablex Publishing, Norwood, NJ.

[Shu, 1988] Shu, N. *Visual Programming.* Van Nostrand Reinhold, New York.

[Stallings and van Slyke, 1990] Stallings, W. and van Slyke, R. *Business Data Communications.* Macmillan College, New York.

[Starker and Bolt, 1990] Starker, I. and Bolt, R. A. A gaze-responsive self-disclosing display. In *Proc. CHI'90: Empowering People*, pages 3–9. ACM.

[Stasko, 1990] Stasko, J. Tango – a framework and system for algorithm animation. *IEEE Computer*, 23(9):27–39.

[Stein, 1991] Stein, R. Browsing through terabytes – wide-area information servers open a new frontier in personal and corporate information services. *Byte*, 16(5):157–164.

[Stewart et al., 1988] Stewart, D., Keegan, D., and Holmberg, B. *Distance Education: International Perspectives*. Routledge, London.

[Sutherland, 1990] Sutherland, I. E. Sketchpad: A man-machine graphical communication system. In *Visual Programming Environments: Paradigms and Systems*, pages 198–215. IEEE Computer Society Press, Los Alamitos, CA.

[Sutherland, 1994] Sutherland, K. Technology is the answer – but what are the questions. In *Proc. Distance Education: Windows on the Future*, pages 174–181. The Correspondence School, Wellington, NZ.

[Swift, 1994] Swift, M. Application of technology and telecommunications in an open learning system: A New Zealand perspective. In *Proc. Distance Education: Windows on the Future*, pages 683–689. The Correspondence School, Wellington, NZ.

[Symantec, 1990] Symantec. *More 3.0 Reference Manual*. Symantec Corp., CA.

[Tanimoto and Runyan, 1986] Tanimoto, S. L. and Runyan, M. S. PLAY: An iconic programming system for children. In Chang, S., Ichikawa, T., and Ligomenides, P., editors, *Visual Languages*, pages 191–205. Plenum, New York.

[Tomek et al., 1991] Tomek, I., Khan, S., Muldner, T., Nassar, M., Navak, G., and Proszynski, P. Hypermedia – introduction and survey. *Journal of Microcomputer Applications*, 14(2):63–100.

[Toolbook, 1994] Toolbook. *ToolBook User Manual*. Asymetrix, WA.

[Tuck and Olsen, 1990] Tuck, R. and Olsen, D. R. Help by guided tasks; utilizing UIMS knowledge. In *Proc. CHI'90: Empowering People*, pages 71–78. ACM.

[Tye, 1991] Tye, M. *The Imagery Debate*. MIT Press, Cambridge, MA.

[Ukkonen, 1985] Ukkonen, E. Algorithms for approximate string matching. *Information and Control*, 64:100–118.

[Umiker-Sebeok and Sebeok, 1987] Umiker-Sebeok, J. and Sebeok, T. *Monastic Sign Languages*. Mouton de Gruyter, Berlin.

[van Dam, 1988] van Dam, A. Hypertext'87 keynote address. *Communications of the ACM*, 31(7):887–895.

[Walker, 1987] Walker, J. H. Document examiner: Delivery interface for hypertext documents. In *Proc. Hypertext '87*, pages 307–323. ACM.

[Wallace, 1991] Wallace, G. K. The JPEG still picture compression standard. *Communications of the ACM,*, 34(4):30–44.

[Watts and Huang, 1976] Watts, A. and Huang, A. *Tao: The Watercourse Way*. Jonathan Cape, London.

[Weeks and Røyrvik, 1993] Weeks, A. and Røyrvik, O. Using e-mail in an English class at NKI. In *Proc. IFIP TC3 Third Teleteaching Conference Teleteaching 93*, pages 925–933.

[Weizenbaum, 1966] Weizenbaum, J. Eliza: A computer program for the study of natural language communication between man and machine. *Communications of the ACM*, 9(1):36–45.

[Wells, 1993] Wells, R. The use of computer-mediated communication in distance education: Progress, problems, and trends. In *Proc. IFIP TC3 Third Teleteaching Conference Teleteaching 93*, pages 79–88.

[Wijngaarden, 1965] Wijngaarden, A. Orthogonal design and description of a formal language. Technical report, MR 76, Mathematisch Centrum, Amsterdam.

[Williamson and Shneiderman, 1993] Williamson, C. and Shneiderman, B. The dynamic homefinder: Evaluating dynamic queries in a real-estate information exploration system. In [Shneiderman, 1993d], pages 295–307. Ablex Publishing, Norwood, NJ.

[Winn, 1989] Winn, W. The design and use of instructional graphics. In Mandl, H. and Levin, J., editors, *Knowledge Acquisition from Text and Pictures*, pages 125–144. North-Holland, Amsterdam.

[Winn, 1994] Winn, W. Designing and using virtual environments: The advantage of immersion. In Ottmann, T. and Tomek, I., editors, *Proc. ED-MEDIA 94*, pages 695–695. Association for the Advancement of Computing in Education (AACE).

[Winterbotham, 1974] Winterbotham, F. *The Ultra Secret.* Dell, New York.

[Witten, 1996] Witten, I. Digital libraries based on full-text retrieval. Invited talk at WebNet 96 — World Conference of the Web Society.

[Witten and Mo, 1993] Witten, I. H. and Mo, D. TELS: Learning text editing tasks from examples. In Cypher, A., editor, *Watch What I Do: Programming by Demonstration*, pages 183–203. MIT Press, Cambridge, MA.

[Wood and Wood, 1990] Wood, W. T. and Wood, S. K. Icons in everyday life. In *Visual Programming Environments: Applications and Issues*, pages 257–263. IEEE Computer Society Press, Los Alamitos, CA.

[Woolf, 1992] Woolf, B. Building knowledge based tutors. In Tomek, I., editor, *Proc. ICCAL92*, pages 46–60. LNCS 602, Springer, Berlin Heidelberg New York.

[Wu and Manber, 1992] Wu, S. and Manber, U. Fast text searching allowing errors. *Communications of the ACM*, 35(10):83–91.

[Yankelovich et al., 1988] Yankelovich, N., Haan, B. J., Meyrowitz, N. K., and Drucker, S. M. Intermedia: The concept and the construction of a seamless information environment. *IEEE Computer*, 21(1):81–96.

[Zaidah et al., 1993] Zaidah, R., Zahran, H., and Witten, I. Supporting operations planning – a multimedia approach. In Hosking, J., editor, *Proc. 13th New Zealand Computer Society Conference*, pages 132–142, Wellington, NZ. NZCS.

[Zhao, 1993] Zhao, R. Incremental recognition in gesture-based and syntax-directed diagram editors. In *Proc. INTERCHI'93: Human Factors in Computing Systems*, pages 95–100, Amsterdam. ACM.

[Zissos and Witten, 1985] Zissos, A. Y. and Witten, I. H. User modelling for a computer coach: A case study. *International Journal of Man-Machine Studies*, 23:729–750.

[Ziv and Lempel, 1977] Ziv, J. and Lempel, A. A universal algorithm for sequential data compression. *IEEE Trans. Information Theory*, 23(3):337–343.

Index